Public Relations For Dummies, 2nd Edition

Cheat Sheet

Employing Important PR Principles

- ✔ **You have to be different.** Conventional publicity strategies get lost in the noise. You have to find a creative way to stand out from the crowd and get noticed.

- ✔ **Publicity should help you reach your market objective.** Getting publicity is fun, but it's a waste of time and money if it doesn't help you achieve your marketing objective. If getting on the front page of *The Wall Street Journal* doesn't help you make more money or increase your firm's market share, it really isn't worth the trouble.

- ✔ **You don't have to have media contacts to get big-time publicity.** You don't have to know Joe TV star to get on his TV show; you just have to come up with an idea that will interest his producer.

Promoting Your Blog

1. **Submit to blog search engines.** Beyond the traditional search engines, such as Google and Yahoo!, there are search engines and directories that track blogs exclusively and which thousands of people search every day. Submit your blog's URL to these sites for free: http://blogsearchengine.com, http://technorati.com, http://www.daypop.com, http://blogdex.net, http://w.moreover.com, http://www.yahoo.com and http://popdex.com.

2. **Ping each time a new post is published.** The blog search engines offer a system whereby you notify (or "ping") them, either manually or automatically, each time a new post appears on your blog.

3. **Use trackbacks and tags.** Look for the "trackback" link at the bottom of a post, next to the permalink and comments link. Trackbacking notifies a blogger that one of their posts has been featured on another blog. It's a non-intrusive way of letting a blogger know you are interested in what they have to say. "Tags" are categories and keywords for blog posts. You will often see keywords on the navigation bar of a blog. If you click on one of the keywords, it will show you all of the blogs that are categorized under one of those "tags." If someone finds your blog and wants to read all of the articles on a particular topic or keyword, tags make this very easy.

4. **Include a growing "blogroll."** You'll see this on the navigation bar of many blogs. It is essentially a list of favorite blogs or related websites. This is one of the ways people hop from one blog to the next and help promote each other's blogs.

5. **Participate on other people's blogs.** Devote a certain amount of your time to actively commenting on and linking to blogs that are related to your industry and topic. Focus especially on blogs that get high traffic. And be sure to include your blog address in your e-mail signature so that your blog will reach many new readers who see your post.

6. **Make it easy for readers to subscribe to your blog via RSS.** Give lots of options so people can choose the one they prefer.

For Dummies: Bestselling Book Series for Beginners

Public Relations For Dummies, 2nd Edition

Getting Editors to Print Your Press Releases

- Offer a free booklet or report. Readers love freebies, and editors love to offer them.
- Set up a hotline for people to call for information or advice.
- Stage a special or timely event or gimmick. A manufacturer of juice machines gained media coverage by holding "juicing seminars" in major cities.
- Introduce a new product or service. Many magazines have special sections featuring new products and services.
- Offer new literature. Many trade journals have sections featuring new sales literature (brochures and catalogs, for example).
- Tie in with a current trend, fad, or news issue and piggyback on that coverage.
- Sound a call to action. Ask people to participate in a boycott, for example.
- Tie your publicity to your high-visibility advertising if it received a lot of attention and created some buzz.

Using Fundamentals to Deal with Media

- **Build a personal contact file.** Keep at it until you have a list of at least 100 media contacts who know you personally and take your call when you have a story you want to publicize.
- **Follow up.** Call everyone to whom you send your press release — several times each, if necessary. Do this and you will get coverage.
- **Become the "go-to guy."** Show the press that you're the one to call for expert interviews in your particular field. For example, Alan Dershowitz is the go-to guy for law.
- **Don't limit yourself.** Broaden your outreach. A CEO reads *Forbes,* but he also watches the evening TV news.
- **Offer an exclusive.** If it's important for you to get into a particular publication, offer the editor an exclusive on the story (meaning you won't send out a press release to other media until that publication has run it first).
- **Go where the cameras already are.** Instead of trying to get media to cover your event, make noise at an event they're already covering. Domino's Pizza gets national TV coverage by bringing free pizza to the post office on April 15 to feed last-minute taxpayers standing in line.
- **Media are not interested in you or your product.** They care only whether your story will interest their readers or viewers.
- **Remember: Media are your customers.** They are buying stories, and you are selling. Meet their needs, and they will run your stories.

For Dummies: Bestselling Book Series for Beginners

Public Relations

FOR

DUMMIES®

2ND EDITION

Public Relations

FOR

DUMMIES®

2ND EDITION

by Eric Yaverbaum with Robert Bly
and Ilise Benun

Foreword by Richard Kirshenbaum

WILEY

Wiley Publishing, Inc.

Public Relations For Dummies®, 2nd Edition

Published by
Wiley Publishing, Inc.
111 River St.
Hoboken, NJ 07030-5774
www.wiley.com

WILEY

About the Authors

Eric Yaverbaum: Eric Yaverbaum co-founded Jericho Communications, a New York City–based PR firm, and served as its president for 21 years before moving to Lime Public Relations and Promotions, where he currently serves as a Managing Partner and Director of Client Services. He has more than 25 years of experience in the practice of public relations and has earned a reputation for his unique expertise in strategic media relations, crisis communications, and media training. Eric has amassed extensive experience in counseling a wide range of clients in corporate, consumer, retail, technology, and professional-services markets and in building brands such as Sony, IKEA, Domino's Pizza, TCBY, Progressive Insurance, and American Express, among many others.

Eric has acted as corporate spokesperson on behalf of dozens of clients, including Domino's Pizza, Hain-Celestial Food Group, Prince Tennis Rackets, and Camp Beverly Hills Clothing. He is a regular on the lecture circuit, speaking to professional organizations across the country on the art of public relations. He has been a guest on many national and regional television and radio programs and networks, including all of the network morning shows, *FOX & Friends,* and *Larry King Live,* to name a few.

Eric has written many articles for trade journals and daily newspapers on various topics in public relations and co-authored the best-selling book *I'll Get Back to You* (McGraw-Hill) and *Leadership Secrets of the World's Most Successful CEOs* (Dearborn). A graduate of The American University, Eric is an active member of the highly selective Young President's Organization, where he served as Chapter Chairman from 2000 to 2003 and founded the "Walk a Mile in My Shoes" initiative that lobbied the U.S. House of Representatives and U.S. Senate to pass the bill calling for increased funding for stem cell research.

Eric can be reached at:

Eric Yaverbaum
LIME public relations + promotion
160 Varick St.
New York, NY 10013
Phone: 212-337-6000
E-mail: eyaverbaum@limeprpromo.com
Web sites: www.limecomm.com
www.jerichopr.com

Robert Bly: Bob Bly is an independent copywriter specializing in traditional and Internet direct marketing. He has written lead generating sales letters, direct-mail packages, ads, scripts, Web sites, Internet direct mail, and PR materials for more than 100 clients, including IBM, AT&T, The BOC Group, EBI Medical Systems, Associated Air Freight, CoreStates Financial Corp., PSE&G, Alloy Technology, M&T Chemicals, ITT, Phillips Publishing, Nortel Networks, Fala Direct Marketing, Citrix Systems, and Grumman Corp.

Bob is the author of more than 45 books, including *The Copywriter's Handbook* (Henry Holt), *Selling Your Services* (Henry Holt), *Business-to-Business Direct Marketing* (NTC), *The Advertising Manager's Handbook* (Prentice Hall), and *Internet Direct Mail: The Complete Guide to Successful E-mail Marketing Campaigns* (NTC). His articles have appeared in *Direct, Business Marketing, Computer Decisions, Chemical Engineering, Direct Marketing, Writer's Digest, Amtrak Express, DM News, Cosmopolitan, New Jersey Monthly, City Paper,* and many other publications. A winner of the Direct Marketing Association's Gold Echo Award, Bob has presented seminars on direct marketing and related business topics to numerous organizations, including IBM, Foxboro Company, Arco Chemical, Thoroughbred Software Leaders Conference, Cambridge Technology Partners, Haht Software, and Dow Chemical.

Bob Bly can be reached at:

Bob Bly
22 E. Quackenbush Ave.
Dumont, NJ 07628
Phone: 201-385-1220
Fax: 201-385-1138
E-mail: rwbly@bly.com
Web site: www.bly.com

Ilise Benun: Ilise Benun is the founder of Marketing Mentor (www.marketing-mentor.com), as well as an author and national speaker.

Her books include *Stop Pushing Me Around: A Workplace Guide for the Timid, Shy and Less Assertive* (Career Press), *Self-Promotion Online* and *Designing Websites:// for Every Audience* (HOW Design Books). Her work has also been featured in national magazines such as *Inc.*, *Nation's Business, Self, Essence, Crains New York Business, Dynamic Graphics, iQ* (a Cisco Systems magazine), *HOW Magazine,* and *Working Woman.*

Benun publishes a free e-mail newsletter called *Quick Tips from Marketing Mentor,* which is read by 7,000+ small-business owners and has been excerpted in many other e-mail newsletters, including Bob Bly's *Direct Response Letter* and *Early to Rise.*

Benun has conducted workshops and given presentations for national and international trade organizations, including American Marketing Association; International Association of Business Communicators; International Association of Business Leaders; American Consultants League; Business Marketing Association; National Association of Women Business Owners; Family Business Council; Downtown Women's Club; American Writers and Artists Institute; American Institute of Graphic Arts; Graphic Artists Guild; NJ Creatives; Association of Registered Graphic Designers of Ontario; New York Designs, a program of LaGuardia Community College/CUNY; the NYU Entrepreneurship Summit; Editorial Freelancers Association; WorldWIT (Women in Technology); the Usability Professionals Association; the HOW Design Conference; New York Public Library; the 92nd Street Y; and ad clubs around the country.

Benun is also a board member of the Usability Professionals' Association (New York chapter) and Women in Cable and Telecommunications (New York chapter).

Benun's Marketing Mentor program is a one-on-one coaching program for small-business owners who need someone to bounce marketing ideas off and someone to be accountable to for their marketing. She started her Hoboken, New Jersey–based consulting firm in 1988 and has been self-employed for all but three years of her working life. She has a B.A. in Spanish from Tufts University.

Ilise Benun can be reached at:

Marketing Mentor
PO Box 23
Hoboken NJ 07030
Phone: 201-653-0783
Fax: 201-222-2494
Email: ilise@marketing-mentor.com
Web site: www.marketing-mentor.com

Dedication

To Wylie — you're always with us all.

Author's Acknowledgments

First and foremost, I must acknowledge that every *I* in the book should have been *we*. Nothing I have ever accomplished in my career would have been remotely possible without some of the great staff and associates I have at our offices in New York City. I thank them from the very bottom of my heart. My office is filled with superstars, but only one member of that great team got his name on the cover.

Huge thank you to Richard Kirshenbaum and Jon Bond who have inspired me to greater heights. It's an esteemed honor to be a part of the kirschenbaum bond + partners. A big thank you to Stephen Fick for making this happen. Deep appreciation to Jennifer Landers for helping to make the transition smooth. Thank you to my new partner, and one of the brightest minds I have ever met in the PR and promotions business, Claudia Strauss. Every once in a while, you meet a business associate whose chemistry with you is akin to catching lightning in a bottle. I am grateful to have the opportunity to partner with someone so gifted at this stage of my career.

Without Ilise Benun, this book never would have happened. What an absolute joy to work with such a gifted, talented, insightful, hard working writer. Every author is happy when the final manuscript is put to bed — I'm not, as I'll miss the daily collaboration with Ilise.

At Jericho and now at LIME, thanks so much to those of you who contributed time and materials to this book, and my longtime shining star Michelle Frankfort. My appreciation to Jim Anstey for his brilliant insights on buzz marketing. Thanks to some of my other incredibly valued staff who had a lot less of my time while I was working on this project, including Anne Giaritta, Andrea Lang, Cheryl Wortzel, Ursula Cuervas, Russell Schaffer, Ron D'Amico, Danielle Bignola, Courtney Cesari, Alison Desena, Caroline Vaughan, Erryyn Gallasch, Greg Mowery, Maryann Palumbo, Janine Brady, Jenna Rosen, Jennifer Rabinowitz, Juliette Jacovidis, Meghan Forbes, Nataki Reese, Nelly Cruz, Shauri Wu, Shoshana Kraus, Felicitas Pardo, Christian Hodgkinson, Gabe Banner, Jenna Marrone, Sean Evans, Yelena Shister, Rachel Wiese and Daniel Teboul. I wish I could list everyone!

Thanks so much to my agent, Lisa Queen, who made sure my career with the good folks at Wiley continued through the second edition of this book. And deep appreciation for my long relationship with Bob Diforio and most importantly, for introducing me to Ilise.

Always a big thank-you for never-ending support to my parents, Harry and Gayle Yaverbaum; to Dana, David, Remy, and Logan Zais; Lori and Michael Berman; Bernie, Noreen, Craig, and Merrill Nisker; Freda and Bessie, Mona and Connie.

Last but far from least, my never-ending appreciation and gratitude to the "Best Friends Club," my greatest and most fulfilling joy in life — my wife, Suri, and kids, Cole and Jace, who gave me up yet again for the extra hours I put in while I rewrote the book.

Ilise and I would like to thank the editorial and production teams at Wiley Publishing for doing the hard work of turning a draft into an acceptable manuscript, and a manuscript into a published book. Their dedicated effort and attention to detail showed us why the *For Dummies* series is so spectacularly successful. Of these folks, we'd like to single out our project editors, Jennifer Connolly and Kristin DeMint, whose knowledge and insight in book writing improved the text as we incorporated their ideas in our revisions. And of course, thanks so much to Kathy Cox for ensuring that *Public Relations For Dummies* lived on and was updated for a whole new group of PR practitioners.

Publisher's Acknowledgments

We're proud of this book; please send us your comments through our Dummies online registration form located at www.dummies.com/register/.

Some of the people who helped bring this book to market include the following:

Acquisitions, Editorial, and Media Development

Project Editor: Jennifer Connolly, Kristin DeMint

(Previous Edition: Norm Cramptom)

Acquisitions Editor: Kathy Cox

Copy Editor: Elizabeth Kuball

Technical Editor: Celia Rocks

Editorial Manager: Michelle Hacker

Editorial Supervisor: Carmen Krikorian

Editorial Assistant: Hanna Scott, David Lutton

Cartoons: Rich Tennant (www.the5thwave.com)

Composition

Project Coordinator: Patrick Redmond

Layout and Graphics: Carl G. Byers, Jonelle Burns, Andrea Dahl, Denny Hager, Joyce Haughey, Stephanie D. Jumper, Lynsey Osborn, Heather Ryan

Proofreaders: Jessica Kramer, Techbooks

Indexer: Techbooks

Publishing and Editorial for Consumer Dummies

Diane Graves Steele, Vice President and Publisher, Consumer Dummies

Joyce Pepple, Acquisitions Director, Consumer Dummies

Kristin A. Cocks, Product Development Director, Consumer Dummies

Michael Spring, Vice President and Publisher, Travel

Kelly Regan, Editorial Director, Travel

Publishing for Technology Dummies

Andy Cummings, Vice President and Publisher, Dummies Technology/General User

Composition Services

Gerry Fahey, Vice President of Production Services

Debbie Stailey, Director of Composition Services

Contents at a Glance

Table of Contents

Foreword

Many years ago, when Jon Bond and I first started our agency, Kirshenbaum Bond & Partners, we launched our agency with one simple ad for Kenneth Cole that stated "Imelda Marcos bought 2700 pairs of shoes. She could have at least had the courtesy to buy a pair of ours." The resulting press and word of mouth taught us an important lesson early on: Create attention. Create a story that captures the public's interest and it could translate into millions of dollars of free press for your client or your own brand. This simple formula helped put our client and agency on the map to fame and fortune. And who can complain about that?

We actually invented a term called *the multiplier effect* because the resulting press attention actually multiplied the client's ad budget, making a few million look ten times larger.

While some, we've heard, argue the PR is all about finding a gimmick, there's nothing gimmicky about creating a famous brand, helping to mold a positive image, or resulting dollars to the bottom line. However, generally good PR is much, much more than just coming up with a one-shot story. Having a proper PR plan, doing targeted PR outreach, and having good press relations can make or break a company's image in the long run.

In fact, we were such big believers in the power of PR that in addition to our ad agency, we also created a PR & Promotions company called LIME, which has become a well-known PR practitioner who always delivers on out-of-the-box PR events and strategies.

When my dear friend and colleague, Eric Yaverbaum, asked me to write a foreword for this book, I was delighted to help him — not only because he's smart, charming, and has run a terribly successful PR business for the last 20 years, but because it's good PR for me and KBP as well.

In fact, Public Relations at its core is exactly that, the relations you or your company have with the public. Hopefully, I have in a few short paragraphs helped relate to you the important ad power of PR. After all, if you've ever bought a pair of Kenneth Cole shoes, a Coach bag, drank a Snapple or a glass of Moet & Chandon, have shopped at Target, used a Citibank American Advantage Card, used Jergens to keep your skin beautiful or Ban deodorant to keep you smelling good, had a sip of Hennessy or fed your cat Meow Mix or ever flown on Song Airlines, you've most likely seen or heard some of our potent PR strategies and advertising. Enjoy this work and remember my golden rule:

The only bad PR is the PR you don't control.

Richard Kirshenbaum
Co-Chairman
Kirshenbaum Bond + Partners

Introduction

*W*hoever you are, wherever you are, public relations makes a difference in your life — believe it or not.

If you're a small-business owner or manager or a wannabe entrepreneur, PR helps level the playing field between you and your bigger, wealthier competitors. You may not be able to afford a 60-second commercial during the Super Bowl, but if you offer a free session at your health club to people who come in *during* the Super Bowl, you can get front-page publicity based on your PR event.

If you're a corporate manager or executive, you've seen ad budgets decline while ad costs skyrocket. With an effective public relations program, you can communicate with your target market *more* often, not less, without increasing ad spending.

And if you're a consumer, public relations plays a role in your education and the formation of your opinions without your even being aware of it. Did you know that half or more of everything you read, see, and hear in the media was put there through the actions of a public relations manager or a PR firm? PR has an enormous effect on the information you get every day of your life.

I wrote *Public Relations For Dummies,* 2nd Edition, precisely because I know that there is no magic to PR and that do-it-yourself is not only viable but also sensible for many businesses. What Wilford Brimley says about Quaker Oats applies equally to doing your own PR for many readers of this book: "It's the right thing to do." And just as eating Quaker Oats is "the right thing to do" when it comes to nutrition at breakfast, *Public Relations For Dummies,* 2nd Edition, shows all you PR do-it-yourselfers out there "the right way to do it."

The key to getting media coverage is to offer them a story that they can't resist. The two key elements are an understanding of the marketing message and the ability to think creatively in terms of PR campaigns. You already understand your business's market, and I am convinced that, with enough practice, almost anyone can learn to think more creatively. The mechanics of PR — and a lot of sample campaigns to inspire you — are laid out in this book. So you already have everything you need to do your own PR, and you don't need to hire an agency if you don't want to.

About This Book

You can think of *Public Relations For Dummies,* 2nd Edition, as "your PR agency in a box." This book gives you all the tools you need to do your own PR — ideas, checklists, forms, documents, and resources — are in your hands right now, presented in a clear, easy-to-use package. With this book, you can get your product or service featured whenever and wherever you want — in newspapers, magazines, and trade journals; on TV, radio, and the Web — so that people find out about what you are offering and come to you to buy it. The result? More fame, recognition, awareness, inquiries, orders, sales — and money!

Can you do your own PR? Yes. Thousands of small- and medium-sized businesses conduct very successful PR campaigns every day, for pennies on the dollar compared to what they'd pay for a similar amount of advertising. Large corporations also are doing an increasing amount of PR in-house. This book is written to help you succeed on your own. You don't need me, my PR agency, or any other PR agency, if you're willing to put in the effort and follow the simple guidelines presented in *Public Relations For Dummies,* 2nd Edition.

You can read through *Public Relations For Dummies,* 2nd Edition, start to finish, or you can start with the chapters that interest you most. It's up to you.

If you want to see quick, immediate results, go to Chapter 8. Follow the press-release strategies presented there, and write a release for your own product following the sample in the chapter. Then distribute the press release to the media by using one of the publicity outlet resources listed in the Appendix, and follow up according to the guidelines in Chapters 11 and 12. The press release is one of the fastest, easiest techniques in this book, and you'll see results fast. I like that because you receive tangible proof that PR works — in the form of press clippings.

My hope is that your newfound enthusiasm for the PR process spurs you to try more and more of the ideas and strategies presented throughout *Public Relations For Dummies,* 2nd Edition. When you do, you'll magnify your results, make your company famous, and get more business than you can handle. What a nice problem to have!

Conventions Used in This Book

To make navigating this book easier, I use the following conventions:

- ✔ *Italic* text emphasizes and highlights new words and terms that I define in the text.
- ✔ **Boldfaced** text indicates keywords in bulleted lists or the action parts of numbered steps.

✔ Monofont is used for Web addresses.

✔ Sidebars are shaded gray boxes that contain text that's interesting to know but not necessarily critical to your understanding of the chapter or topic.

Foolish Assumptions

Whether you want to put out a single press release to announce your grand opening, or plan an ongoing PR campaign, I made the following assumptions about you as I wrote this book:

✔ You may plan on keeping your product name in the public eye for many years to come through your own efforts.

✔ You may prefer to have someone do your PR for you.

✔ You may have a big budget and special contacts with the media.

✔ You may have a special budget and no contacts with the media.

✔ You may have little or no experience.

✔ You may have substantial experience.

✔ You have a telephone, a desk, a word processor, and your wits — this book supplies most of the rest or tells you where to get it.

How This Book Is Organized

The *For Dummies* series was conceived as books for smart people who are absolute beginners, and that's the approach I use in *Public Relations For Dummies,* 2nd Edition. Part I covers the basics. Part II discusses the process we use to create successful PR campaigns. Part III covers the PR materials you need and how to create them. In Part IV, you discover how to work with the media to get your material published. Part V gives you power techniques for getting the media to notice and cover you. And Part VI is a collection of useful tips. The appendix gives you a list of useful resources.

A detailed breakdown of each part follows.

Part 1: PR: What It Is, How It Works

Everybody has heard of PR but surprisingly few people have a clear picture of what it really is and what it involves. Part I supplies the big-picture overview of the public relations field. Chapter 1 defines what public relations is and how it fits into an overall marketing campaign. Chapter 2 examines PR uses and applications, answering the questions "Who needs PR?" and "How can it benefit me and my company?" Chapter 3 deals with the "make or buy" issue: Should you always do your own PR, or does it ever make sense to hire outside help? It also covers the alternatives available (PR firms, ad agencies, graphic design services, and freelancers), including where to find them and how to evaluate and hire them.

Part II: Brainstorming and Thinking Creatively

PR is largely a business of creative ideas, and this part shows you how to think more creatively about PR and come up with breakthrough ideas that make your product or service stand out and get media attention. In Chapter 4, I show you how to set up your own in-house PR capabilities, so you can do just what the big PR agencies do, only without the big PR agency bills. Chapter 5 gives you techniques for producing PR ideas. Chapter 6 is my arsenal of PR "weapons" — tactics used with extraordinary success to publicize my firm's clients.

Part III: Putting the Wheels in Motion

Sitting around cooking up ideas for PR campaigns is fun, but a lot of hard work is involved in turning the plans into a working campaign that gets your name in the papers and your company on the evening news in a favorable light. Chapter 7 covers the details of setting up that workhorse of PR programs, the company newsletter. In Chapter 8, you see how to churn out press releases and media kits. Chapter 9 explores writing and placing feature articles. And Chapter 10 shows you how to deliver your message in person with confidence and persuasiveness at interviews, press conferences, media tours, and other presentations.

Part IV: Choosing the Right Medium for Your Message

The ideas you come up with and the PR materials you produce won't generate one thin dime of extra revenues or profits if you don't get the media to run them. Part IV shows you how to pitch your ideas to the media so that you get the coverage you want. Chapters 11 and 12 give you a crash course on how to deal with media types effectively. Chapters 13 through 17 focus on specific media: radio, TV, print, the Internet, and new technology like blogs, webcasting, and podcasting.

Part V: Creating Buzz

If things about your business aren't exciting enough to get the media's attention, you have to stir things up a bit — to create "buzz," as PR professionals are fond of saying. Chapter 18 gives you tips on getting the most from buzz marketing. Chapter 19 shows how to create events that generate tons of free publicity for you and your organization. Chapter 20 shows you how to exploit events and activities originated by others. Chapter 21 covers how to handle events when things don't go your way and a crisis pops up, whether it's a toxic spill at your plant or a defect in your product. Chapter 22 suggests ways to monitor and measure PR results so that you can determine the return on your PR investment.

Part VI: The Part of Tens

Here you can find a large amount of very useful little items, arranged in groups of ten: the ten greatest PR coups of all time (Chapter 23); the top ten PR myths debunked (Chapter 24); ten reasons for doing PR (Chapter 25); the ten things you should never do in the quest for more publicity because they're illegal, unethical, immoral, or in the long run unproductive (Chapter 26); and ten steps to writing better PR materials (Chapter 27).

Appendix

Lots of resources exist to help you with your do-it-yourself PR efforts, and this section puts them at your fingertips. The appendix tells you all about the dozens of resources to aid you in your PR efforts.

Icons Used in This Book

As if this book weren't already easy to use, I also include some icons that flag different pieces of information for you.

The Win/Win Medal highlights best practices — things you should regularly do as a PR practitioner.

The bomb warns you about potential mistakes you want to avoid.

The string around the finger marks important items you don't want to forget.

This icon is a flag for special tips and insights.

The zinger gives you tricks and twists that you may not find in standard PR texts.

Where to Go from Here

You may use *Public Relations For Dummies,* 2nd Edition, to create the one or two PR programs you want to do, execute them, and get great results — and that may be it. That's okay, and it's the beauty of PR. With its low cost and the ease with which you can do your own PR without professional help, even a single PR effort can generate tremendous returns, paying back your investment in this kit a hundred times over.

But I hope you aggressively embrace and pursue the many PR opportunities available to your organization on a regular basis. Why pay the media a fortune every time you want them to carry your message with a paid advertisement, when in essence you can get them to do all your advertising for you absolutely free?

The bottom line: PR can communicate your company's message and help you achieve your marketing objectives at a fraction of the cost of paid advertising. Any business or organization that sells or markets but doesn't take advantage of the incredible leverage of free publicity is pouring marketing dollars down the drain. But it's never too late to start. So dip into *Public Relations For Dummies,* 2nd Edition, put the ideas to work, make your organization or product famous, and get rich. If you become a millionaire or celebrity in the process, more power to you!

Part I

PR: What It Is, How It Works

The 5th Wave   By Rich Tennant

"I think I know what your problem is. Not enough PR."

In this part . . .

Many people have heard of public relations but very few people know what it actually means. Part 1 gives you the umbrella perspective of the industry. Chapter 1 tells you the role of public relations in the overall marketing campaign. In Chapter 2, gives you clear guidelines to establish your goals and the realities of budgeting. And in Chapter 3, we provide you with guidelines and insights so you can determine whether it makes sense for you to do your own PR or hire someone to help (and what the alternatives are if you decide to hire help).

Chapter 1

The Power of PR

*W*hen I was a young man of 24 and almost a complete beginner at public relations, I got on the front page of *USA Today* with a feature story about the baseball strike and a color photograph of my partner and myself. That piece put my then-fledgling PR firm on the map, so to speak, and helped advance my career in the PR business.

At the time, no one had heard of my agency or me, and I had no press contacts with *USA Today* — or any other major media. That lack of contacts could easily have become a major stumbling block for our PR firm in getting new clients: The agency did good work, but larger corporate prospects would naturally — and in my opinion, naively — ask, "Who are your key media contacts?" When I confessed that I didn't know the editor in chief of the *New York Times* and wasn't invited to Oprah's dinner parties, potential clients could have easily lost interest and chosen other firms. This problem was one I wanted to solve as quickly as possible.

So how did I get *USA Today* to put my picture on the cover? At the time, a Major League Baseball strike was the news of the day. My partner and I sent out a press announcement and called the media to announce that we had formed a new organization, called Strike Back, to protest the baseball strike. The premise was simple: For every day the Major League players refused to play, we would boycott their games for one day when the players did return to work.

Did I do this for the love of the game? Yes — partially. But it certainly wasn't lost on me that turning ourselves into a national news story would (1) demonstrate the type of PR we practice, (2) showcase our ability to get media exposure, and (3) attract new business. *USA Today* was the first big media placement for my agency, and it got potential clients to pay attention to the new kids on the PR block.

This anecdote illustrates three basic PR principles that form the core of our agency philosophy and the how-to PR techniques in this book:

- ✔ **You have to be different.** The media and the public are drowning in data but starved for amusement. Conventional publicity strategies get lost in the noise. You have to find a creative way to stand out from the crowd and get noticed — and Strike Back is just one of dozens of examples I show you throughout this book.

- ✔ **Getting publicity is fun, but it's a waste of time and money if it doesn't help you achieve your marketing objective.** If getting on the front page of the *Wall Street Journal* doesn't help you make more money or increase your firm's market share, is it really worth the trouble? In the case of Strike Back, the campaign did achieve a specific objective: getting corporate PR clients to take our PR firm seriously and hire us, despite the fact that we had fewer clients, fewer years of experience, and a fraction of the media contacts of the big PR firms.

- ✔ **You don't have to have media contacts to get big-time publicity.** (Strike Back certainly helped us communicate this principle to our own potential clients!) A creative idea, a clear marketing goal, and effective implementation are what count. You don't have to know Joe TV Star to get on his TV show; you just have to come up with an idea that will interest his producer. So what if you're a small business and you don't have time to schmooze the press? In *Public Relations For Dummies,* 2nd Edition, you find out how to get all the publicity you need to achieve your marketing objectives — without making public relations your full-time job.

Who Needs PR, Anyway?

If you have all the business you will ever want and are rich beyond the dreams of avarice, you may not need public relations.

A crisis is an obvious exception. A lot of my work as a PR professional is in response to clients who have an immediate PR crisis to solve, like a tainted shipment of food products or a toy posing an unexpected safety risk to children because of a product defect. So in some cases, even if your sales are skyrocketing and you don't need to promote yourself, you may want to engage in PR activities to avoid negative publicity or correct any bad press that comes your way. (See Chapter 21 for crisis management.) Other reasons a business or person may want to use PR are

- ✔ To grow the business
- ✔ To make more money
- ✔ To increase sales

Doctors, lawyers, dentists, chiropractors, therapists, and other professionals can promote their practices with public relations. PR is used with virtually every product category, from construction equipment and industrial goods to food, health and beauty products, healthcare, travel, tourism, real estate, and investments. In high-tech industries, everyone from hardware manufacturers to software companies, e-commerce Web sites, and service providers has benefited enormously from the power of PR.

So one perspective of PR concerns a person's goals, where she is now, and where she wants to be. Good PR can turn marginal businesses into profitable ones and ordinary folks into millionaires.

Another perspective of PR has to do with resources. If a business has an advertising budget that approaches infinity (or say, 20 million dollars or more) and it won't miss the money if it's spent, the business can probably get its message across without relying on the subtler medium of PR. That doesn't mean it *shouldn't* use PR as part of its marketing mix, however: Many clients find that a relatively modest investment in PR greatly extends the reach of their total promotional program.

And cost, frankly, is one of the great appeals of PR to both small businesses and large corporations alike. Small businesses with limited budgets simply can't come close to matching the ad budgets of larger competitors. PR can help them level the playing field and get the same or better promotional bang for a lot fewer bucks.

As for the big corporations, if you work for one, you know that getting more money in the marketing budget is always an uphill battle. With PR, you can achieve the objectives senior managers want even if they don't give you the money you think you need to do it.

Beyond Stunts: The Real Value of PR

It's fun to see stunts like Calvin Klein's models swimming in a perfume bottle in Times Square and hot products like the iPod get truckloads of front-page and prime time coverage. Obviously, PR can work wonders for those who seek publicity for publicity's sake. (See Chapter 19 for more on staging publicity events.)

Actually, that's the easy part of public relations. The real value of PR is using it to solve a real-life marketing situation for a real product, service, organization, brand, or image. PR can work for any and every industry, from florists to funeral directors, software to soft ice cream. Any organization or individual with a message to deliver or a goal to achieve can benefit from a PR effort. You don't even need a license or special certification to practice PR — this book shows you how.

You don't need a creative or unusual product to gain publicity; you just need a creative idea that meets two criteria:

- ✔ It's newsworthy.
- ✔ It communicates the marketing message.

Creative PR, with proper execution, can work wonders for manufacturers, wholesalers, distributors, retailers, resellers, agents, service companies, and professional practices in any industry. I delve into marketing messages in detail in Part II of this book, but here's a quick example.

British Knights wanted a way to sell more of its sneakers to kids. As a seasonal promotion, the company sent out press releases announcing an unusual "Summer Exchange" program: Parents who were concerned that their kids were spending too much time indoors watching TV and playing video games, rather than getting wholesome exercise playing outdoors, could mail British Knights their TV remote control and receive in return a brand-new pair of British Knight sneakers. (The remote control was mailed back to participants with the sneakers at the end of the summer.)

In another PR campaign, also successful, British Knights sponsored a World's Smelliest Socks Contest. The top ten winners — individuals who sent in the stinkiest socks — won free British Knights sneakers for three years.

Stinky socks? Joseph J. Kelley, a speechwriter for President Dwight Eisenhower, once said, "There is a kernel of interest in everything God created." How true! Every product or service, no matter how mundane, contains a PR hook or angle if you think creatively. Even sneakers.

Make a graph of your sales by week. If the graph is smooth and your sales are consistent, your marketing is probably steady and continual. But if the sales curve has peaks and valleys, you may need to increase the frequency of marketing communications to smooth out the bumps and eliminate the lows. PR is perhaps the best means of getting your message out on a continual basis and eliminating periodic sales slumps.

The Relationship between PR and the Media

Publicity certainly is free advertising, but it's also legitimate news. By alerting the media to newsworthy events, products, services, and people, you can prompt an editor to cover everything from the opening of a new restaurant to the publication of a new catalog, from the techniques of an acupuncturist to the makings of a new trend.

In the early days of public relations, many PR practitioners held the belief that their job was to get the client's name in the papers as prominently and frequently as they could. George M. Cohan, the famous composer, knew how PR worked. "I don't care what they [the media] call me," he said, "so long as they mention my name." Actress Katharine Hepburn gave that idea a twist, remarking, "I don't care what is written about me so long as it isn't true."

A more recent and, to my mind, relevant definition states, "Public relations is the business of creating public opinion for private advantage." At my PR agency, Jericho Communications, we think of PR as "using the media to achieve a client's marketing objective." By practicing what you find in this book, you can use PR to communicate your message, build your image, motivate desired behavior, and generate greater revenues and profits.

Instead of putting up signs, sending banner ads across people's computer screens, or holding sales rallies, PR practitioners persuade the media to publish and distribute stories, articles, news, and information that promotes our clients' goals — whether it's to attract venture capital to a dot-com start-up or help Domino's Pizza sell more pizzas. I have sometimes cynically told new clients that we exploit the media on their behalf. But strictly speaking, that isn't true, because it's the media — not the publicist — who is the final judge of what appears in print or on the air.

More accurately, public relations is, at its best, a win-win partnership among publicists, the clients whose products they promote, and journalists. Here's how that partnership works:

The journalists have too much to do and not enough time to do it. Every day they must fill pages or airtime with stories that interest, entertain, and inform their readership, viewers, or listeners. The deadlines are too tight, and the editors and reporters are overworked.

The publicists step in and offer assistance by providing what journalists need — ideas, information, interviews, and even ready-made stories — in abundant supply and absolutely free. The media choose from among the press releases, use them as is or reworked, and discard the rest — with no cost or obligation to the publicists who supply the releases. The media can fill their pages and airtime, meet deadlines, keep their audiences happy and entertained, and thereby deliver a large audience to the advertisers. (To find out how to write a press release that the media will use, see Chapter 8.)

Publicity Plus: The Many Components of PR

Public relations is more than just pitching stories to the media or mailing out press releases. The PR umbrella covers a number of related activities, all of which are concerned with communicating specific messages to specific target audiences. If you're the PR person at ABC Enterprises, you're responsible for managing communications between your company and your public.

The label *public relations* typically encompasses the following:

- **Research:** You have to thoroughly understand not only your company but also your customers and potential customers. What do you offer that is unique or special? What are customers looking for? And how well do you fill those needs? Market research and an internal company audit are the starting points of successful PR campaigns. For more on the research and audit processes, see Chapter 2.

- **Strategic planning:** Define each target audience, your marketing objectives for that group, and the messages you must communicate in support of those marketing objectives. Chapter 2 outlines this planning process.

- **Publicity:** For most small businesses, the central public relations activity is publicity — getting visibility for your products, the company, and the owners in print and broadcast media. I define *publicity* as "proactive management and placement of information in the media used to protect and enhance a brand or reputation." Simply put, this means getting ink and airtime. (See Chapters 13 through 19.)

- **Community relations:** Recently, I saw a TV news report about local citizens protesting a big retail chain that wanted to build a store in their town, because it would wipe out a popular wooded area with a pond. That chain has a community relations problem in that town, and the PR professional's job is to find a favorable solution that will get the store built while preserving the store's goodwill with the citizens.

- **Government relations:** Community relations often involves relations with the local government, and PR people are often called upon to help companies improve their relationships with local, state, federal, and even foreign governments.

- **Internal relations:** Employees are the internal audience. With the unemployment rate at an all-time low, good employees are hard to find, and a good public relations program job can help improve loyalty and retain more of them.

- **Investor relations:** With the incredible stock market volatility of 2000, or more recently, the events of September 11, 2001, and the hurricanes in 2005, we've all seen how emotion and public perception have the power to send stock prices soaring or plummeting. Investor relations is the aspect of PR that communicates the company story to stock analysts and other financial professionals.

✔ **Stakeholder relations:** A *stakeholder* is anyone or any organization that holds a stake in how well your company performs. A key vendor is a stakeholder; rumors that you are financially shaky may cause them to restrict your credit terms. Other key stakeholders can include top consultants, board members, your bank, suppliers, sales representatives, distributors, and industry gurus.

✔ **Charitable causes:** When a company gives to charity, it wants to help the cause, but it also wants to be recognized for its contribution. PR specialists can help you get maximum publicity and goodwill from the time, effort, and funds you donate.

✔ **Communications training:** In large corporations, PR specialists may spend a lot of time coaching senior executives in dealing with the media and other communications skills. The specialists may also advise the executives on strategy for day-to-day PR as well as PR crises.

What PR Is Not

Public relations is a business tool that often gets confused with marketing and advertising, two related but very distinct activities. In the following sections, I clear up the differences for you.

Marketing: The four Ps

Marketing is typically defined by the Four Ps — product, price, place (channels of distribution), and promotion.

✔ **Product** refers to the physical product and its packaging. With many products — fruit juice, for instance — the packaging is a key product differentiator: Juice boxes are a separate product category from frozen concentrate. Service can also be an integral part of a product. For example, L.L. Bean has gained widespread fame publicizing its lifetime guarantee on everything it sells.

✔ **Price** is what you charge for the product.

✔ **Place** refers to channels of distribution — in other words, where the product is sold. Do you sell at a retail store or on a Web site? Do customers buy the product directly from you or through an agent or distributor?

✔ **Promotion** consists of advertising, sales promotion, personal selling, and, of course, public relations.

So as you can see, public relations is a part of promotion under the larger umbrella of marketing.

Paying for advertising while PR is (practically) free

Several characteristics separate public relations from advertising, but one fundamental difference is this: Advertising is paid; public relations is free. When you run an advertisement for your company, you pay for the space; when your press release prompts a newspaper to write an article about your company, you don't pay for that coverage.

Of course, PR is not absolutely free of cost. Your public relations staff member or your outside PR agency has to be paid for services. But compared to the megadollars of advertising campaigns, PR is quite a bargain. Many small- and medium-size businesses that can afford only limited advertising (with limited results) can do much more PR — and get better results — on a fraction of the budget they'd spend on paid advertising.

So the difference in cost is fundamental. But another distinction between PR and advertising gets less attention, though I think it's equally important: Advertising is clearly identified in the media as a paid promotion — readers and viewers know that it is a promotional message paid for by a sponsor. Publicity, by comparison, is not identified as a paid promotion. Even though a story about a product or organization may have resulted from a publicity campaign, the article or report never acknowledges that fact. (For instance, you almost never see an article in a newspaper or a magazine say, "According to a press release sent by the PR department of So-and-So Corporation. . . .")

Thanks for the lousy press coverage!

Clergymen across the United States denounced actress Sarah Bernhardt (1844–1923) as the "whore of Babylon," which, much to their dismay, generated massive attendance at her performances. After a Chicago bishop delivered a particularly critical speech against Bernhardt, which was widely reported in the press, the actress sent him a $200 check along with the following note, as recounted by Clifton Fadiman in *The Little Brown Book of Anecdotes:* "I am accustomed, when I bring an attraction to your town, to spend $400 on advertising. As you have done half the advertising for me, I enclose $200 for your parish."

Four other key differences between PR and advertising are

- ✔ Control
- ✔ Repetition
- ✔ Credibility
- ✔ Attractiveness

Sometimes these distinctions mean an advantage for PR, sometimes not. In the following sections, I go into more detail on each of these differences.

Control

When you advertise, you have almost total control over the content, format, timing, and size of your message. You specify how big your ad is and when it runs. You write the copy and design the layout, and your material appears exactly as you created it. With public relations, on the other hand, you have almost no control over the content, format, timing, and size of your message as it appears in the media. You can write whatever you want in your press release, but you can't dictate to the newspaper how it is printed or used, nor can you review or approve any changes made. You provide the press with written materials that they use (or don't use) in any way they see fit. Your press release may appear verbatim in one magazine but may be rewritten almost beyond recognition in another. One industry trade journal may write a cover story based on your material; another may not publish it at all.

Repetition

Advertising is repeatable; PR is not. The same advertisement can be repeated as many times as you want in a given publication; the same TV commercial can be broadcast night after night. With PR, a media source is going to run a given press release or cover a publicity event only *once*. To get covered again, you have to provide the media with a new story, or at least come up with a different angle or new spin on the old topic.

Credibility

Consumers are skeptical of advertising. They tend not to believe the claims made in advertising — at least that's what many consumers say. Many people believe that if your service or product is as good as you say it is, you don't need to advertise. On the other hand, people tend to take at face value what they hear on radio, see on TV, or read in the paper. They believe that if the newspaper printed it, it must be true. Because publicity is promotion in the guise of editorial, feature, or news material, people do not identify it as promotion and are, therefore, not skeptical of it; indeed, they believe it.

In many instances, media coverage of your event or story can appear to the public to be media endorsement of your organization or product — for example, a favorable story about your charity on the evening news or a good review of your software package in a computer magazine. What's more, comments or claims that would sound conceited, self-serving, and not credible if you said them about yourself in an ad seem complimentary, flattering, and impressive when the media say them about you.

Attractiveness

Publicity must have an *angle* — that is, a hook or theme that engages an editor's attention — in order for it to have a decent chance of being noticed, read, and used. Therefore, it must appeal to editors and program managers, as well as to the consumers (your sales prospects and the people who read the magazine or listen to the radio show).

An ad has to appeal to only one audience: your sales prospects. You don't care whether the media like or are interested in the ad, because they have already agreed to run it in exchange for a given amount of money.

Key Audiences PR Can Reach

How far does PR reach? Public relations can connect you with anyone who reads a publication, listens to radio, watches TV, or rides the Internet — in short, anyone who is exposed to the media, which in the United States means just about everyone.

PR, therefore, has the broadest reach of perhaps any element of the marketing mix. Web sites and banner ads reach only those people connected to the Internet, which amazingly is fewer than 5 percent of the world's population. Direct mail reaches only people whose names are on mailing lists, and in many countries, mailing lists are not available for rental.

But almost everyone, everywhere, reads a newspaper or magazine, or watches TV. That's why PR is effective at targeting both business and consumer audiences. The best publicity outlets for reaching consumers are radio, television, newspapers, and consumer magazines. For business, use these as well as business magazines, associations, and the Internet. If you want to appeal to a particular industry or profession, target the trade publications they read.

I like to hit a broad target, because you never know exactly what your prospect may be reading. Once, when I was with the CEO of a large corporation, I was amazed to see that when he had a copy of *USA Today,* he went to the Life section first and the Money section last — and often he never got around to reading the Money section. I like to "surround" my prospect by being in all the media he is likely to see; that way, I have a better chance of getting my message to him with greater frequency and repetition.

Employees, of course, are a well-defined audience and reachable at any time. One of the best PR vehicles for employee communication is a company magazine or newsletter. Some large corporations even have in-house TV stations that broadcast the latest company news and information via closed-circuit TV.

Investors and members of the financial community are an important PR audience for publicly traded corporations, and press releases are the way to reach them, says *Business Week*. "Once a relatively mundane communication device, a press release now has the might to dramatically drive the price of a stock," says the respected business magazine. (Underscoring the power of press releases, the Securities and Exchange Commission has even sued companies for posting fake press releases containing recommendations to buy their stock.)

Again, PR's high credibility takes the credit. The financial community and potential buyers are much more apt to believe and act upon a column in the *Wall Street Journal* than yet another image advertisement by a dot-com company. And a survey by the Public Relations Society of America shows that investors rate a story in a financial or business newspaper as second only to a company's own annual report (also a PR vehicle) when it comes to credibility.

The Changing Role of PR in the Marketing Mix Today

The public relations industry is evolving, driven by new market realities. PR is finally taking a step forward, stretching its capabilities and its role in the overall marketing mix that consists of PR, advertising, Internet marketing, direct marketing, and sales promotion.

From the day I started my PR firm in 1985, I have believed that public relations can play a greater role in clients' good fortune than tradition dictates. The reason my agency has delivered so much media exposure to clients is that I'm not afraid to break the "rules" of traditional PR, which is more worried about churning out paper (for example, routine press releases such as "Joe Smith Appointed Product Manager") than contributing to the bottom line. While other marketing genres have shown how to invent successful new ways to do business, many public relations professionals have seemed to care more about following rules. And let's face it: Same-old same-old doesn't get anyone's audience excited.

Where public relations is routine, frankly, I blame PR professionals who are too willing to accept a back seat for the successes of their art. In fairness, I should say that some of them have it tough, receiving very little credit for anything good and all the blame for everything that goes wrong at a company. And that being the case, when PR executives grow averse to risk and creativity you can chalk it up to human nature. Going beyond status quo simply holds nothing for them. The bad part is they often give their outside PR counselors very little room to move, too.

But today, in the fast-paced e-commerce world — where online and offline clients must reach out to grab their target audiences and the investor community — public relations has risen in importance. With this new importance comes more freedom. All of a sudden, the value of creative public relations is apparent. The ability to use what I consider the most credible form of marketing in ways that extend way past the standard is now revered.

So, for the first time in a long time, PR practitioners who can do more than just communicate to an audience — people who can create an emotional effect that *motivates* an audience — are free to ply their craft to its fullest potential.

As you can see, I'm passionate about PR. You're using this book because — just maybe — you're passionate about public relations, too. My goal is to give you all the tools you need to turn that passion into results.

Assessing Your Situation: How to Tell When PR Is the Missing (Or Weak) Ingredient

What are the telltale signs that PR is the weak point in your company's marketing communications chain? Ask yourself the following questions, and if you answer yes to any of them, I highly recommend that you read through this book and focus for a bit on getting your PR department in shape.

✔ **Do your competitors seem to get all the exposure in newspapers, magazines, and the trade press? Are you consistently left out of industry roundups, product listings, and vendor resource guides?** Maybe the press omits you because they don't know about you. Maybe it's time to let them know. (See Chapter 6 for ideas about which tactics to use to get the word out.)

✔ **Do your mailings unleash a stampede of responses? Is your Web site choked with traffic?** PR works hand in hand with other kinds of promotions. The better your PR visibility, the more your other marketing communications efforts will pull in responses. Low response rates may not be the result of a bad ad or mailer. That deafening silence could mean that the people reading your ad or receiving your mailing have never heard of you. (See the overview of a PR plan in Chapter 2.)

✔ **Do your people in the field find it easy or hard to get deals done (or doors opened)? Do they hear "I've never heard of your company" from prospects?** Good PR establishes your firm as a player in the prospect's mind before the salesperson calls. If you don't have good PR, your people may meet with increased resistance. (Placing feature articles is great for wide exposure. Find out how in Chapter 9.)

✔ **Do your vendors list you as one of their customers?** If not, maybe they don't think your name is big enough to impress other potential customers. That's a sign you need to strengthen your corporate brand in the marketplace. (And public speaking will help you do that. Check out Chapter 10.)

✔ **If you're a public company, do major brokerages follow your stock?** When you tell your company story to analysts, do they eagerly take notes or stare at you with blank looks? When Wall Street doesn't understand the value in your company, the investor relations side of PR can help fix the problem. (See Chapter 11 for more ideas about getting your message out.)

✔ **Do audiences see your company the way you are today or the way you want to become tomorrow?** Or do they see you as you used to be? PR can help to change your image in the marketplace. (Using the newest media tools can bolster your image. You find out which ones to focus on in Chapter 17.)

✔ **Do headhunters try to woo you away to other companies?** Especially in high-tech industries, headhunters raid the hot companies first. You don't want headhunters recruiting your employees (unless it's you and the pay is fantastic!), but you do want to be considered a hot company, don't you? (See Chapter 23.)

Cold-call classic

A classic McGraw-Hill ad shows a prospective customer sitting in a chair, staring straight at the camera and saying, "I don't know you, I don't know your company, I don't know your product. Now — what is it you wanted to sell me?" Better visibility through public relations can warm up cold prospects like this one, making the salesperson's job much easier.

Chapter 2

X-Raying the PR Process

....

In This Chapter

▶ Starting out with research and plan objectives

▶ Establishing a PR plan and budget

▶ Making the most of essential PR elements

▶ Taking steps toward creative and successful promotions

▶ Figuring out if your PR ideas will work

▶ Factoring in time and chance

....

The key to good public relations creative thought is understanding that it's more than pulling good ideas out of the air. Quality creative public relations concepts come from a deliberate planning process.

In this chapter, I outline the basic preparation and execution of a PR Plan. Successful PR concepts tend to have a few things in common, so I also cover the four elements that, if you give them proper consideration during the planning stage, will take you a long way on the road of PR success. I provide you with some advice for crafting an innovative and creative concept and help you assess whether your plan is a real winner.

Pre-Planning Steps

Set a strong foundation for the planning process by doing some initial research and identifying your objectives.

Using Research to Shape the Process

Planning begins with research. At my PR agency, we begin the PR planning process for a particular project by conducting an audit (or assessment) of both internal and external factors:

- ✔ The **internal factors** include the company environment, marketing objectives, and product features and benefits.

- ✔ The **external factors** include the audience, marketplace, channels of distribution, and competition.

What am I looking for? I want to know where the company and its products are positioned in the marketplace and what people — customers, prospects, and the press — think of them.

I also want to understand what messages the consumer should be getting but isn't. In other words, what story does the company want — or need — to tell in order to change market perception and increase or preserve market share?

Some of the methods I use to gather information on the internal and external factors related to a project include the following:

- ✔ Interviews with key company executives

- ✔ Mail or phone surveys with customers and potential customers

- ✔ Personal interviews with customers and potential customers

- ✔ Interviews with industry analysts, consultants, journalists, and other experts

- ✔ Reviews of all current and past PR and marketing materials, including article clippings, ad tear sheets, press release archives, product brochures, catalogs, and other promotional documents

- ✔ Thorough searches of Internet and print sources such as articles, case studies, product literature, and other relevant publications

Your questions should be tailored for each audience. For your internal audience, you want to know: What is the current perception of the company? What do they believe the customer's perception of the company is? What additional information would be helpful to do a better job?

For your external audience, ask: What is the number one reason you bought the product or service? Why did you decide to buy the competitor's product over ours? What is your perception of the quality of our product? Have you ever seen or heard any of our advertising or other forms of marketing? What was the message that you received?

Another external audience to query is the media itself. Questions to ask include: Have you ever heard of our company or product? Do you have positive or negative feelings about our company or product? Do you actually use our product or service? Would you be interested in hearing from our company when we have news? In what format would you prefer receiving that information?

Defining Your Goals and Objectives

After the audit is complete, you should have a pretty good idea about the following:

- ✔ **The key messages you want to communicate:** Often these key messages revolve around the product's benefits or its advantages over the competition. But not always. For example, your key message may be that the company cares about the local community or environment, or you may want to focus on the fact that a product is organically grown and has no preservatives or artificial ingredients.

- ✔ **The marketing objective:** Is the objective to increase sales revenues or market share? One client may ask us to sell as many juicing machines as possible. Another may want to become the dominant Internet portal for small business. In order to get the most for your PR efforts, you have to identify the end result you want PR to help you achieve.

- ✔ **The audience:** Is the audience for your key message the end user or the channel of distribution (retailer, wholesaler, dealer)?

    - • **If you're targeting consumers,** picture your ideal audience in terms of age, income, marital status, lifestyle, career, socioeconomic status, hobbies, interests, and spending patterns.

    - • **If you're targeting a business audience,** identify what industry those people are in and their job functions, titles, and responsibilities.

  Geography is important, too: Determine whether your audience is local, regional, national, or global.

- ✔ **The response you want to generate:** Just saying that your goal is to "increase sales" isn't specific enough. Dig deeper: What do you want your target prospect to do, say, think, or believe after being exposed to your key PR messages?

- ✔ **The media you want to reach:** To best reach your target audience, what publications do you want to carry your story? These media outlets can include TV shows, radio programs, newspapers, newsletters, magazines, trade journals, and any other media your target prospect is likely to read, see, or hear.

Working Out the Plan Details

When you're putting together a PR Plan, before you get too broad, you have to be specific. There are some really important things to establish to make sure you're dealing with reality. First is the budget. I can write an incredible plan to sell a million widgets if my client has millions of dollars, but usually they don't. The most important thing to know is how much money you'll have available. What you can and can't do has everything to do with how much money you have to spend. Not all tactics are expensive, and when you don't have money, you spend time. But it's essential to know the limit at the beginning.

Putting together the PR plan

Most PR Plans follow the same basic format. I've provided here not only the format but also a sample of a PR Plan for this book, to show you how it can be fleshed out:

1. **Overview:** An executive summary of the marketing challenge you're facing that the PR campaign is designed to help you meet.

2. **Goals:** What you want the PR campaign to achieve for your firm.

3. **Strategies:** The methods by which you will achieve your goals. (See Chapter 6.)

4. **Target audiences:** The types of people you want to reach.

5. **Key target media:** The specific publications and programs toward which you will direct your PR efforts. (See the chapters in Part IV for ideas on how to use radio, television, print and the other media.)

6. **Recommendations:** Which of the PR tactics presented throughout this book you will use; other ideas you have; and the theme, hook, or angle for each tactic.

7. **Next steps:** An action plan for who does what and when.

Check out this sample plan for *Public Relations For Dummies*, 2nd Edition:

1. **Overview:** To create mass media exposure for yet another how-to business book, with a distinct challenge: to get the press to write about how to get press.

2. **Goals:** As a result of mass media exposure, this book becomes a bestseller.

3. **Strategies:** Add a creative and newsworthy element to the book, which adds an enticing reason for journalists to cover it, beyond the value of the content.

4. **Target audiences:** Primary audience: entrepreneurs and owners of small and mid-size businesses who want to incorporate public relations into a marketing program. Secondary audience: experienced PR professionals who have a continuing desire to look at PR in different ways.

5. **Key target media:** Lifestyle and business print publications, radio talk shows, morning TV talk shows, television and radio news.

6. **Recommendations:**

>   Hide a clue within this book. The first person to find the clue gets a prize: an opportunity to pick my brain for one hour. The clue is a cell phone number in the 917 area code.

>   Send book to reviewers at major publications with personal notes from Eric Yaverbaum.

>   Look for a breaking story for which the press would be interested in the opinion of a PR expert and approach as "author of *Public Relations for Dummies*, 2nd Edition."

7. **Next steps:**

>   Assign a writer to write press materials.

>   Clear creative concept with publisher.

>   Creative brainstorm to determine logistics of stunt: how to hide clue, deliver prize, and so on.

>   Develop targeted media lists.

>   Set up initial call with publicity department at publishing house to clearly establish who's doing what.

Budgeting to get the job done

PR costs a small fraction of other marketing methods — often less than $\frac{1}{100}$ of what you'd spend for paid advertising — yet it's not 100 percent free. True, media don't charge you for featuring you in their publications and programs, but you still have to factor in the time involved in planning the campaign and writing the PR materials, plus the cost of printing and distributing those materials and following up with the press. And certain public relations tactics, such as *b-rolls* (raw free-flowing footage) and *VNRs* (prepared segments for television) for television, can actually be pretty expensive! (Check out Chapter 14 for more coverage of b-rolls and VNRs.)

Given the number of different types of costs involved in a PR program, sitting down with pencil and paper (or your PC and a spreadsheet) and calculating a reasonable budget before you start spending money is important. The main expenses are

✔ The staff time of your employees who handle PR responsibilities

✔ Fees paid to outside vendors (such as graphic artists, freelance writers, PR agencies, media lists or directories, and clipping services)

✔ Out-of-pocket expenses (such as printing and postage for mailing press kits)

Devising Winning PR Concepts: The Four Essential Elements

Every public relations concept or tactic should be constructed from four elements: newsmaking, commercial message, media target, and advance target. The following sections explain these elements.

Newsmaking

Strangely enough, newsmaking is the element that most PR firms aren't good at. Most people think it's who you know, but it's not who you know but how you create newsmaking elements, which requires a broader and deeper understanding of what makes a good news story. Here's the irony: You can study this every day when you watch the daily news. Concepts don't get media coverage simply because you want them to, and they don't get broad-scale coverage because of "good contacts" in the media. Basically, a PR concept gets coverage because some part of that concept makes it newsworthy.

What makes an element newsworthy? Well, the answer can involve many factors. Some people, such as Bill Gates, make news just because of who they are. But for the majority of PR tactics, you need to add a variety of spices to the stew in order to make the tactic of interest to the media. The number-one spice is emotion: A newsworthy element is effective if it makes people happy, makes them laugh, allows them to channel their anger, or appeals to their personal greed or concerns about home, family, and career.

Newsworthy elements that are most effective in PR are usually *quantitative,* meaning that they have to do with some sort of measurement. For example, a PR concept would state, "Studies show that 82 percent of people who use this nasal spray can smell roses better." In contrast, an advertising concept, which uses the art of the *qualitative,* would state, "This product is great" or "This product clears your nose the fastest."

A potent PR news element also usually moves from the audience's needs (such as "We need a better mousetrap because there are a lot of mice") to the product's assets, explaining how the product fills the needs you've identified. In advertising, that process is reversed so that you move from the product's assets out. Essentially, you harp on what the product can do, and then you relate it to the consumer's needs.

Elements that make campaigns newsworthy are usually demonstrative, not stated. Again, I compare to advertising: Advertising is the art of statements. You make brazen statements about your product or service, but because those statements are usually very commercial, the media won't run them for free.

You make an advertising-type statement about a product and then take the PR approach of demonstration in order to get it in the media. The way to get around that is to demonstrate your key message points. So if the product is perfume, the advertising message would be, "It smells really good" because that isn't something the media would respond to. To get media coverage for the perfume, that message would need to be translated into the language of news and provide a demonstration that brings the aroma of the fragrance to life. One idea is to create a "smell taste" (like a taste test) to demonstrate and animate the advertising message in a way that is more appealing to the media.

Here's another example: British Knights was launching a new line of canvas basketball sneakers, the key feature of which was that the canvas construction resulted in maximum ventilation, and the better ventilated the sneaker, the fewer the foot odor problems. To demonstrate the main asset of maximum ventilation, we developed a search for the World's Smelliest Sock. The campaign asked people to send in their socks, and the person with the worst-smelling sock won a lifetime supply of British Knights canvas sneakers. (I talk about another British Knights campaign in Chapter 1 — the "Summer Exchange" program designed to unglue kids from the TV set. You may want to check it out. For more on this topic, see Chapter 5.)

Commercial message

The thought that any PR is good PR is nonsense and the type of belief that can lead to a great waste of money and time. In reality, good PR is PR that gets wide exposure and maintains a clearly communicated commercial message of what you want to sell to your audience. Sometimes you can build a campaign that funnels attention to a clearly stated commercial message, but more often, that commercial message must be demonstrated rather than stated directly.

For instance, if the agency that I manage wanted to promote itself and we sent out a press release saying, "Lime Public Relations and Promotions Now Handles PR for Dot-Com Companies," nobody would have cared. I could have said, "We're dot-com experts," but that's a self-promoting boast, and people wouldn't have taken an interest.

So what we did at my former agency to bring this message to life and make it far more appealing to the media was a survey based on the TV show *Survivor,* asking CEOs questions such as "What would you bring with you if you were stranded on an island?" Our published survey results showed how dot-com CEOs think differently than brick-and-mortar CEOs about survival issues. When the *Washington Post* ran a feature story on the campaign and mentioned that our PR firm did the survey, we became positioned as experts in the way dot-com executives think. Our biggest achievement with this project, however, was that we animated the message in an engaging way instead of stating the message directly.

Media target

Nothing in PR happens by chance, so if you're targeting an area of the media, you must put an element in your campaign that tempts the attention of that specific area of the media. That advice may sound obvious, but PR firms often overlook this step. The result is that you end up trying to sell a story to your target media that really doesn't fit their needs.

This is a good time to bring up a very important factor in public relations: Targeting your effort is very cost-effective. If you were running an advertising campaign, creating a separate ad for each media vehicle would be very costly. Not so in PR. To maximize results, create media tactics that seem to be created specifically for each key media outlet. (To see the media target element in action, check out the nearby sidebar "Zeroing in on your media target.")

For example, an author hired my former firm to promote a book of toll-free consumer hotlines. We created different press releases, each containing sample listings of hotlines focused on excerpts from different chapters: healthcare, gardening, travel, hobbies, and child care. We sent the press release with the gardening hotlines to gardening magazines and home sections of daily newspapers, and we sent the press release on child-care hotlines to parenting magazines and lifestyle editors. The pickup was substantial because (I'm convinced this is the reason) my former firm took a general book and targeted it by topic to appropriate media.

Audience target

As you target the media (see the preceding section), you should also target your audience — either as a whole or any key subset that you're concentrating on. Therefore, you need to let your audience know that you're speaking directly to them. The audience target element may sound like the same task as targeting areas of the media, but it's not. In PR, there's no reason why you can't use the lifestyle media to sell a business product or the sports media to sell beauty products to women. We're all multidimensional people who have many different interests. Therefore, you can use all sections of the media to sell your message as long as an element clearly lets your audience know that you're speaking to them.

For instance, one of my co-authors, Bob Bly, was publicizing a book he wrote on toll-free hotlines. He created one press release featuring all the toll-free hotlines for sports fans and sent it to sports editors. Another press release summarized the toll-free lines for leisure and entertainment and was picked up by lifestyle section editors.

The audience target element brings up another important difference between PR and advertising — one that makes it so difficult for advertising people to grasp how PR works. Advertising has a concept of *waste,* which refers to buying an ad that reaches a lot of people but only a few members of your particular audience. Advertisers see this action as wasteful because you pay a premium to reach a great number of people, but you don't get value because only a few of those people are in your targeted scope.

In PR, waste has little meaning (some, but little). The size of the media outlet doesn't affect your expense because you're not paying for each media outlet in which you appear. Therefore, you should broaden your range and go after every media outlet, even if only a small percentage of those outlets reach your core customers. Of course, when the tactic is over, you must be able to show that you've reached a large number of core customers, but you can achieve that communication by going after:

✔ **Nonlinear media:** Those broader and peripheral publications not directly targeted at your core audience

✔ **Linear media:** Mainly journals, trade publications, and newspapers directly targeted at your core audience

Zeroing in on your media target

Pick up the Sunday *New York Times* and look at each section. See how each section — Sports, Arts and Leisure, Business, and so on — targets a different consumer interest. By targeting your PR materials to the specific slants and interests of the media you mail to, you significantly increase the chances of the editors using your material. I call this kind of media targeting "the Sunday *New York Times* approach."

In fact, taking your message out of the expected media often makes it stand out more and makes you appear bigger than your particular industry. This technique is very effective.

Sharpening Ideas to Form Creative Promotions

The first draft of any document is never the best effort (that's why it's called a *draft*), and the first draft of your PR Plan is no different. You may have been deliberately vague or general in the first go-around, so now's the time to go back and sharpen the recommendations of which PR tactics you plan to use. Doing so involves some hard work and creative thinking — it's definitely not a five-minute job — but it's worth the effort. ***Remember:*** The more complete and specific your plan is now, the easier your job will be later when it's time to implement the plan.

To make your tactics as creative, sharp, original, and engaging as possible:

✓ **Understand that the media is looking for news.** *News,* by definition, is anything that is new, different, and creative. Nowhere does that exclamation *"Vive la difference!"* hold more true than in securing the media's interest.

✓ **Accept that, often, the most successful PR ideas aren't totally unique.** They may be just old ideas with a new creative slant, so don't beat yourself up if you're stumped for something new. For example, one of my clients, a major restaurant franchise, initiated a food drive for the homeless. The company's officers believed that such a large-scale undertaking was enough to attract national attention, but they were wrong, and the franchise received minimal press coverage. Another client instituted a similar promotion, but instead of doing a typical food drive, we called the promotion "Pound for Pound for the Homeless." The difference was this creative twist: The company donated a pound of food for every pound of chicken sold during a particular month. The media coverage was staggering.

✓ **Don't lose sight of who you're creating publicity for.** When writing a press release, be careful not to write it as an advertisement because the media doesn't run advertisements without getting paid to do so. If you want your publicity to work, you must design your campaign from the public's point of view, not your own.

✔ **Use the radio-show test.** If you have an idea for a promotion, ask yourself, "Would this work for a call-in radio show?" Call-in radio shows need stories that are informative and induce the audience to strike up an interaction with the issue at hand. So if your campaign works for them, it will work for all media.

✔ **Tie into hot news stories.** Whenever a big news event hits, you can always find coordinated support stories to use for your own publicity. Years ago, I handled PR for Domino's Pizza. During Operation Desert Storm, we began monitoring Domino's Pizza orders to the White House, CIA, and Pentagon, and we noticed that orders went up before any major event or crisis. By announcing this correlation, we were able to get incredible publicity, ranging from stories in *Time* magazine and on *Nightline* to a comedy sketch on *Saturday Night Live.* A similar tactic worked on another occasion; during a presidential election, we offered a free pizza topping to anyone who came into a Domino's to register to vote. Not only did we use a hot news story to get coverage, but also we did it in a way that drove up store traffic.

✔ **Tie into seasons or holidays.** Try making up recipes that are appropriate for certain holidays. For example, my former firm created a Halloween promotion for Chop Chop Chinese to You, an Atlanta-based Chinese-food franchise, by distributing scary-titled recipes for kids' Halloween parties. The recipes were innovative and creative and received tons of press for the franchise. If you do it in a creative way, you're almost guaranteed success.

✔ **Tie into an emotion.** Your promotion usually works if you can make the media laugh, cry, or even feel anger. When one client wanted to publicize the winning of an independent taste test over its biggest competitors, the emotion we chose was humor. Using the slogan "The good-taste-for-good-taste swap," we offered the client's chicken free to anyone who showed their good taste by taking the plastic covers off their furniture and sending them to the client. The campaign worked simply because the media found the whole idea of trading plastic furniture covers for chicken humorous.

✔ **Research your media.** If you want to get into a certain column of the newspaper or on a specific TV program, read it or watch it every day and pay attention to the types of stories the journalists like to do. Next, fit your news item into that medium. For instance, one of my co-authors, Bob Bly, saw that a columnist writing about retirement liked to tell his readers about ways to make extra money in their spare time to supplement their retirement incomes. Bob sent the columnist a pitch letter (see Chapter 9) about a book he had written on freelancing. The columnist liked the idea and featured Bob's book in his next column.

✔ **Take stock of your assets when going after the media.** Never lose sight of how your product can be manipulated to move the public and get the attention of the media. If you're an e-business, your greatest asset is probably your customer database. If you're a restaurant, your greatest asset may be your food. For the latter example, feeding the hungry is easy to implement, food is an emotionally effective asset, and the emotional ties that people have to food is also an effective asset. We had great success when we worked with Domino's because pizza is more than sustenance — to many people, it represents fun. We were able to use Domino's Pizza as an inducement for everything from good attendance in school to registering to vote.

✔ **Use swaps to grab attention.** A campaign that involves some sort of exchange is a popular, effective way to get publicity. Long before urban areas began sponsoring days during which the populace could turn in guns for cash, we came up with a guns-for-sneakers exchange PR campaign. We also have done successful swap campaigns that included television remote controls for sneakers. The media is very high on swaps these days, but as they become more common, the swap must become more creative and innovative.

Assessing PR Ideas: Will It Work?

As a PR professional, I'm at a disadvantage compared to many of the readers of this book: My clients ultimately decide what PR concepts and campaigns they will run, which makes me the adviser, not the decision-maker. I may have strong opinions, but I'm working with the clients' money, and they ultimately determine what I launch.

If you're a business owner or manager, however, you may not only come up with the PR ideas but also decide which campaign to implement. Here are some questions to help you assess whether a particular idea just sounds good on paper or may actually work in the field:

✔ **Does the campaign have emotional strength?** *Emotion* — a compelling sense of understanding and feeling — is the fuel that drives the influence of PR. It secures media placements, shapes decision-making, generates awareness, builds interest, increases response rates, and gets the target audience to believe the messages intended for them.

✔ **Does it demonstrate the message?** Creating publicity initiatives, events, or promotions that demonstrate rather than state commercial messages is what makes them newsworthy.

✔ **Can the intended audience relate to it?** A winning campaign focuses not just on what you do but also on what your product does for the audience. This focus on the customer guarantees newsworthiness; but it also encourages audiences to take notice of the message and change their attitudes, opinions, beliefs, or behaviors.

✔ **Is it a step above the ordinary?** Public relations tactics are at their finest when they give you a superior position in your industry or marketplace. PR should showcase your natural strengths and assets so that you stand head and shoulders above the competition.

✔ **Does it answer the basic questions of** *who, what, when,* **and** *where?* A good PR campaign plan determines what the exact message is, to whom that message has the greatest relevance, and in what aspect of the target's life the message is best communicated. Know precisely why you have a PR program, what you expect from it, and when you expect to see results.

✔ **What results do you want?** Determine a budget based on how much you want to achieve, and decide how you will measure your progress: inquiries, market research surveys, focus groups, increased market capitalization, and/or key accounts acquired.

Because all PR concepts are a sum of elements, you can forecast how a concept will succeed by examining the idea not as a whole but as individual elements. You can discern which elements will carry the emotion, which will maintain the commercial message, which will create the newsworthiness or interest, and which will point the concept at the exact target media or audience. By knowing the specific effect that each element will have in directing a concept, you can build a PR campaign that is much more likely to achieve the success you want.

Controlling Time and Chance

Motivational expert Dr. Rob Gilbert once told me, "The way you control timing is to be there all the time." Here's how that works. Suppose that you own a collection agency and are an expert in collections, and you want to get some press attention for your business. Problem is, you can never tell in what month a particular editor at your city's largest business magazine will want to do a story about the collection problems faced by small businesses and how to solve them. But one thing is certain: If you send this editor a press release on collections strategies and tactics every month, eventually your material will wind up in his lap *in the month he decides to do that story.* And when that happens, who do you think he'll interview, you or your competitor whom he's never heard of?

One more homey example: My wife and I once took our son to a town carnival. At one game of chance, you could win a small stuffed animal by placing a quarter on one of ten numbers and then hoping, when the wheel of chance was spun, that the pointer would end up on your number. It occurred to me that if I wanted to be certain of getting a stuffed animal for Alex, I could do so by spending $2.50 and putting a quarter on each of the ten numbers simultaneously: I'd *have* to hit with one of my ten bets. (In fact, we bet normally and won a stuffed animal on the first spin!)

In PR, the same principle applies: Keep putting yourself out there in the media — with query letters, pitch letters, press releases — and you *will* hit the winning number. The prize is publicity for your company or service. It's inevitable.

Does this mean that a one-shot press release or PR promotion won't work? Not at all. Even a single press release or media appearance on TV or radio can generate scads of press coverage and hundreds or even thousands of inquiries and sales. But on the other hand, your first effort may bring little or nothing. When you treat publicity as a one-shot event, you're gambling. When you have a consistent, ongoing program, with efforts going out monthly or on some other regular basis, you'll almost certainly get the result you want sooner or later (sooner if you follow the suggestions in this book).

Chapter 3

Hiring Professional PR Help

. . . .

In This Chapter

▶ Considering and finding which type of outside PR help to use

▶ Using PR professionals to your best advantage

. . . .

My fellow PR professionals may hate me for saying this, but PR is something that many companies — especially small businesses — can and should do on their own.

The question then arises: If you can do it yourself, why pay someone else to do it for you? Sometimes it's just a matter of the advantages inherent in outsourcing: Your staff is already too busy to do PR, and you don't want to add to your overhead by hiring your own PR department, adding a PR person to your marketing department, or expanding your already overworked in-house PR people. An obvious answer is to outsource PR. In addition to giving you access to outside expertise, hiring a PR professional frees your employees to concentrate on their core business.

Companies also hire outside PR counsel for a fresh point of view and original, creative thinking. In-house people may have been working on a product line for so long that they're bored and can't see any excitement in it. To the outside PR professional just brought onboard to handle the account, promoting the product is a fun challenge that gets the creative juices flowing.

Another reason that companies hire PR firms is to benefit from the PR firm's impressive list of media contacts. But you already know what I think of that.

Getting Help

Few people in small business have the time to become experts in PR and promotions, even though they may be quite decent at it. So should you hire an advertising agency or public relations firm to handle all this, or can you do it yourself?

Some small businesses use their ad agencies to handle their PR. Others hire PR firms or PR counselors — independent PR advisers, usually one-person shops. Another alternative is to hire a freelance PR writer to create your press materials. In this section, I take a look at each of these options.

Advertising agencies

Advertising agencies provide advertisers with a wide range of communications services: copywriting, art, production, media planning and buying, market research, sales promotion, and public relations, both online and off.

Many ad agencies promote themselves as "marketing communications" firms and include both advertising and PR in their roster of services. Should you engage separate firms for advertising or PR, or is it better to have them both handled by a single shop?

The argument in favor of hiring a PR firm for PR, and an ad agency for advertising, is simple: They are two different disciplines requiring very different skill sets. Advertising agencies can say practically whatever they want in an ad, because they simply pay the media to carry their message. In PR, we have to convince — sometimes subtly — the media to carry our message for us, because we're asking for a "free ride" — we are not paying for the coverage. It's a different art and not one that all ad agencies practice well.

The argument in favor of having one firm do both advertising and PR is synergy between the campaigns. One danger of having separate agencies for advertising and PR is that they won't communicate well and work in tandem, resulting in ad and PR campaigns that communicate different messages. Integration is absolutely and vitally important and will stretch your investment farther.

But you don't need to take the single-agency approach to solve that problem. Just make sure that your ad agency and PR firm — if you have one of each — talk to each other frequently and are aware of what the other is doing. At my current agency, we are fully integrated with advertising, which is what makes the most sense and is often the elusive holy grail of marketing. When true integration exists, the client gets the greatest investment for their dollar.

Public relations agencies

Public relations agencies are the professionals to turn to when you want to get coverage in the media. Now, sending out a press release or calling up a local editor are two things anyone can do — you don't need to be a specialist to practice public relations. So why hire a PR agency? One reason is that PR firms are PR specialists.

At Lime Public Relations and Promotions, the PR firm where I am currently the Managing Partner, the PR group is made up of experts at writing, planning, timing, and executing PR and promotional campaigns. A big reason is that doing PR is the priority. We treat it as a critical task, and we spend the vast majority of our time doing PR. Although novices tend to be unstructured and haphazard in their PR efforts, professionals can plan and execute a campaign that supports a marketing strategy.

Many public relations firms charge their clients a monthly retainer for their services; a typical monthly retainer can be $5,000 to $15,000 a month or more, depending on the scope of the work. Larger and mid-size PR firms usually require a retainer of at least $10,000 to $25,000 a month or more. Smaller PR firms are more flexible, with minimum monthly retainers in the $5,000 range. You can even find solo practitioners — one- or two-person PR firms, often working out of someone's home — who will take you on for $4,000 to $5,000 a month. If you find someone who wants to charge less than that, just remember that you get what you pay for.

Deciding whether to hire a PR firm

Do you need the highly professional and somewhat costly services of a PR agency? Or can you do things less expensively and better yourself? Here's a list of do's and don'ts to help you decide:

- ✔ Do use an agency if effective PR is crucial to your success and if you feel that you can afford the going rates.

- ✔ Do consider using an agency if you spend $3,000 or more a month on PR. That's probably the minimum amount it will take to interest even the smallest agency in handling your account.

- ✔ Don't hire an agency because you're trying to cut costs. Getting outside help is almost always more expensive than doing it yourself.

- ✔ Don't hire an agency solely because you think you don't have time to do it yourself. Yes, the agency will free your time for other tasks. But when you hire an agency, you're hiring creativity coupled with PR expertise — and not just another pair of hands.

- ✔ Do hire an agency if your company is marketing oriented.

- ✔ Do hire an agency if you intend to use its services to full advantage.

- ✔ Do hire an agency for fresh thinking, outside objectivity, and a more creative approach to PR.

- ✔ Do hire an agency if you need help planning promotions, introducing new products, and selecting target markets.

- ✔ Do hire an agency to do things first-class.

- ✔ Don't hire an agency if you're certain that only you know the best way to promote your business and that outsiders can never make useful suggestions in this area.

Most important, hiring an agency is an investment in your time. You must have a partnership with the agency and a person within your organization who will champion the program.

If you decide to hire an agency, you need to know how to select the one that's right for your business. I cover this in the following section.

Selecting a PR firm

Here are seven useful tips for selecting the PR firm that can best serve your company:

- ✔ **Opt for a PR agency with expertise in your area.** All else being equal, accountants, brokers, and bankers should select a PR agency that specializes in financial accounts. A manufacturer of globe valves for petroleum refineries should choose an agency with industrial expertise. A designer of men's swimwear would do best to seek counsel from a PR agency with other fashion accounts. By choosing an agency that already has some experience in your industry, you save yourself the costly and time-consuming process of educating its staff from scratch.

Make sure that the agency does not have any of your competitors as clients. A conflict would surely arise. Another warning: Take my caveat "all else being equal" seriously. A more important factor than expertise in your area is whether the PR firm is good at getting PR for its clients. All else is usually *not* equal, and I'd rather have a great PR firm that didn't have experience in my industry than a mediocre one, with weak results, that did.

- ✔ **Do not hire an agency with more capabilities than you need.** Do you really need an agency with overseas branch offices, television production capabilities, a market research department, and clout with the White House? All of an agency's clients pay to support its complete operations — so, to save money without sacrificing service or quality, select an agency that offers only those communications services you need, which will likely be account management, PR writing, and media relations.

- ✔ **Make sure that the agency is the right size for you.** A $20,000 account represents only 0.01 percent of a $200-million agency's income and consequently receives only 0.01 percent of its management attention and 0.01 percent of its creative effort. Make sure that your agency is small enough to consider your account profitable and worth its best efforts, yet large enough to have the resources to get the job done.

- ✔ **Ask to see the agency's work.** Examine a prospective agency's portfolio of press clippings and client case studies. Do you like what you see? Is it the kind and caliber of work you want done?

Avoid agencies that "talk the talk" but haven't "walked the walk." Lots of PR firms say they can get you in the media you want. But have they constantly delivered on this promise for their existing clients? More important, do they just get a bunch of press clipping for their clients, filling up portfolio books? Or do they execute targeted campaigns that have actually helped build major brands and achieve a significant improvement in the client's bottom line?

✔ **Get the names of some current and past clients and talk with those clients.** Find out what the PR agency did for them and whether the results were worth many times the fees paid in terms of increased business results.

Also ask the PR agency for the names of two or three clients who fired them. That's right, ex-clients who left them. Find out why the PR firm was fired. If it was for lack of results, that's bad. If it's because the PR firm's ideas were too daring and the client was afraid to try them, maybe you're more daring and won't be so afraid.

In reviewing my career, I have found that the number-one reason I have lost accounts is that I gave the clients my opinion and they disagreed with it. If you're simply looking for someone to parrot your own ideas, don't waste your money on an outside PR firm or consultant. A large part of what you pay an outside service for is a fresh point of view and ideas different from what you would come up with on your own.

I tell my own employees, "It's okay to have an opinion different from mine; it is *not* okay to have no opinion." As a client, you should give your PR advisers the same instructions I give my employees.

✔ **Make sure that the agency is sympathetic with the needs of small business.** Especially if you're a small business on a limited budget, explain to prospective agencies that your goal is to create PR campaigns that increase sales — and not to win PR industry awards. Tell them that your money is limited. Tell them that you want a PR campaign to generate traffic or boost sales, not to get your picture in the paper just to please your mother.

✔ **Check the personal chemistry.** PR is a people business. My PR agency's most precious assets all leave the building in the elevator every night: my employees. If you don't like the people who will be working on your account, or if you sense they don't like you, look for another PR firm; it's not a good fit.

✔ **Be clear about fees.** Check out the price. What is the average monthly retainer the PR firm's clients pay? The minimum monthly retainer? How much do they propose to charge you? And what do you get in return? Have them spell out what they will do and the level or degree of activity you can expect for your investment.

My agency has hourly rates established for me, my partner, and every other employee. We keep track of everyone's time and bill it against the retainer. So if Joe bills at $100 an hour and does 10 hours of work this month for Client X, $1,000 of that client's $12,000 monthly retainer has been spent on Joe's services.

How many PR agencies should you interview when making your selection process? I recommend you meet with at least three different agencies so that you can see the different perspectives from which they approach PR in general, and your business problems in particular. You may find it helpful to spell out what you're looking for in a PR firm and what you want it to do for you in a Request for Proposal (RFP).

Review the proposals that the PR firms submit. A good proposal should give you, the client, insight into how the agencies think, the strategies they use, their costs, and their time line for implementing your campaign. Although their fee is paid monthly, you usually need at least six months of working with a PR firm before you can accurately evaluate results.

After reviewing the proposals the PR firms submit, ask the ones you like to come in and do a presentation. That means a presentation of their capabilities and what they can do for you, not actual creative work on your account. You shouldn't ask for that until you've made your decision and hired one of the agencies.

Freelancers

Many creative types of people — especially writers, artists, photographers, and publicists — are skilled in areas of promotion and work as freelancers, serving both advertisers and advertising agencies. Freelancers are capable of delivering the same high-quality work as advertising and PR agencies at a fraction of the cost. Using freelancers can be the least expensive way of getting professional help to create your promotions.

Before hiring a freelancer, check his résumé, portfolio, and client list. Find out his rates and get a written estimate in advance. Most important, make sure that you like (or at least can tolerate) the freelancer as a person. With advertising agencies, an account executive separates you from the writer or artist. With freelance help, you deal with the creator of your promotion directly. To have a successful collaboration with the freelancer, you must be able to work well together.

Some freelance PR writers may say they can also do PR placement, but be wary of this claim. Part of the reason I can follow up so effectively is that if I send a press release to a thousand editors at a thousand publications, my staff personally calls every one of them — some several times — to follow up and get more placements. Now, if each call takes ten minutes, a thousand calls would take one person seven consecutive days if he worked 24 hours a day without a break. A lone freelancer with limited time and no staff cannot duplicate this level of effort from a home office.

Graphic design studios

Most small businesses rely on print promotions — posters, signs, pamphlets, ads, point-of-purchase displays, coupons, media kits, and brochures — to reach their customers and prospects. Graphic design firms can often meet this need with great quality at a reasonable fee.

Graphic design studios do not, as a rule, offer media, marketing, writing, and PR services. They are simply the experts in designing and producing print material.

Some small-business managers have a good grasp of sales and marketing, know their business well, write lucid copy, and understand the basic promotional tools. They just need help turning their ideas into polished print material, and a graphic design studio can provide that help.

The rates for graphic design services vary according to where your business is located. In Manhattan, a city that may have more working graphic artists than anywhere in the United States, the design rate ranges from $100 to $150 an hour.

Web designers

The Web is an important part of any PR campaign (read more about that in Chapter 16) so you need a professional Web designer to create a site that is both useful and usable for your press contacts. When it comes to hiring a Web designer, beware that there are generally two types: designers who understand technology and technologists who understand design. It's rare (but possible) to find someone who does both well. To find out what kind of designer you're talking to, ask, "Who is doing the design and who is doing programming?"

Search engine specialists

It is also rare to find a Web designer who understands search engine optimization, but when you do, they're usually the technologists. If being found by the search engines is a key component in your campaign, be sure that the Web designer or firm that you hire has someone in place or on staff who not only understands search engine technology but also stays up-to-date on it, as the technology is constantly changing.

Getting the Most out of Hired Help

You've looked at your checkbook, looked with dismay at your current promotion campaign, and made a major decision: You want your promotions to be first class, and you've decided to get professional help — an advertising agency, a PR firm, a freelancer, or a graphic design studio. Here, then, are some helpful hints for getting the best work out of your outside supplier with the least amount of trouble:

✔ **Brief your agency.** The more your PR firm or advertising agency knows about your product, your company, and your markets, the better. Tell your agency what makes your product unique. Explain its advantages over the competition's products. Explain your marketing strategy. Provide background material in the form of current ads and press releases, brochures, articles on your industry, and market-research reports. The best clients prepare comprehensive agency briefings in writing.

✔ **If you use separate agencies for advertising and PR, brief them both at the same input meeting.** Doing so further helps ensure integration between your advertising and PR campaigns. It also saves you from having to present the same background briefing twice.

✔ **Do not compete with your agency in the creative area.** You certainly can disapprove of the brochure copy or the press kit that your agency turns in. Make helpful criticisms and turn it back for a revision. But don't tell outside talent how to do the job. If you can write better than the writer and take better pictures than the photographer, fire them and do the work yourself.

✔ **Don't strain your promotions through many layers of approval.** You, and possibly your business partner, should approve or disapprove the work that the outside agency submits. But don't look for approval from your purchasing agent, your accountant, your cashier, and your mother-in-law. Too many levels of approval muddy clear writing and water down the impact of the message. Worse, they dampen the creative spirit of your writers or artists so that the next thing they do will be mediocre enough to get your company's instant approval.

> ✔ **Be reasonable about paying.** Making a good profit in PR or advertising is difficult, and many agencies and freelancers have gone out of business waiting for late payments from their clients. Be fair to your agencies and freelancers and pay them promptly.

By all means, watch expenses carefully, and don't pay for something you never asked for in the first place. On the other hand, too much haggling over money can cause your outside professionals to put forth less effort on your account. You will get a competent promotion, but not a great one.

That said, when you hire a PR agency to work with you, it's essential that you stay in charge of the process. If the agency is making the decisions, it's akin to the tail wagging the dog. Your practitioner is there for advice (and you should hire someone who will give you the best advice), but you are the one who knows your company best. You are the one with daily and one-on-one contact with your customers. That's why you must be the ultimate decision-maker when it comes to how you implement your PR campaign.

> ✔ **Create a budget.** Before talking to an agency, know what you can afford to spend on PR. Your budget will depend on where you are in your business cycle. A mature business will have different needs from those of a new business. In a major corporation, the PR budget will be 5 to 10 percent of the entire marketing budget. You must determine the parameters before you speak to an agency or a PR practitioner.

> ✔ **Set sensible expectations.** This is the number-one key component in establishing a successful, long-term relationship and must happen from the beginning. The most realistic expectation is that the process takes time. Steer clear of any agency that promises to get you on *Oprah* next month. Create communication documents with time lines that spell out what will happen — not just the tactics but, for example, every little task that goes into writing a press release and getting it out to the press. Assign every item to a person so you see who's doing what and when it's due. Update these documents weekly, adding new assignments, checking off what's finished, and using red flags to indicate where you're late.

> ✔ **Understand who does what from the beginning.** Hiring a PR firm doesn't make your work easier. If you want PR to work, you have to keep in mind that it is a partnership and will require a commitment of your time. You need to know how PR works (reading this book is a good start, of course). Typical tasks you should expect to do include talking to the press, taking incoming calls, sending product samples to the press, and so on.

> ✔ **Establish and maintain direction in the process.** Set up a weekly conference call to review the weekly update so you see exactly what goes on. The decision-makers for your company need to be on the call, so schedule the conference call around them, if necessary.

Where to find help

You want to hire a PR firm, ad agency, or free-lancer, but you don't know where to turn. The following mini-directory of creative talent should be of some assistance:

➤ *The Agency Databases,* **published by Lexis Nexis,** 121 Chanlon Road, New Providence, NJ 07974, Phone: 800-340-3244. www. redbooks.com. Contains detailed profiles of nearly 14,000 U.S. and international advertising agencies, including accounts represented by each agency, fields of specialization, breakdown of gross billings by media, contact information on agency personnel and much more. Available in most libraries.

➤ *O'Dwyer Directory of Public Relations Firms,* **271 Madison Ave., New York, NY 10016.** Lists 2,900 PR firms. Available in most libraries.

➤ *Public Relations Tactics,* **a monthly magazine published by the Public Relations Society of America, 845 Third Ave., New York, NY 10022.** Many PR agents offer their services each month in the classified ads section of this journal.

Also check your local Yellow Pages for listings under "Advertising Agencies," "Public Relations Agencies," "Graphic Design Studios," "Illustrators," "Writers," "Copywriters," "Artists," and "Photographers."

Part II

Brainstorming and Thinking Creatively

The 5th Wave   By Rich Tennant

ANOTHER BEAUTIFUL DITCH DUG BY **BILL FOWLER**

LOOK FOR MY OTHER DITCHES ALONG RTE 682

YOU CAN ALWAYS TRUST A FOWLER DITCH

In this part . . .

PR depends on creative ideas, and Part II equips you to hatch those ideas by the truckload. The first step is to set up your own PR program (Chapter 4). In Chapter 5, you get a process for formulating creative ideas, and Chapter 6 gives you some creative PR tactics you can apply to your own campaigns.

Chapter 4

Setting Up Your PR Department and Program

*T*o win the Super Bowl, you don't just show up that day, play, and hope for the best. Long before you get there, you put together a team and a plan. You also review your strategy, practice your moves, buy the equipment you need, and train your players.

Winning in PR is similar — early preparation leads to lasting success. This chapter covers the steps to follow whether you're planning to do your own PR campaigns in-house or manage the activities of an outside PR specialist or agency you hire (as covered in Chapter 3).

Picking the PR Team

One person in your organization should be responsible for PR, serving as a liaison between your company and your PR specialist or agency, as well as coordinating communication between your firm and the press.

If you're a self-employed professional or a small home-based business, the PR coordinator or manager will probably be you. You probably can delegate a lot of the administrative work to an assistant, and if he is bright, maybe he can take on some strategic and creative responsibility as well.

Large corporations usually have a separate PR department or at least one or more managers who have PR as a full-time job responsibility. They go under a variety of names, including PR manager, corporate communications director, and media relations manager.

In mid-size firms, the sales manager, marketing manager, or advertising manager may handle PR as part of the company's overall marketing communications mix, which may also include trade shows, advertising, a Web site, and direct marketing.

Whoever you select, that person — whether PR is a full-time responsibility or just one of many responsibilities — is in charge of PR and is accountable for getting programs done on budget, on time, and in synch with communications objectives.

Defining the Scope of Your Authority

Unless the PR manager is also the owner of the business, he may have the responsibility for PR but probably does not have the final authority. That is, the PR manager reports to someone else who has approval authority over all major PR activities, including copy for press releases, decisions about event planning or special promotions, and what to say to the press.

Because effective PR depends on being able to give the media a fast, accurate, honest response when reporters have questions, the PR manager cannot operate effectively if everything said in PR — in print, in person, and on the phone — has to go to a half-dozen people to get approval. By the time the response is approved, the story has grown cold and the media is alienated. And it's your competitors you will be reading about, I can promise.

To make PR efforts effective, the PR manager needs to be able to make decisions quickly. That means a simplified chain of command. For approval on major PR documents, the PR manager should have to circulate copy to no more than two or three people — the product manager, a technical expert for accuracy, and perhaps the CEO or marketing director. For media contact, the appropriate spokespeople within the company, such as the CEO or marketing manager, should be committed to giving priority to media response and to understanding that the press can't wait.

Integrating PR with the Rest of Your Business

As I discuss in Chapter 1, PR is an essential element in an overall marketing scheme, but remember that it's only one component of many. PR should be part of an integrated marketing communications strategy. When deciding when and how best to use it, consider the following:

- ✔ PR should be fully integrated into other forms of marketing when launching a new product or service.

- ✔ PR should always be "in the loop." Having a PR practitioner present during strategic brainstorming is vitally important.

- ✔ PR should work synergistically with other components of the marketing mix whenever possible — the more the better.

- ✔ PR should lead in a crisis situation (of course, the lawyers will disagree). In a best-case scenario, the two disciplines — PR and the legal department — work together. (See Chapter 21.)

In an organization large enough to have a PR manager or department, the danger is that these PR specialists may operate in a vacuum and become removed and remote from the day-to-day business. Ironically then, those assigned the task of communicating company messages and information to various outside audiences (the media, the public, shareholders, the community) risk becoming the least informed.

Half the job of a full-time PR professional is disseminating information to the media; the other half is understanding what the company is really doing.

Don't sit at your desk all day. Get out and walk around the factory, the warehouse, the shipping department, and the product managers' offices. Ask people what's important, what's interesting, and what messages they want to communicate to the outside world. Your job is then to understand these stories and package them in a way that's appealing to the media and their audiences.

Every PR manager, full time or part time, should do the following to keep up-to-date with a company's activities:

- ✔ Read industry trade journals.

- ✔ Attend major trade shows at which your company is exhibiting.

- ✔ Frequently review your own Web site to make sure that it's current. (See Chapter 16 for more on getting the most out of your own Web site.)

- ✔ Frequently visit competitors' Web sites and see what they're up to.

- ✔ Read all new sales literature that your company publishes.

- ✔ Respond to competitors' ads in magazines and request their sales literature.

- ✔ Talk with sales reps to see what customers are saying about your products versus the competition.

- ✔ Go with sales reps on actual sales calls to prospects.

✔ Read the daily newspaper to follow journalists who may write about you or your competitors.

To follow and track your competitors in the news, make sure to set up news alerts on each of them. (Read more about this in Chapter 18.)

✔ Become a student of the media. Analyze your evening news from the perspective of the person being interviewed. How well is she getting her message across? What could she be doing better? How could she be clearer?

Before you start a flurry of PR activities, have a PR plan in place that clearly defines audiences, objectives, and key messages you want to communicate. The PR planning process is covered in detail in Chapter 2.

Setting Up the PR Command and Control Center

To be an effective and efficient PR professional, you need to create a "PR Command and Control Center" — a place in your business where you can, from a single location, develop and implement all your PR campaigns.

Getting in gear

Fortunately, your workspace needn't be elaborate or expensive; all you really need is a desk, a phone, a computer with Internet access, a fax machine, a good photocopier, a postage meter, and some reference directories. Here are some suggestions to help you transform your own desk into a tiptop PR command and control center in short order:

✔ **Invest in a set of media directories.** If you do any sort of regular PR campaign, I recommend owning one or more of these directories, such as *Bacon's Media Directories* or *Gebbie's All-In-One Media Directory*. If you are truly only going to do a one-shot press release once or twice a year, you can often find some of these books in the reference section of your local library.

✔ **Develop a good media list — a list of media contacts to call when you want to get a story in print or on the air.** Ideally, your media list is a work in progress that is comprised of contacts from a current media directory in addition to personal contacts. A thorough media list contains not only contact and outlet information but also information on deadlines, preferred means of contact, and other useful notes. A media list is an invaluable tool when you're sending any announcements or responding to queries.

- Keep your lists updated. Reporters commonly switch beats or even outlets, so keeping in touch with your contacts is important so you know whom to call or where to send your releases.

- As the years go by, your media contacts will change jobs. Keep your media contact list up-to-date, and follow these contacts as they move from job to job. Failing to do so means you have lost valuable contacts you have spent time and effort in building.

- As people make career moves, they often climb the corporate ladder. As a result, the young journalists I knew when they and I were in our 20s are now in their 40s. Many are media big shots, and by keeping in touch, I now have personal access to high-level producers and editors at media outlets I did not have before. *Remember:* One easy way to get to the top of the oak tree is to plant an acorn and sit on it.

- For more information on building a media list and working it to your advantage, refer to Chapter 11.

✔ **Use a monitoring service.** A monitoring service, also known as a clipping service, helps you track your media placements. Monitoring services provide two benefits: They track the stories you place and the news you don't as well. For example, if you sent a release to the *Wall Street Journal,* and the service finds nothing about you in the *Journal,* you know your release didn't get used. In addition, reporters don't have time to clip and mail you the stories they write about you when they're published. So without a monitoring service, you may not even know that a story has come out.

Monitoring services are a great safety net when reporters can't give you a publication date on a story they're writing about your company or when a television station picks up an announcement as soon as you release it. Several free but very limited services, such as Google Alerts (www.google.com/alerts), Yahoo! Alerts (http://alerts.yahoo.com), and Northern Light (www.northernlight.com), do a better job monitoring an industry than a specific company. Fee-based services such as Factiva are online and have a comprehensive list of publications and radio and television stations that they monitor through company- or keyword-specific searches. Also fee-based are traditional clipping services such as Luce or Burrelle's, which send you photocopies of newspaper or magazine clippings but have a longer delivery time. Broadcast monitoring services such as Video Monitoring Services or Media Link monitor both radio and television programs for clients.

✔ **Become acquainted with the media outlets.** The media directories are a great starting place and an ongoing resource for getting to know the media. But the best way to fully understand what a newspaper or television or radio station covers or to find out about a specific reporter's beat is simply to read the newspapers in the morning, turn on your radio on your way home from work, and catch the evening news on television. Doing so helps you to better frame your stories and to avoid PR blunders — such as pitching a reporter on a story that he covered only two days ago. Building relationships with reporters is key.

✔ **Collect and maintain editorial calendars for key media.** Magazines and special sections of some national daily newspapers have yearly editorial calendars that note upcoming topics or issues they will be covering. To obtain a calendar, log on to the publication's Web site or call its advertising sales department.

✔ **Assemble a complete list of vendors.** You will deal with many different vendors on different projects. From printers for press kits to release distribution services (services that distribute your press release to the media for you via mail, fax, or e-mail), many vendors can enhance your activities. Some vendors excel at making color media kits, while others are known for broadcast faxing out a press release. Helpful sources for finding vendors include your local Yellow Pages and networking with other businesspeople in your city or town.

✔ **Do your homework.** Research your competitors on the Internet, while daily keeping abreast of breaking news, trends, and new developments. What's the best way to do this? Go to the library and search a database of past news stories in your industry (some clipping services come with this option) and read as much as you can every day.

✔ **Develop a standard kit of core press materials.** A good press kit consists of the following elements:

- **Company fact sheet:** This one- to two-page document gives a brief description of the company, its primary activities, products and services, and any other relevant facts, such as sales/revenues, number of employees, and names of key management personnel.

- **Biographies:** Prepare short biographies of your company's key management, usually the CEO, chairman, president, and other key executives, such as the CFO or senior vice presidents. The bios should discuss their current position and responsibilities in addition to a brief professional history.

- **Key releases:** Depending on your objectives and your audience, key releases can be anything from quarterly results to product or service announcements.

✔ **Sharpen your writing skills.** PR professionals write everything from press releases, media alerts, and letters pitching ideas, to speeches, strategy plans, and client correspondence. You may want to consider taking a PR writing or journalism course at a local college to find how to write for your different audiences. You should always have at your fingertips these three writing resources — a dictionary, a thesaurus, and the *Associated Press Stylebook* to guide you on matters of grammar and style. And remember, professionalism is critical in your relationships with both clients and media, so always carefully proof your materials. Or better yet, ask someone else to look over the material for mistakes.

Sometimes you can easily fail to see errors in documents that you've written yourself. For more tips on how to write better, refer to Chapter 27.

✔ **Network.** Try to continually meet other PR professionals and journalists to help you develop and maintain relationships. Here are some ways to do this:

- Join industry trade groups like the Public Relations Society of America (PRSA; www.prsa.org) or the National Investor Relations Institute (NIRI; www.niri.org). They offer seminars that provide access to some of the most well-respected PR professionals and key media people. They also offer invaluable training and informational seminars on a wide range of areas (for example, crisis management, media relations, buzz marketing, and writing skills).

- Invite reporters out to lunch, not to pitch a story to them, but rather to give a general background on your company and to find out more about what stories they're interested in covering.

Creating and maintaining a media contact list

As an alternative to formal networking, a business owner or manager who has part-time responsibility for public relations can build up a list of media contacts slowly, over time. You do this by creating and maintaining a list or database of any media contact or outlet that runs a story or short item about you based on PR materials you sent. Your media contact list consists of the names, titles, publications or stations, addresses, phone numbers, e-mail addresses, and fax numbers of editors, writers, reporters, program directors, hosts, and other media people who have previously given coverage to your PR efforts. Putting together your personal media contact list is outlined in Chapter 11.

Every time you get media coverage, send a thank-you note to the reporter or editor who used your material. Your note should thank the person for taking the time to write about you, while also briefly mentioning one or two other story ideas that may be right for the publication and that you could help with by providing more information. The letter should be short and primarily focus on a sincere thank-you; the mention of new ideas should be a soft sell and take only one or two lines.

Don't offend the media! Members of the media are extremely sensitive about the symbiotic relationship between the press and PR people. Be extremely cautious not to suggest in any thank-you letter that the journalist is doing you a favor or helping to promote your product.

Also, enter the media person's name, publication, and other contact information (address, phone, and so on) into a card file, your Rolodex, or a computer database. Whenever you get coverage from a media source that hasn't written about you before, add that name to your database.

In a short time, you will have a contact database of media people who have covered you or used your PR materials in some way and, therefore, have some familiarity with you and your company.

Just as in direct mail, sending letters to your *house list* of existing customers will almost always produce a greater response than mailing the same letter to a rented list of *cold names*. Sending PR materials to your house list of media contacts will result in greater use of your materials than mailing the same press releases to a list of editors or program directors taken from one of the media directories listed in the appendix.

Does this mean that you should send your PR materials only to your house media contact list and not to other sources? No. Any release you distribute should go to your house list as well as to all other appropriate publicity outlets listed in whatever media directories you're using.

The purpose of maintaining a media contact database is to ensure that these people get all your materials and are not accidentally left out. Make sure that your media contacts get all your PR mailings because these people are most likely to give you coverage.

To sum up: For the small and part-time PR practitioner, it is not cost-effective to "court" the press for purposes of making personal connections to increase the odds of media placement. The better strategy is simply to keep track of and maintain constant contact with every media source who *does* cover you, based on the assumption that any editor or program director who has featured you once is likely to want to do so again if you present a story or angle of interest.

Targeting Your PR Efforts

You can target your market in any of several ways (or a combination of ways). The nine major ways are: industry, company size, location, job function or title, product application, distribution channels, affinity groups, specific users, and buying habits. After you select your target market, you must then seek out, identify, and collect information on the publicity outlets reaching your various market segments.

Industry

You can target by industry, specifying industry segments by name or by Standard Industrial Classification (SIC). The SIC system uses a series of eight-digit codes to organize U.S. businesses into 15,000 categories and subcategories. The definitive reference work to SIC is Dun & Bradstreet's *SIC 2 + 2 Standard Industrial Classification Manual.*

Here is an example of targeting by industry for a company that sells plastic diaphragm pumps: The PR manager creates two different press releases describing the same product. Why two different releases? Because the users in different markets are interested in different performance features. Buyers in the chemical industry are interested primarily in corrosion resistance; buyers in the pharmaceutical industry are more concerned with purity and cleanliness. Press releases sent to the editors at top trade journals covering these markets stress these different themes. The advantage of doing this? Editors respond better because the press materials they receive talk about what is of interest to their readers.

Many of the available directories of publicity outlets are organized by industry segment or cross-referenced by industry segment or at least allow you to specify industry-specific publications when ordering mailing lists. The volume of Bacon's Media Directories covering business magazines is especially helpful when you're looking for the publications covering a particular industry segment. For details, contact Bacon's PR Service, listed in the appendix.

Size of company

Your market can be segmented according to the size of the company. I see American business divided into three basic markets: small business, medium-size companies, and large corporations. How you define *small, medium,* and *large* for your marketing and PR purposes is really up to you. But here's how I think of it:

- ✔ **Small companies** are generally privately owned and usually family-run businesses, with anywhere from 1 or 2 employees up to 30, 40, or maybe 50 employees. For a manufacturer, this means sales under $10 million; for a service firm, sales under $2 million.

  The small company is usually run by an owner who keeps a tight rein over all aspects of the business. Entrepreneurs are skeptical, pressed for time, not terribly interested in technical details, bottom-line oriented, and cost conscious.

Home-based businesses are a distinct submarket within the small-business market. Many computer, fax, copier, telephone, furniture, and office supply companies are aggressively targeting this market segment because of the rising popularity of working at home. The disadvantage in targeting this market, however, is that home-based businesspeople are usually frugal and on a limited budget, and they rarely offer opportunities for repeat business or volume sales. They tend to buy only one of everything, and that only after much deliberation. And they also tend to require a lot of after-sale support and service.

✔ **Medium-size companies** may have from several dozen to several hundred or more employees, with sales usually above $10 million if a manufacturer (or above $2 million to $3 million if a service provider) but less than $100 million. Your prospect here is probably not the owner, but he may very well report to the owner. Some prospects have a lot of autonomy and authority; others have to check with the boss to spend $50 on office supplies. This market segment is difficult to put neatly into a single category, because it is so big: There's a lot of difference, for example, between a firm with $10 million in sales and a firm with $150 million in sales.

✔ **Large corporations** typically include the Fortune 500 firms and those of similar size: big companies with thousands of employees and annual sales in the hundreds of millions of dollars.

Typically, managers in these firms are part of a chain of authority and must consult with others in their company to make a purchase decision of any consequence. Prospects at big corporations frequently are as concerned with making an "acceptable" buying decision (one that pleases the immediate supervisor or top management committee) as they are with bottom-line results. Many hesitate to take risks.

What publicity outlets reach businesspeople? These would include the following:

✔ General business magazines

✔ Local and regional business magazines

✔ Chamber of commerce magazines and newsletters

✔ Industry-specific trade journals

✔ Industry-specific newsletters

✔ Business sections of major daily newspapers

Readership overlaps among these publications, so you can't strictly target publicity outlets by the size of the business in your PR mailings. For example, *Business Week* is written for corporate executives, but I'm sure that many small-business owners read it, too.

The best you can do when targeting PR by the size of a company is to give a little extra attention and focus to those publicity outlets known to concentrate on your market segment. For example, I'd probably devote a separate effort to getting my material into *Inc.* if targeting small to medium-size businesses; for reaching top executives in large corporations, I might concentrate on *Across the Board, Forbes,* and *Fortune.*

You can get a good feel for the audience of any business publication simply by flipping through a recent issue. Or you can read the descriptive listings of these publications in *Writer's Market,* available at your local library and most bookstores.

Although *Writer's Market* is published primarily for freelance writers as a guide to where they can sell their work, businesspeople seeking publicity also find it useful: The listings are more detailed than in the standard publicity outlet directories, especially concerning the readership of each publication and the types of articles sought by their editors.

Location

Some marketers target PR geographically; others do not. Most of my clients in the food business, for example, sell to customers across the country, and geography does not affect their marketing efforts. Regional or local chains, on the other hand, might market only in their immediate and surrounding states because they can offer delivery that is both fast and economical only to prospects who are nearby.

Many companies selling professional, consulting, and technical services to businesses are often similarly restricted to serving markets within the immediate geographic area of their headquarters or branch offices. Companies that sell to businesses from retail outlets — resellers of computer systems, for example — also serve a market within driving distance of the shop or store, as do firms that offer on-site repair services.

Even some companies that sell products may do target marketing based on location. One company, a vitamin chain, finds that marketing efforts do better in some states than others, and it deletes the poorer states when targeting PR efforts.

In today's global marketplace, many U.S. firms are looking to expand into overseas markets. Most certainly, a separate international campaign will be developed; larger, more sophisticated marketers may even have separate campaigns aimed at different regions (Europe versus Asia) or even countries.

To target by location, you can select from *Bacon's Media Directories* and many of the other media directories listed in the appendix those newspapers, business magazines, and consumer magazines with circulations limited to a specific town, region, or state.

Job function or title of prospect within the company

Another means of targeting prospects is by job title. By concentrating your marketing efforts on those people who are responsible for buying, recommending, or specifying your type of product or service, you eliminate the waste of marketing to people not involved with your product or its purchase.

Although PR mailing lists are not categorized by job title, certain publications are aimed at people with specific job titles. *CEO,* for example, is written for chief executive officers; *Purchasing,* for purchasing agents. If I want to reach female consumers, I arrange for the CEO of my client to give a speech at a women's group, such as female entrepreneurs. To reach teens, we might offer a free print or Internet newsletter written specifically for high schoolers. Consult the publicity directories listed in the appendix to research publications that are job-title specific.

Application or use of your product

You can target your marketing efforts based on how the prospect uses your product. Good examples are the pocket planners, daily calendars, time management systems, and other pocket schedulers and diaries sold to businesses.

Some companies sell them to be used personally by the buyer. Their catalogs and mailings go into elaborate detail about how the time management systems work, how they save you time, make your life more efficient, and so on.

Other companies market these items as gifts to be bought by businesses and given to customers, prospects, and colleagues. When selling these same items as a gift, rather than for personal use, copy is much shorter and doesn't detail how the systems work. Instead, it stresses the high value, elegant look, leather cover, personal imprint, and other aspects that make the books and diaries an appealing gift item.

Press releases should be slanted similarly, depending on how you want your product to be positioned in the marketplace. Example: One client sells a software package used by systems analysts to develop applications, but saw that they needed software to help them generate reports in different formats. Because the client's product could handle this function well, a separate marketing and PR campaign positioned the product as a first-rate "report generator."

Take a look at the Sunday *New York Times* and how the different sections reach different readers with different interests. Your releases should be similarly targeted so that people who use a particular product (for example, computers) for a particular application (for example, a home-based business) are attracted by your message.

Channels of distribution

You can target different promotions aimed at getting response from different people in the distribution channel — end users or customers, distributors, agents, resellers, wholesalers, agents, reps, original equipment manufacturers (OEMs), value-added resellers (VARs), stores, and catalogs.

Campaigns aimed at end users or customers naturally stress the benefits of using the product, while promotions aimed at the distribution channel tend to stress how much money or profit the distributor can make by carrying the item in his line and selling it aggressively.

Marketers sometimes use the term *push* to describe marketing to the distribution channel and *pull* to describe marketing to the end user or customer. This is because promotion to dealers is aimed at pushing the product on them and getting them to push it onto their customers, while marketing to customers creates demand that pulls the product through the distribution chain from manufacturer to distributor to end user.

PR aimed at pushing the product through the distribution channel by promoting it to the trade should be sent to trade publications, while PR aimed at pulling the product or service through the distribution channel should be sent to magazines read by consumers and other end users.

For example, to promote a book such as this one to the trade, press releases may be sent to *Publishers Weekly, Library Journal,* and other magazines read by those in the book trade. To promote this book to potential buyers such as business owners, managers, executives, and marketing professionals, press releases may be sent to such publications as *PR Journal, Advertising Age, Business Marketing, Inc.,* and *Business Week.*

Is it better to concentrate your PR efforts toward end users or the distribution channel? It depends on the market and the timing. If customers tend to buy the product directly from the manufacturer and distribution channels account for only a small percentage of sales, then naturally you concentrate your PR efforts on the end user.

In other markets, distribution channels are pretty important. Take books, for example. If bookstores don't buy a particular book from a particular publisher and put it on the shelves, it has very little chance of selling. And with 50,000 new books published each year, most get little or no shelf space in bookstores. So selling the distribution channel is essential.

A similar situation exists in supermarkets. With too many products competing for limited shelf space, many packaged goods manufacturers actually pay the supermarket a fee to stock and display their products.

The same situation affects many PC software packages. Thousands of software packages are on the market, yet most computer stores have room on the shelves for only a few dozen titles. If they don't carry yours, you either have low sales or must direct sales through other channels, such as catalogs, space ads, or direct mail.

How do you overcome this resistance? At first you may think that heavy marketing to the distribution chain is the answer. But suppose that you do this, and the bookstores carry your book. Readers may see it and snap it up. But perhaps they've never heard of it, so they walk right by it. With no demand from the end user, the title will be pulled quickly.

Often, creating a heavy customer demand is effective in getting the distribution channel to buy your product: After all, if your book gets rave reviews and dozens of people ask for it every hour, the bookstore will naturally want to carry it and order many copies from you.

For products where the distribution channel is important, then, you will probably target both the customer and the distribution chain. In most cases, the bulk of your effort will go toward end-user marketing; a much smaller portion will go toward dealer and distributor promotion. Exceptions? Of course.

If you study the publicity outlets as described in the media directories listed in the appendix, you will see that many industries have different magazines aimed at various segments in the distribution channel. In the computer field, *VAR* magazine is aimed at value-added resellers who customize, repackage, and resell software for specific applications, while *Dr. Dobb's Journal* is written for people who design and write software.

Affinity groups

An *affinity group* is a group of prospects with similar interests. These might include classical music buffs, computer gurus, bodybuilders, health and fitness enthusiasts, and other people who vigorously and enthusiastically pursue specialized hobbies, interests, or activities.

When you market a product that appeals to their common interest, you can get much higher results than with mass marketing of the same product to the general population because the people in the affinity group have a demonstrated interest in your product category or in the benefits your product provides.

This is a good example of marketing made more efficient through targeting. "Preaching to the converted" is always easier — it makes more sense to advertise your steaks to beef lovers instead of trying to convince vegetarians that meat is good for them. Targeting to an affinity group assures that your audience is already converted before you start preaching to them.

PR lends itself very well to affinity-group marketing, because in today's publishing industry, the general-interest magazine has given way to the special-interest magazine. Most successful magazines today cover a niche: They report on a specific topic for an audience composed of people with a strong interest in the topic. Examples include bodybuilding magazines, karate magazines, gun magazines, pet magazines, computer hobbyist magazines, car magazines, gourmet magazines, and home magazines. By selecting these publications from the media directories listed in the appendix, you can easily build a list of publicity outlets that reach your affinity-group audience.

Users of specific devices, products, machines, systems, or technologies

Targeting members of this category is a simple, sensible strategy. Its premise: If you're selling fax paper, you'll do a lot better selling to people who own fax machines than to those who don't.

A good example is in the computer field: If you have software that runs only on a Macintosh, you can go to a source of publicity outlets such as *Bacon's Media Directories* or *Media Map* and select publications written specifically for Mac users. This increases the odds for success and eliminates waste; the editor of a magazine for PC users isn't going to run a story on your Mac software (no matter how great the program) because readers can't run the software because they don't have the right machine.

Buying habits

Although this is not a major method of targeting the market, there is some evidence that you can increase marketing results by tailoring your marketing efforts to fit the buying habits or patterns of the target prospects.

In consumer direct marketing, for example, results show that mailings using a sweepstakes do best when mailed to lists of people who have previously responded to sweepstakes mailings. Apparently, these people enjoy sweepstakes and will go through the trouble of entering, more so than the general population that contains a number of people who do not have patience for sweepstakes and do not respond to mailings.

So, if your company is running a big contest or sweepstakes as a promotion, make sure that, in addition to announcing the promotion to all the regular media, you hit publications such as *Contest News* and any others that highlight sweepstakes and contests.

Or, if most of the orders for your product or service are placed with credit cards, you might contact the person at American Express responsible for producing the newsletter mailed with its monthly bill and see whether you can get a mention in one of its service articles or resource lists.

In recent years, companies have begun targeting customers by the buying habit of online purchasing. PR campaigns are targeted to Internet surfers based on their (often) younger age and technical proficiency.

Chapter 5

Formulating Ideas

After spending my entire professional life in public relations, I am convinced that PR — unlike, say, brain surgery or local area network (LAN) design — does not require special education, knowledge, or background for success. Anyone can do it. In fact, to succeed in PR, here's all you need:

✔ **A knowledge of the basics** — the formats, techniques, and methods typically used to communicate with the media. There's nothing mysterious or difficult about them, and they're all in this book.

✔ **The ability to think creatively** — to come up with ideas that are clever, compelling, and relevant to the marketing message.

I hire a lot of creative people at our agency, and yet you may not feel that you're strong in this area. I'm often asked, "Can creativity be taught, or is it something you either have or you don't?"

The answer is: Although some people are more naturally inclined toward promotion and creative marketing, anyone who tries can come up with good PR ideas for his business on his own.

Giving New Ideas a Chance

Many businesspeople, especially managerial types, develop their critical faculties more finely than their creative faculties. If creative engineers and inventors had listened to these people, we would not have personal computers, cars, airplanes, light bulbs, or electricity.

The creative process works in two stages: The first is the idea-producing stage, when ideas flow freely. The second is the critical or "editing" stage, where you hold each idea up to the cold light of day and see whether it's practical. Many people make the mistake of mixing these stages. During the idea-producing stage, they're too eager to criticize an idea as soon as it's presented. As a result, they shoot down ideas and make snap judgments when they should be encouraging the production of those ideas. Many good ideas are killed this way.

A common idea killer is, "We did that already and it didn't work." Yes, but with the rapid pace of change, it's a different marketplace than when you last tried the idea. Maybe the idea can be dusted off and altered a bit to make it work now.

Even more dangerous (and perhaps absurd) is the often-voiced objection, "We don't do things like that around here." My answer: Perhaps it's time to try something new. In over two decades of working as a PR professional, I have discovered one indisputable fact about public relations: When you do the same old thing, you are likely to get the same old results. The only way to get new results is with a new idea.

Creating Profitable PR Programs

Just as public schools are remiss in not teaching how to study, degree programs in marketing and business are remiss in not teaching how to think creatively. If I were to create such a course, I would include idea generation as a series of simple and repeatable steps.

Step 1: Clearly establish the goals of a PR program

Many people forge ahead without knowing what it is they're trying to accomplish. You can use PR to accomplish many different goals, but if you don't establish your goals at the outset, you're unlikely to achieve them.

Goals will vary from industry to industry. For example, when we worked with Domino's Pizza, the goal was simple: Sell more pizza. That's why all the PR was focused on the customer. When we worked with Subway, the goal was to grow the company swiftly, so the PR program was more business-to-business and focused on trade press.

You should be able to state the marketing objective in a single sentence — for example, "Convince people that they should read books on e-book readers and download them off the Internet instead of reading paper books bought in bookstores."

Step 2: Assemble pertinent facts

In crime stories, detectives spend most of their time looking for clues. They can't solve a case with clever thinking alone; they must have the facts. You, too, must have the facts before you can solve a problem or make an informed decision.

Professionals in every field know the importance of gathering specific facts. A scientist planning an experiment checks the abstracts to see what similar experiments have been performed. An author writing a book collects everything she can on the subject: newspaper clippings, photos, official records, transcripts of interviews, diaries, magazine articles, and so on. A consultant may spend weeks or months digging around a company before coming up with a solution to a major problem. When I took on a cigar club as a client, I began smoking expensive cigars and socializing in the cigar culture to get a deeper understanding of that world.

Keep an organized file of the background material you collect on a project. Review the file before you begin to formulate your solution. If you're a competent typist, use word processing software to rewrite your research notes and materials. This step increases your familiarity with the background information and can give you a fresh perspective on the problem. Also, when you type notes, you condense a mound of material into a few neat pages that show all the facts at a glance.

Step 3: Gather general knowledge

In business, specific facts have to do with the project at hand. They include the budget, the schedule, the resources available, and the customer's specifications, plus knowledge of the products, components, and techniques to be used in completing the project. General knowledge has to do with the expertise you've developed in your life and includes your storehouse of information concerning events, people, media, culture, science, technology, management, and the world at large.

You can accelerate your own education by becoming a student in the many areas that relate to your job. Subscribe to the journals that relate to your field. Scan them all, and clip and save articles that contain information that may be useful to you. Organize your clipping files for easy access to articles by subject.

Read books in your field and start a reference library. Take some night school courses. Attend seminars, conferences, and trade shows. Make friends with people in your field and exchange information, stories, ideas, case histories, and technical tips. Most of the successful professionals I know are compulsive information collectors. You should be, too.

Step 4: Look for combinations

Someone once complained to me, "There's nothing new in the world. It's all been done before." Maybe. But an idea doesn't have to be something completely new. Many ideas are simply new combinations of existing elements. By looking for combinations, for new relationships between old ideas, you can come up with a fresh approach.

The clock radio, for example, was invented by someone who combined two existing technologies: the clock and the radio. The Earl of Sandwich, who invented the sandwich, did so because he wanted to hold his meat in his hands and eat while gambling.

Look for synergistic combinations when you examine the facts. What clever promotion can you think of that ties in with your marketing objective and demonstrates your message in a creative way? For Empire Kosher Chickens, we wanted to dramatize how carefully each chicken is inspected. Our promotion was to offer a free chicken to anyone whose income tax form was being "inspected" (audited) by the IRS. The press ate it up (excuse the pun).

Step 5: Sleep on it

Putting the problem aside for a time can help you renew your idea-producing powers just when you think that your creative well has run dry. But don't resort to this method after only five minutes of puzzled thought. First, you have to gather all the information you can. Next, you need to go over the information again and again as you try to come up with that one big idea. You'll come to a point where you get bleary, punch-drunk, hashing the same ideas over and over. This is the time to take a break, put the problem aside, sleep on it, and let your unconscious mind take over.

A solution may strike you as you sleep, shower, shave, or walk in the park. Even if that doesn't happen, when you return to the problem, you will find that you can attack it with renewed vigor and a fresh perspective. I use this technique in writing: I put aside what I've written and read it fresh the next day. Many times, the things I thought were brilliant when I wrote them can be much improved at second glance.

Step 6: Use a checklist

You can use checklists to stimulate creative thinking and as a starting point for new ideas. Many manufacturers, consultants, technical magazines, and trade associations publish checklists that you can use in your own work. But the best checklists are those you create yourself, because they're tailored to the problems that come up in your daily routine.

For example, Jill is a technical salesperson who is well versed in the technical features of her product, but she has trouble when it comes to closing a sale. She could overcome this weakness by making a checklist of typical customer objections and how to answer them. (She can cull the list of objections from sales calls made over the course of several weeks. She can garner possible tactics for overcoming these objections from fellow salespeople, from books on selling, and from her own trial-and-error efforts.) Then when faced with a tough customer, she doesn't have to reinvent the wheel but is prepared for all the standard objections because of her familiarity with the checklist.

Keep in mind that no checklist can contain an idea for every situation that arises. ***Remember:*** You use a checklist as a tool for creative thinking, not as a crutch.

Step 7: Get feedback

Sherlock Holmes was a brilliant detective. But even he needed to bounce ideas off Dr. Watson at times. As a professional publicist, I think I know how to plan an effective PR campaign. But when I show a draft to my partner, he can always spot at least half a dozen ways to make it better.

Some people — maybe you — prefer to work alone. But if you don't work as part of a team, getting someone else's opinion of your work can help you focus your thinking and produce ideas you hadn't thought of.

Take the feedback for what it's worth. If you feel that you're right and that the criticisms are off base, ignore them. But more often than not, the feedback provides useful information that can help you come up with the best, most profitable ideas.

Of course, if you ask others to take a look at a piece, you should be willing to do the same for them when they solicit your opinion. You'll find that reviewing the work of others is fun; critiquing someone else's work is easier than creating your own. And you'll be gratified by the improvements you think of — things that are obvious to you but would never have occurred to the other person.

Identify a gem

A gem is a great idea that makes you look like a star. The problem with gems is that they're only obvious after the fact. Coming up with them and identifying them in your plan is where the talent lies in PR.

Actually, a gem is only a gem if the timing is right. A good idea too late doesn't qualify as a gem. Speed — acting quickly when you have a good idea — is crucial. That's why you must be always on the lookout for stories in the news that your company or your client can become a part of. Then you must move on it right away (and don't let the press release get caught in the editing process) or the issue will disappear and it will be too late.

Step 8: Team up

Some people think more creatively when they work in groups. But how large should the group be? My opinion is that two is the ideal team. Any more and you're in danger of ending up with a committee that spins its wheels and accomplishes nothing. The person you team up with should have skills and thought processes that balance and complement your own. For example, in advertising, copywriters (the word people) team up with art directors (the picture people).

In entrepreneurial firms, the idea person who started the company often hires a professional manager from a Fortune 500 company as the new venture grows. The entrepreneur knows how to make things happen, but the manager knows how to run a profitable, efficient corporation.

As an engineer, you may invent a better microchip. But if you want to make a fortune selling it, you should team up with someone who has a strong sales and marketing background.

Finding Other Ways to Turn on the Light Bulb

Thomas Edison said that genius is 1 percent inspiration and 99 percent perspiration. But sometimes you need more inspiration to get your creative juices flowing. Here are a few ideas that have worked for me and people I know:

- ✔ Go to a toy store and look around. Can you create a game to publicize your message?

- ✔ Keep a *swipe file* — a file of promotions that you especially like or that at least caught your eye. Use them for inspiration when planning your own PR.

- ✔ Ask employees for suggestions. Reward the winning idea with a $100 gift certificate.

- ✔ Browse the library or bookstore. Or hang out at a museum. Inspiration often strikes in places where you're surrounded by ideas.

- ✔ Look outside your industry. What is a common, successful promotion in one industry may be creatively copied and applied to your industry, in which it is unheard of and, therefore, novel.

- ✔ Read literature on creative thinking. I recommend *A Whack on the Side of the Head* by Roger von Oech and anything on creativity by Michael LeBouf.

- ✔ Keep a pad and pen with you at all times to record thoughts as they occur to you. People have ideas all the time, but they lose them when they don't write them down.

- ✔ Whenever you write down a creative idea, drop it into a paper file or enter it into your computer. Keep a central idea file that you can dip into when you need a new creative promotion.

Thoughts on creative thinking

Here are a few of my favorite quotations about creative thinking:

- ✔ "The best way to have a good idea is to have lots of ideas." — Linus Pauling

- ✔ "The best ideas come from jokes. Make your thinking as funny as possible." — David Ogilvy

- ✔ "When in doubt, make a fool of yourself. There is a microscopically thin line between being brilliantly creative and acting like the most gigantic idiot on earth." — Cynthia Heimel

- ✔ "If you want to make something happen, you have to be outrageous. You have to go beyond what is acceptable. Unwillingness to do that is the biggest risk of all." — Mike Vance

Chapter 6

Using PR Tactics

*I*n the old cartoon *Felix the Cat,* Felix was able to win the day by reaching into his "bag of tricks." All PR practitioners have a similar bag of tricks — favorite PR tactics that they have used with success and often resort to when creating campaigns. This chapter presents a miscellany of some of the best tricks in my own bag.

A well-rounded PR campaign will not target only TV or only print. It will go after all types of media (as you can see in our sample PR plan in Chapter 2). Use multiple "tricks" or tactics simultaneously. Take the same subject matter and make it visual for TV, make it "how-to" for radio, and so on. For print, come up with ways to pitch the same story to different sections of the newspaper. I like to tell my staff, "If they close the doors, go in through the windows." And the only way is if we have multiple ways to get into the house.

Going Where the Cameras Are

Look for creative ways to tie in your product with current news or trends. If you use a news tie-in, you don't need to create a news story from scratch and then attempt to get the media to cover it. Piggybacking on an existing news story with a relevant promotional tie-in — one that is both credible and favorable to your product — is much more cost-effective. As the event is already happening, it won't be on your dime to create it.

The idea: If you get involved in a story the press is already covering, you'll find getting *yourself* covered is that much easier. When one of our clients, Earth's Best, introduced a new line of organic baby food, the safety of eating genetically engineered foods was making headlines. We grabbed our share of these headlines for our client when we sent out a press release (reprinted in Chapter 15) announcing that Earth's Best baby foods would not contain any genetically engineered ingredients.

Although organic foods had been around for a long time and were of interest in themselves, promoting the new baby foods as "100 percent pure" and "made without GMOs" (genetically modified organisms) was a new twist that allowed us to grab some of the media attention already focused on the controversial issue of genetic engineering.

We also sent free pizza from Domino's Pizza to last-minute taxpayers. By sending free pizza to the post office on April 15 at midnight, we didn't have to call the TV camera crews and try to convince them to film the event — they were already there filming last-minute taxpayers standing in line trying to make the filing deadline. When our pizza-delivery team showed up, how could the TV crews do anything but turn the cameras on our client's product, which was right in front of them?

Creating a Tie-in to a TV Show or Movie

You know that the hot motion picture — usually the one that was number one at the box office over the weekend — gets an incredible amount of public attention for a short period, usually a few weeks. The highest-rated new TV show of the season gets a similarly disproportionate share of buzz for a somewhat longer period — up to several months. By creating a campaign that ties your product to these popular big- and little-screen attractions, you can siphon off some of their buzz and apply it to your own story for greatly expanded media coverage.

For example, when the movie *Coneheads* was hot, we created a promotion for a chain of sandwich shops in which any customer coming in to a store and claiming to have seen an alien would get a free sandwich.

When Regis Philbin's *Who Wants to Be a Millionaire* became a hit, we did a promotion for a client that linked *Millionaire* to fitness — by offering to make you fit enough and strong enough to beat up a millionaire.

Spotlighting the Product

You can use many products as props or devices to add visual and tactile interest to PR and promotional campaigns. This is both a better way to connect with your target audience and leave a lasting impression on viewers. In addition, you'll increase the number of placements that you get.

One publisher who advertised his magazine as the "hot" publication in its field sent a handsome tin containing a pound of chili powder to potential advertisers.

Once, my agency staff scotch-taped press releases for a client — a pizza chain — to pizza boxes containing hot pies and delivered them to local broadcast media 20 minutes before the evening news. The broadcast personalities not only talked about the promotion on the news but also actually ate the pizza on camera!

What made this strategy effective was the combination of timing and humor. Delivering deep-dish pizza right as they were going on the air is not so unique. But the fact that it was hot food meant it was delivered directly into the newsroom. (A salad probably would have sat on a desk somewhere.) What we added to that was humor. The entire campaign was a preposterous theory, which we elaborated on in the press release. It was all tongue in cheek.

Every local affiliate used it on the same night, which is unheard of. They didn't use it simply because of the timing but also because it was so funny.

Staging a Contest

Contests can generate an enormous amount of media coverage. Public relations history clearly shows that making your contest new and different from any others can yield great results. Of course, the contest should also relate to the product.

For example, thanks to the First in Line Contest, IKEA store openings have people camping out nights before as if it were a rock concert. This is not your run-of-the-mill contest. It generates tremendous excitement, not to mention local media coverage (plus a cover story in a national business magazine). And the prize for the contest not only relates to the product, the prize **is** the product. The winner gets $3,000 of home furnishings.

Figure 6-1 is the release we did as a promotion for Jose Cuervo. It's a takeoff on the old message-in-a-bottle theme. The contest was that if you found the bottle, you won a lifetime supply of tequila. The tongue-in-cheek style was appropriate both to the nature of the promotion and to the fun-oriented image of the product.

PLEASE HELP US FIND OUR BELOVED BLOW-UP BOTTLE

Jose Cuervo Offers Lifetime Supply* of Tequila as a Reward for Safe Return of Promotional Bottle

Last seen wearing a red and gold Jose Cuervo label at the CozyMel's Bar and Restaurant in Westbury, Long Island on the night of May 5, 2000. Various witnesses reported last seeing the bottle at 1:30 AM (EST) on the morning of May 6, 2000.

At the time of the disappearance, the bottle was only four days old. It weighs approximately 300 pounds when deflated and stands 3 stories tall. Often full of hot air and known for occasional "outbursts," the bottle had been partying all night in celebration of Cinco de Mayo and reportedly disappeared between 1:30 AM and 1:50 AM on the night in question….

 "Although only four days old, we were very attached to the bottle," explained Velvet Mickens, Director of Marketing, Tequila Portfolio at UDV-NE, Jose Cuervo's parent company, as she held back tears. "It may be big, and even a bit clunky… but it has a lot of heart." Other employees at Jose Cuervo have been holding a candle vigil at their corporate offices in Stamford, CT, since the incident.

All information given will be confidential and we will be not be pressing charges. The person that comes forward with information or the bottle itself will receive a lifetime supply of tequila.*

For additional information contact: Lara Hauptman at 212/645-6900.

The lifetime supply of tequila is equivalent to 1 bottle every four months for 25 years.

Figure 6-1:
Message-in-a-bottle release for Jose Cuervo.

WARNING!

Before running any promotional contest, run all the copy and materials by your attorney. Contests and sweepstakes are regulated by laws, and noncompliance can give you the kind of PR you wish you never had.

Working for a Worthy Cause

If you're going to help others, do so creatively. Merely giving sums of money to charity — even if you're giving large sums — gets you little PR bang for the buck. It's best to avoid commonplace charitable acts and invest your time and energy creating other, more unique ways to give that can help a group or cause and provide a great benefit for the recipient while promoting your brand or corporate image.

Here's one example: Domino's Pizza in Washington DC wanted to raise money for, and awareness about, the growing homelessness in that market. The main tactic used in their PR campaign was to print — directly on the pizza boxes — educational information about homelessness plus contact information to encourage donations to several large shelters in the area. But that effort alone was not enough to generate mass media coverage.

We also recruited the late Frank Meeks, the local Domino's franchisee who owned and operated 60 extremely successful franchises in that market, to spend a couple nights in one of these homeless shelters. The media covered that, every night and morning he was there, raising both funds and awareness.

Rhinotek, a manufacturer of ink cartridges for laser printers and fax machines, based its brand on the rhinoceros. Rhinos are featured on product packaging and promotional giveaways, such as rhino mouse pads. Even when it comes to charitable donations, Rhinotek reinforces its brand by donating a percentage of the profits from every product purchased to help preserve the rhino as a species. By detailing its charitable contributions in brochures given to dealers, not only does the charity benefit, but the brand benefits as well.

If you choose a worthy cause because you really do want to help, not because you want the publicity, you may wonder whether you should follow through with publicizing the donation. The question to ask yourself is this: Will the media exposure help the charity? If so, then you should follow through. Often, a charity values the simple exposure it gets, because it's more exposure than it would receive otherwise.

Tying In to a Holiday

Relating your campaign either to a holiday (Valentine's Day, Halloween, Thanksgiving, Christmas) or to an event (National Secretary's Week, Elvis Presley's birthday) works because it increases your odds of getting coverage. You must be talking to the press at a time when the press cares, is looking for material, and will listen. So if you reach out with an idea related to Valentine's Day on February 12 (not the 17th) you're more likely to be covered.

The aphrodisiac survey campaign (reprinted later in this chapter) tying in with Valentine's Day for AllHerb.com, an herb and nutritional supplement e-commerce Web site, is a good example of a holiday tie-in. We also did a tie-in for AllHerb.com with Cancer Awareness Month called "Stop Smoking, Mon, for Pokémon."

Conducting a Survey

By definition, the news media are interested in news above everything else. And it's not always easy for PR people to come up with something that is news — or even new. Surveys are my secret weapon in PR; they're one of the easiest ways to provide the news media with the news they crave. The reason is simple: There is very little new information in the world. But a survey, by definition, always creates new information. If you survey 1,000 business executives and 87 percent answer yes to your survey question "Do you feel stress on the job?", then you have created a fact — "Eighty-seven percent of 1,000 executives surveyed by XYZ Company say that they feel stress on the job" — that you and no one else owns.

For a trade association of pet manufacturers, we did a survey showing that pet owners were more successful than those who didn't own pets at keeping their New Year's resolutions — promoting the value of owning a pet. Another survey for the same association promoted pet ownership by showing that 73 percent of companies surveyed said that having pets in the office increases productivity.

For Calyx & Corolla, a direct marketer of flowers, a survey indicated that corporate CEOs like flowers, and sending flowers to your CEO may help you land a raise.

We also did a survey for a client who sells nutritional supplements over the Internet. Again, we tied in with a holiday. The holiday was Valentine's Day, so we used the theme of romance. How to relate nutritional supplements to romance? By linking foods (which are nutrients) to their roles as aphrodisiacs. Figure 6-2 shows the press release for this campaign.

AllHerb.com

Contact: Marisa Milo
Jericho Communications
212-645-6900 x126

THIS VALENTINE S DAY, DON T SAY IT WITH FLOWERS, DIAMONDS, OR WORDS FROM THE HEART SAY IT WITH GARLIC???!!

Do oysters really get you in the mood? Or does chocolate actually make you romantic?? People have always questioned whether or not aphrodisiacs really work. Well, finally someone has actually put aphrodisiacs to the test. According to the study conducted by AllHerb.com, an online herbal resource, **the number one foods that couples who spoon frequently ate during the week they were surveyed were made with garlic, followed by dishes prepared with shiitake mushrooms, chocolate, and lemon.**

The survey, which queried 314 couples nationwide for a week to determine what aphrodisiacs make you feel sexy, romantic and cuddly – had couples fill out a form documenting how many times they had sex, orgasms, felt romantic, and did different "nuzzling" activities comparable to what they ate that evening. The study also discovered that couples who cooked regularly with certain ingredients found themselves to be "in the mood" more often: **the top five spices that couples who had sex the most often during the week cooked with were: cayenne pepper, followed by rosemary, garlic, onion, and basil.**

"Food is a source of many natural ingredients that can do anything from curing a headache to stimulating your hormones," explained Ken Hakuta, CEO of AllHerb.com. "Many of the foods we eat everyday affect us in ways we're not even aware of, and with Valentine's Day approaching, we wanted to take a look to find natural ingredients that act as aphrodisiacs"….

Figure 6-2: Valentine's Day aphrodisiacs press release.

Staging an Event

Create news worth covering by staging an event. But first, you must decide what your goal is for the event. Is it all about awareness or sales? Do you want to get a thousand people in attendance, 5 million to read about it, or 5,000 to buy? And if you don't get any ink, but you get 1,000 people to show up, is that enough exposure for the price of the event? (By the way, you don't have to have a big budget to do this. Sometimes it can cost you only the price of the product you provide.)

The National Hockey League (NHL) hired the PR firm I founded to create excitement around the playoffs. To accomplish this objective, we worked on an event called the "Cup Crazy" traveling festival. The event was like a traveling carnival show. It included a range of hockey-related and other games, such as an in-line hockey tournament, slap-shot contests, and ticket raffles. The event, which was capped off by the appearance of the Stanley Cup in each playoff city, was covered in *Sports Illustrated, USA Today,* and *Newsweek* and on *Hard Copy* and *Extra.* More than half a million people attended the event during the playoffs.

For more information on using events as PR promotions, see Chapter 19.

Making Them Laugh

Don't overlook humor as a source of PR inspiration and ideas. If you can play off something familiar in a fun and different way, you can get people smiling. Many editors and producers look for light material and filler to run between harder news stories, and you can gain a lot of media coverage by providing material for this feature.

As an example, several comedians joked in their routines about removing the DO NOT REMOVE UNDER PENALTY OF LAW tags from furniture. To announce a bedroom furnishing sale for IKEA, we created a campaign in which we offered a discount to anyone who removed and brought us the DO NOT REMOVE tags from their pillows. As an added creative element, the tags became entry tickets to a sweepstakes, the grand prize for which was a trip to Alcatraz. The campaign received extensive media exposure nationwide.

Humor is often an effective way to make a serious point, too. In a campaign for Empire Kosher Chicken, for example, the objective was to communicate how carefully the company inspects its chickens. In the campaign, people who sent in proof that the IRS was auditing them got a free chicken. We said that if the IRS audits you — an excruciating process for most consumers — you have some idea of how Empire's chickens feel after they're inspected! The campaign got wide media play, and even the *Wall Street Journal* ran a feature on it.

Waging a Trade-in Campaign

As Chapter 15 outlines more fully, trade-ins — while clearly a gimmick — can catch the media's attention if you do them in a clever way.

For British Knight, for example, the objective was to promote its shoes to the youth market. We created a special promotion to encourage kids to play outdoors rather than watch television. If the parents sent in a TV remote control (which we actually returned, so they lost nothing), the child would get a pair of free sneakers. In another campaign for British Knight, we had consumers trade in smelly socks for new sneakers.

To promote Domino's Pizza as comfort food, we offered a free pizza to anyone who turned in a pink slip (termination notice) or layoff notice from work or a rejection letter from a college. The tie-in with pizza? The creation of "Eat Your Rejection Letter" month. Pizza sales soared the day after Johnny Carson started his monologue with this story on the *Tonight Show*.

Creating a Character

Who doesn't know and love Mr. Whipple, Aunt Jemima, Sam Breakstone, Colonel Sanders, Ronald McDonald, or the Dunkin' Donuts "Time to Make the Donuts" guy? Creating characters has proven successful in advertising for decades. Now we're finding that it can work in PR, too.

Empire Kosher Chicken once asked us to stimulate sales during the winter months. We created a character named Bubby and dubbed her "America's Jewish Grandmother." Bubby offered people a chance to treat their colds by trading in their modern cold medicine for a free soup recipe and a free kosher chicken. Thousands of people wrote in to Empire Chicken to take advantage of this offer, putting the chickens (and the attitude of an Empire Chicken being nourishing and even medicinal) in the households of many first-time users.

Using Viral Marketing

Viral marketing is a term used to describe techniques that harness the power of the Internet and existing social networks to produce exponential increases in brand awareness.

It's called "viral" marketing because it spreads like a virus, mostly through e-mail (sometimes called *word-of-mouse*), and can be used to reach a large number of people quickly — if you've targeted well and have creative ideas. Much of what gets spread is the printed word — jokes and letters — but video clips and games are being passed around the Internet more and more and have become hugely popular for corporate PR.

How it works is quite simple: one person sends it to everyone in their address book, maybe 10 or 100 people. They, in turn, do the same. It's organic, not manufactured, so there is no list of names that the marketer can access. For example, Road Rage Rendezvous is a videoclip from IKEA Home Furnishings that spread exponentially around the Internet and hit the top of the viral marketing charts. People passed it along because it was so clever.

This tactic is popular because, compared to other tools, it's relatively inexpensive. Anyone can do it. One weakness, however, is that the messages, delivered via e-mail, can be mistaken for spam, which can put the brand at risk. One way around that is to make sure the From and Subject lines are recognizable to the recipients so they know the message isn't unsolicited.

Part III
Putting the Wheels in Motion

The 5th Wave   By Rich Tennant

BEEKS
Bird Supplies

"Tell the PR department I love the new client newsletter. It's interesting, informative, but more than that, it's absorbent and fits into the bottom of most bird cages."

In this part . . .

A large part of PR is creating the variety of documents that deliver your story to your various audiences, including the media, the public, customers, and employees. One of the most versatile of these documents is the company newsletter, and Chapter 7 shows how to produce a newsletter and use it to promote yourself. Chapter 8 shows how to write and format the most commonly used weapon in the PR arsenal, the humble but powerful press release. In Chapter 9, I give you complete instructions for writing and placing articles that promote your business, as well as getting the press to write articles about you or quote you in their pages. But PR isn't all paper; sometimes you've got to get on the phone or even dress up and go out of the office to sell your story to the media. Chapter 10 deals with delivering your message in person through public speaking.

Chapter 7

Creating a Company Newsletter

*E*ven a regular, frequent program of public relations, as described throughout this book, cannot guarantee consistent exposure of the target audience to your key messages. There are several reasons for this: Not every effort is certain to yield equal results, you cannot control the exact timing and placement of PR pickups, and the media outlets are widely dispersed and read by different people, so not every prospect will see every pickup.

There is one marketing communications tool that you can use to assure regular, repeat, consistent exposure for your company name, message, and information: the promotional newsletter.

These newsletters, magazines, tabloids, or other regular publications are published primarily as marketing tools. They range from simple sheets published in-house to elaborate, four-color company magazines with photography and professional writing rivaling the quality of newsstand magazines. More and more newsletters are published electronically, due to the vast savings on printing.

In this chapter, find out how to create a newsletter that addresses different audiences, internal and external, how often to send it, how to send it (both printed and via email), plus how it should be designed and marketed.

Meeting Internal Needs: The Employee Newsletter

An employee, or "internal," newsletter can be created and used by a company of any size, but if you have 100 or more employees, you definitely need one. It's not a frill or something you do for fun. It is a strategic PR tool — without it, you won't maintain control of the communication within your company.

People want to work for a company they believe in and feel a part of. They want to work in a positive environment. An employee newsletter can support and reinforce your positive message, communicating the same message in the same voice at the same time.

Include the following ideas when deciding what you want to communicate to your employees:

- ✔ **Celebrate the victories of the company.** Everyone needs to know what has happened in the past month. For example, the receptionist (or anyone else answering the phone) must be briefed on the company's successes and be able to answer basic questions. Our company newsletter has featured new clients and accounts we've recently won, as well as recognition we've received within the public relations industry.

- ✔ **Devote space to employee profiles and announcements of internal awards.** Your employees like to see themselves in print as much as any client, and they want to hear about their colleagues. Who brought in a new piece of business? Where has the company been recognized and for what? Who got married? Who had a baby? We've done that with regular sections such as "Placement of the Week" and "Best Campaign of the Month."

- ✔ **Communicate the official message about difficult situations.** When things go wrong, the official message needs to be communicated to everyone in the company and the employee newsletter is the perfect place to do that. When addressing a difficult situation in writing, be brief and provide only the facts. *Remember:* The spoken word should precede the written word, so be sure to make a verbal announcement as soon as possible. Don't let employees get the bad news for the first time in your newsletter.

Where cost is an issue, you can use the same newsletter for both internal and external audiences. But because they're two distinct audiences with very different needs, it's best to have two separate newsletters.

Staying in Touch with Your External Audience

The main purpose of a promotional newsletter is to establish your image and build your credibility with a select audience (the people who receive the newsletter) over an extended period of time.

Reaching a busy audience

Instinctively, most marketers recognize that they should be in touch with their customers and prospects far more often than they actually are. You know, for instance, that you may not think about, see, or talk to certain people in your life for long periods of time simply because you're busy and not thinking of them.

Your customers and prospects are busy, too. And although you may be agonizing over why Joe hasn't placed an order with you recently or called your firm to handle a project, Joe isn't even thinking about you because he has so much else on his mind.

You know that you should be doing something to keep your name in front of Joe and remind him of your existence. You may want to call or send a letter, but you think doing so is too pushy. And besides, you don't have a real *reason* to call, and you don't want to seem as though you're begging for business. The newsletter solves this problem. It regularly places your name and activities in front of your customers and prospects, reminding them of your existence, products, and services on a regular basis. And you need no excuse to make this contact, because the prospect *expects* to receive a newsletter on a regular basis. The newsletter increases the frequency of message repetition and supplements other forms of communication such as catalogs, print ads, and sales letters.

Knowing what's newsworthy

The definition of news is just that: It's new. Something gets added to yesterday's news to make it new today. But that's not necessarily the case with your promotional newsletter. People often need to be reminded of stuff they already know but have forgotten. Sometimes it makes them feel good to read something they already know.

Your external audience cares more about the success of the PR campaigns you're running and less about the individual people in your company. They care about trends in the industry, the way world events affect the industry. They want to hear your perspective on other PR campaigns, as well as new areas of expertise you've developed, new services you offer, new technologies and techniques you're using. All that content can also go a long way toward generating leads for your company.

What your customers and prospects read in your promotional newsletter must, however, be fresh — a fresh take on an old idea, a different angle on a tried-and-true technique, an update on a story you're following. All these subjects are newsworthy in the context of a promotional newsletter.

Deciding on Size and Frequency

How often should your newsletter be published? Four times a year — once every three months — is ideal. Publish fewer issues, and people aren't aware you're sending them a newsletter per se; they feel as though they're just getting a piece of mail from time to time. Four times per year is enough to establish credibility and awareness. Publishing six times or more per year is unnecessary, because some months you may prefer to make contact with your prospects by using other media, such as the telephone, direct mail, or catalogs.

What's more, my experience indicates that most companies don't have enough news to fill six or more issues each year. If your schedule is too frequent, you may find yourself putting unnecessary fluff and filler in the newsletter just to get something in the mail. Your readers will be turned off by the poor content and lack of quality, and your newsletter will eventually hurt rather than help you.

How long should your printed newsletter be? In my opinion, four to eight pages is the ideal length for a printed promotional newsletter. More than that is too much reading, and two pages seems insubstantial — more like a flyer or circular (which is perceived as junk mail) than a newsletter (which is perceived as a useful publication).

You may wonder whether you should keep printing your newsletter or send it electronically, but we haven't arrived at the completely electronic age yet. This choice, while based partially on budget considerations, should also depend on the industry and the demographics of your audience. The younger your market, the higher their expectations for and openness to anything electronic. See "Using the Company Newsletter as a Marketing Tool" later in this chapter for more information on using an electronic newsletter.

Creating a Mailing List

Basically, your company newsletter should go to anyone with whom you want to establish a regular relationship. These people can include the following:

- ✔ Current customers
- ✔ Past customers
- ✔ Current prospects
- ✔ Past prospects
- ✔ Employees
- ✔ Vendors
- ✔ Colleagues
- ✔ Consultants, gurus, and other prominent members of your industry
- ✔ Referral sources (influential people who can refer business to you)
- ✔ Trade publication editors, business columnists, and other members of the press who might use material in your newsletter in their own writings

All your current customers should receive your newsletter. The newsletter is an important vehicle for keeping in touch on a regular and predictable basis. It confers automatic high visibility and does so in the best possible way: by reflecting you as a knowledgeable and competent professional. This not only builds your image but also helps to ensure that current customers will remain responsive to your recommendations.

Also send the newsletter to customers who use your services or products in a very limited manner and to those with whom you haven't visited recently. You may not think of them as current customers, but, of course, they are. What's more, the newsletter offers the kind of visibility that prompts many marginal customers to expand their use of your products and services instead of drifting away from you.

Here are some ways to build your subscriber list:

- ✔ **Include all current and past prospects and customers on the list.** But don't use names that are too old. For example, include past prospects and customers that are no more than two or three years old.

- ✔ **Add all the names of the people your company's salespeople call on regularly.** Salespeople have their own favorite prospects who may not be in the corporate database. Ask your salespeople to give you these names. You essentially want to convert the dozens of individual names from Blackberries or other address books, electronic or otherwise, kept by various salespeople and sales reps into a single, integrated subscriber list for your newsletter.

✔ **Add the people on your media list.**

✔ **Automatically add all new inquiries and new customers to your subscription list.** Include every response and every sales lead generated by your ads, direct mail, and other lead-generation programs.

✔ **For trade shows, create a subscription application form and offer a free one-year subscription to anyone who stops by your booth and completes the form.**

✔ **Don't forget to include the names of your immediate supervisors, your product and brand managers, your sales and marketing managers, your CEO, and any other key personnel whose support you need in order to run an effective PR effort.** Company managers enjoy getting the newsletter and often offer ideas for articles and stories you can use.

Designing Your Company Newsletter

You want your newsletter to stand apart and be easily recognized by those who receive it. But newsletters don't have to be elaborate to get readers' attention. The design, however, should be attractive, easy to read, and consistent from issue to issue in order to build recognition and awareness. After a time, many recipients will come to welcome your newsletter, even seek it out from among the pile of mail in their inbox. But you'll get that result only if the newsletter has a distinctive, recognizable, and consistent design.

Making some design decisions

Although many paid subscription newsletters are simply pages of typewritten text, a more graphically pleasing design that uses some color and artwork will enhance your image and make your newsletter stand out from the rest.

You need to make several decisions as you begin the design process. Do you want a two- or three-column layout? Do you want *rules* (lines) between the stories? Do you plan to use white or colored paper stock? Are you going to use one or two colors of ink? What *font* (type style) is appropriate for your audience? What size will your headings be? Another important design element that you need to develop is the nameplate highlighting the name of the publication. In some cases, you may want to use the services of a graphic designer or artist to help you with some of these design issues.

You need to determine the look, content, and feel of your newsletter long before you even publish the first issue. In addition to the basic format, you also need to decide approximate length of copy, the type of graphic elements (photos, line drawings, graphs, and so on) needed, the technical depth of the content, and the types of articles to be featured.

For instance, you may decide that each issue will contain two feature articles, one biographical profile, a regular question-and-answer column on technical issues, one product-related story, three or four short news tidbits, and a box with short previews of the next issue. Your newsletter may be different, of course, but the point is, you'll eventually find a formula that works and stick with it from issue to issue.

Readers like this consistency of format because they know what to look for in each issue. For example, when people open the Sunday newspaper, some readers turn to the sports section first; others go to the comics; still others read *Dear Abby* first. In the same way, some readers may check your technical tips column first, while others will read the profile. Make these features look and read the same in each issue (even position them in the same spot) so that readers gain a comfortable familiarity with your publication.

Putting together your newsletter

After you have a newsletter design, putting together each issue is not terribly difficult.

The first step is to make a list of any possible story ideas. (See the "Newsletter story ideas" sidebar, later in this chapter.) Then narrow the list to only the ones to be featured in the next issue. If you're unsure about how much room you'll have, you're better off selecting one or two extra ideas than too few. You can always use the extra material in a future edition.

Don't reinvent the newsletter wheel

The material in your promotional newsletter doesn't have to be original, nor must it be created solely for the newsletter. In fact, a company newsletter is an ideal medium for recycling other promotional and publicity material created by your company, such as speeches, articles, press releases, annual reports, presentations, and so on. Try to get maximum use out of material you've already created while minimizing the time and expense of writing and producing the newsletter.

Create a file folder for each article and collect the information that will serve as background material for the person writing the story. This background material typically includes sales brochures (for product stories), press releases (which are edited into short news stories), and reprints of published trade journal articles on a particular topic (which are often combined and compiled into a new article on a similar topic).

The next step is to write each story based on this material. Many businesses hire freelance writers to write and edit their company newsletters. Others do it themselves. A few hire their PR or ad agency to do it. Using freelancers is usually more cost-effective. Besides, although most freelancers relish such assignments, most ad agencies don't like doing company newsletters because they find them unprofitable.

Some articles may require more information than is contained in the background material. In this case, supply the writer with the names and phone numbers of people within your company whom he can interview to gather the additional information. Notify these people in advance that a freelance writer will be calling to interview them for the newsletter. If they object, find substitutes.

After you get the copy, the next step is to edit it, send it through for review, and make any final changes. The shorter the review cycle, the better. An article on a new product, for instance, should go to the product manager, an engineer, and maybe the company president for comment. But don't give it to ten people for review; too many cooks spoil the broth.

Then give the final copy to your graphic artist or printer, who will create a layout. Carefully proofread and review this before it is printed. Many companies today use desktop publishing systems in-house or hire outside desktop publishing services for newsletter layout and creation.

When the copy is approved, make any final changes and send the revised layout to the printer. Find out whether your printer prefers to work with hard-copy originals or computer files and what resolution is required.

If your subscriber list is small — say, only a few hundred names — you can have your computer generate gummed mailing labels and affix them on the newsletters in-house. After you have a thousand or more subscribers, you may want to use a letter shop, fulfillment house, or similar mailing service to handle the mailing and distribution on a regular basis. Get an estimate from an outside service. Then compare this estimate against the time it takes to do it yourself in-house. This comparison will give you an idea of whether outsourcing newsletter circulation makes sense.

Using the Company Newsletter as a Marketing Tool

You can do several things to promote your newsletter (and to use the newsletter offer as a promotion).

Consider offering the newsletter as an extra incentive to people who respond to your direct mail. You can do something as simple as adding a line to the business reply cards that you include with your mailings with a box that says, "Check here if you would like a free one-year subscription to our quarterly newsletter." You can also emphasize the newsletter offer in the P.S. of your sales letter.

You can offer the newsletter as an extra incentive for responding to your company's print advertising campaign, especially if you use print ads to generate sales leads. You can generate inquiries from ads by including a coupon the reader can fill out and return to request a free catalog or product brochure. You can get more coupons returned by adding another check box to the response coupon that says, "Check here for a free one-year subscription to our newsletter." Although a *brochure* or *catalog* sounds purely promotional, people perceive *newsletters* as valuable information. So offering a subscription to your company newsletter will get more people to respond to your ads.

At speeches, seminars, and presentations, your company representatives can use the newsletter offer to get listeners involved in conversations with them, which in turn can help turn listeners who are qualified prospects into sales leads. Ask your company's presenters to say something like this at the end of their talks: "Our quarterly newsletter will give you more information on this topic. Just give me your business card, and I'll see to it that you get a free one-year subscription." This way, the presenter collects many more business cards for follow-up than she might otherwise have received.

Creating an e-mail newsletter

Because an e-mail newsletter is so much less expensive to produce, there are a lot of them, so you must use this tool properly. Otherwise, your newsletter will be considered spam, which can annoy people and ruin your relationships with them before those relationship have even gotten off the ground.

Whether to create a promotional e-mail newsletter depends on the industry and the expectations of your market. For the entertainment industry, for example, your newsletter needs to have fancy graphics or the recipients won't even notice it. For a technical audience, there is no need for fancy graphics. They care most about the value of the information. Marry the format to your readers. Also, if you know your audience is getting most of their messages via tiny screen cell phones or PDA's, text is best.

A few points to remember:

- ✔ **Never sell e-mail addresses.** Ever. Prove you are trustworthy.
- ✔ **Keep your message concise and useful.** Content should be useful to the reader.
- ✔ **Keep your product mentions to a minimum.** Product-driven newsletters with paragraph after paragraph of sales copy are a drag. A sidebar with a "Product of the Month" is acceptable, but don't overdo the product mentions.

Integrating print and e-mail newsletters

For an internal newsletter, you don't need to do two versions — print and e-mail. But to make sure your promotional newsletter (the one you send out to potential customers) is read by the most people, you should create both a print version and an e-mail version.

You may think you can get around doing both by e-mailing a PDF version that recipients can print out themselves. But I don't recommend that approach, because many corporations have e-mail filtering systems that prevent your messages from getting through. They filter certain types of documents or sometimes they simply block all messages with attachments.

Having both types of newsletters is most effective. Even if your e-mail version *does* get through to your prospect's inbox, the prospect may not read it right away. If you follow up with a print version, it'll jog the prospect's memory and make it even easier for him to read your newsletter.

Making your e-mail newsletter a must-read

In thinking about what kind of content to include in your e-mail newsletter, think about what kind of information will help the recipients do their job better. What will make them smarter in their environment, give them inside information they wouldn't otherwise get, or get it in advance. In essence, what adds value to their day? Provide it and they will read.

Don't just rehash what everyone else is writing and saying. Develop your own viewpoint. Listen to your customers, listen to their common questions, listen for what they don't seem to understand, and then address those issues in your newsletter. Employing that strategy will make your newsletter more relevant to their lives.

Newsletter story ideas

Stuck for ideas for your newsletter? Use this checklist for inspiration:

✔ **Product stories:** New products, improvements to existing products, new models, new accessories, new options, new applications

✔ **News:** Joint ventures, mergers and acquisitions, new divisions formed, new departments, industry news, analyses of events and trends

✔ **Tips:** Tips on product selection, installation, maintenance, repair, and troubleshooting

✔ **How-to articles:** Similar to tips, but with more detailed instructions — for example, how to use the product, how to design a system, how to select the right type or model

✔ **Previews and reports:** Articles about special events such as trade shows, conferences, sales meetings, seminars, presentations, and press conferences

✔ **Case histories:** In-depth or brief stories about product applications, customer success stories, or examples of outstanding service or support

✔ **People:** Company promotions, new hires, transfers, awards, anniversaries, employee profiles, human interest stories (unusual jobs, hobbies, and so on)

✔ **Milestones:** Events such as "1,000th unit shipped," "Sales reach $1-million mark,"

"Division celebrates tenth anniversary," and so on

✔ **Sales news:** New customers, bids accepted, contracts renewed, satisfied-customer reports

✔ **Research and development:** New products, new technologies, new patents, technology awards, inventions, innovations, breakthroughs

✔ **Publications:** New brochures available, new ad campaigns, technical papers presented, reprints available, new or updated manuals, announcements of other recently published literature or audiovisual materials

✔ **Explanatory articles:** How a product works, industry overviews, background information on applications and technologies

✔ **Customer stories:** Interviews with customers; photos; customer news and profiles; guest articles by customers about their industries, applications, and positive experiences with the vendor's product or service

✔ **Financial news:** Quarterly and annual report highlights, presentations to financial analysts, earnings and dividend news, reported sales and profits

✔ **Photos with captions:** People, facilities, products, events

(continued)

(continued)

- **Columns:** President's letter, letters to the editor, guest columns, regular features such as "Q&A" or "Tech Talk"

- **Excerpts, reprints, or condensed versions:** Press releases, executive speeches, journal articles, technical papers, company seminars

- **Productivity stories:** New programs, methods, and systems to cut waste and boost efficiency

- **Manufacturing stories:** Statistical process control/statistical quality control (SPC/SQC) stories, computer integrated manufacturing (CIM) stories, new techniques, new equipment, raw materials, production line successes, detailed explanations of manufacturing processes

- **Community affairs:** Fund-raisers; special events; support for the arts; scholarship programs; social responsibility programs; environmental programs; employee and corporate participation in local, regional, and national events

- **Data processing stories:** New computer hardware and software systems, improved data processing and its benefits to customers, new data processing applications, explanations of how systems serve customers

- **Overseas activities:** Reports on the company's international activities; profiles of facilities, subsidiaries, branches, people, and markets

- **Service:** Background on company service facilities, case histories of outstanding service activities, new services for customers, customer support hotlines

- **History:** Articles about the history of the company, industry, product, or community

- **Human resources:** Company benefit programs, announcement of new benefits and training and how they improve service to customers, explanations of company policies

- **Interviews:** Q&A with key company employees, engineers, service personnel, and so on; with customers; with suppliers (to illustrate the quality of materials going into your company's products)

- **Forums:** Top managers answer customer complaints and concerns, service managers discuss customer needs, customers share their favorable experiences with company products and services

- **Gimmicks:** Contents, quizzes, trivia, puzzles, games, cartoons, recipes, computer programs

Chapter 8

Putting Your Message in Writing: The Press Release

*W*hat you say and how you say it can greatly influence the media and your audiences. Revolutions have been started with nothing more than a quill and parchment. Even today, a few postings on the Internet can cause a stock's price to plummet or even take a nosedive in the entire market. Similarly, you can sometimes do more to build awareness with a single simple press release than with a million-dollar ad campaign.

When publicists place companies' self-promotional PR stories in the media, the companies, in effect, get free advertising for their products. For example, a Canadian company wanted publicity for a home-safety device it manufactures — a breathing hood to wear in case of fire. It positioned its press release as a kind of public-service announcement. The release describes the product and its advantages, but it also offers fire-safety tips that editors can run in their newspapers or magazines.

If you can write, you can write PR materials — as long as you follow a few simple rules of style and the accepted formats, examples of which abound throughout this book. In this chapter, you find out how to write press releases, media kits, and other printed PR materials. If you want to know how to write for the Web, see Chapter 16.

Writing a Press Release That Gets Picked Up by Media

Although a press release may be e-mailed, the typical press release is a one- or two-page, typed document of news or information about a company and its activities. A press release is, in essence, a mini-article that you prepare and send to the media for their use. Sometimes they use it for background information and sometimes they use it verbatim.

The parts of a press release include the following:

- ✔ **Contact information:** The company name, the name of the individual the editor should contact for more information, and the phone number of that person

- ✔ **Release date:** The specific date on which the information can be released (If timing is not critical, just type the words "For Immediate Release.")

- ✔ **Headline:** Designed to get the editor's attention and get him to start reading

- ✔ **Body:** What you want the media to know about your product or service

- ✔ **Response information:** How the reader can get in touch with you for more information on your product or service

PR firms sometimes include a *tip sheet* with the press release. A tip sheet, typed on a separate sheet of paper, highlights extra information that may catch an editor's eye.

Because the press release is not an *exclusive* (although it may be offered that way to a major outlet as part of your initial strategy), you can send the same press release to hundreds of publications and stations. (Wondering what an *exclusive* is? In an exclusive, one publication or outlet is given the first opportunity to write the story. This is the publication you would most like to be in. The only time you offer an exclusive is if it is genuinely a hot news story.) I've had a single press release picked up by hundreds of publications and generate thousands of inquiries. No marketing method is more cost-effective than the humble press release for getting your message out to a wide audience.

Preparing a press release is simple and straightforward. Just print it out double-spaced on regular letter-size (8½-x-11-inch) sheets of paper.

You can photocopy your press releases at a local copy shop, or you can run off copies on your office copier if the quality of reproduction is good. You can print the press releases on plain paper, business stationery, or special PR letterhead with the words *news release* or *press release* printed across the top. Special paper isn't necessary — plain paper does the job.

At the top

Follow the format of the samples presented in this chapter. At the top of the first page, type **FROM:** or **SOURCE:** followed by the name and address of your company. Underneath this, type **CONTACT:** followed by your name and telephone number.

If you use a public relations agency, it will list its own name and address (under FROM: or CONTACT:), followed by the name and address of the client (which is you).

Below the contact address, type **For immediate release.** This tells editors that your story is timely, but it doesn't date the release. That way, you can keep a supply on hand and send them out to editors as the opportunity arises. If the release is tied to an event that takes place on a specific date, or if it contains breaking news or other timely or dated information, type **For release: Monday, August 22, 2002** (substituting the actual date, of course). Underneath this comes the headline and then the story. (See the following section for information on writing headlines.)

The headline act and the lead role

The *headline* and the *lead* (first paragraph) of your press release need to grab an editor's attention. After all, you may be competing with hundreds of other press releases that cross an editor's desk. You certainly don't want yours ending up in the circular file!

The best press release headlines summarize the unique nature of the story and grab the editor's attention without being blatantly promotional. Inject news into the headline whenever possible. Type the headline in boldface; it can be as short as one line or as long as three lines. The better the headline, the better your chances that it will be read.

Leave some extra space between the headline and the first paragraph of the story. The first paragraph can begin with a dateline, such as "New York, NY, October 2000 —" with the first sentence of the first paragraph coming immediately after that dash. The city and state given in the dateline are usually the city and state where your company is headquartered.

Press releases use one of two basic types of leads:

> ✔ **News leads:** The news lead is the prototypical *who, what, when, where, why,* and *how* opening of a straight news story as taught in Journalism 101. The advantage of using the news lead is that, even if the editor chops the rest of your story and prints only the first paragraph — a common occurrence — the gist of your story still gets across. Here is an example of a straight news lead:

Kingston, NY — PLATO Software recently released an upgraded version of its modifiable business and accounting software package, P&L-Pro Version 6.0.

"What makes P&L-Pro unique is that it's the only affordably priced accounting software that can be modified by the user with no programming required," claims Richard Rosen, president, PLATO Software.

To see more examples of news leads, pick up any major daily newspaper and study the first paragraphs of the stories.

✔ **Feature leads:** The feature lead is written in an entertaining, attention-getting fashion similar to the opening of a magazine feature article. The purpose is to grab the editor's attention by being clever, startling, or dramatic, so that more editors read and use your release.

Figure 8-1 shows a good example of a feature lead. To see more examples of feature leads, pick up any issue of your favorite magazine and read the first paragraph of each of the major articles listed on the content page.

Body building

After the lead comes the *body,* or text, of the story. If you're coming to the end of the page and it looks as if the paragraph will have to continue onto the next page, move the entire paragraph to that page. Don't divide paragraphs between two pages.

Why? Because some editors may want to use scissors to cut your release into paragraphs, and then tape it together in a different order. (This is how some editors edit.) For the same reason, releases are always printed on one side of a sheet of paper, never on two sides.

You may say at this point, "But I don't want the editor to edit my story. I want it to run as is!" This attitude is understandable, but it's self-defeating. In public relations, the editor is in clear control and is the "customer" for your stories, and you must meet the editor's needs and standards first if you are to have any chance of reaching your final audience — readers.

If editors want to edit, make it easy for them, not difficult. If they want a new angle on your story, don't protest — help them find it. The more you cooperate with editors and give them what they need, the more publicity you'll get.

The last paragraph of your press release contains the response information, including name, address, and telephone number. For example, "To get Smith Widget Company's new 32-page Widget catalog, contact: Smith Widget Company, Anytown, USA, 123-456-7890."

For Immediate Release

CONTACT: Kathy Bell
Jericho Communications
212/645-6900 x117

Worried About Paying For Your Child's College Education? You Could Start A Trust Fund, Get A Part-Time Job ...Or Shop For Car Insurance

"Insure Our Future" Provides A Way To Start Your Child's College Fund

Mayfield Village, OH, January 24, 2000 -- For many parents, the thought of funding their child's college education occurs as early as the time of birth, sometimes even the moment of conception. If you think you can't possibly save enough to fund your children's college education, think again. The money could be right in front of you -- in the form of your auto insurance premium.

Progressive Insurance has announced a program, "Insure Our Future," designed to help consumers better understand the savings available to them if they only shopped around for their auto insurance. The fact is, rates vary widely. The potential savings are enough to significantly contribute to a child's education. **Details of the program can be found on progressive.com.**

Progressive's research shows that the average difference between the highest and lowest auto insurance premium available to the same consumer from different companies is $522 every six months...Most consumers don't understand that they may be leaving money on the table by not shopping around for auto insurance.

If a person shopped for auto insurance and realized savings equal to the average variance every six months and put this 'found money' ($522) into an interest-bearing account (averaging 6 percent interest compounded annually), in 18 years, the savings on auto insurance would accrue to more than $34,000 (without considering taxes). This could be a big step toward paying for the college education for the more than 15 million American children under the age of three.

Figure 8-1:
Press release with feature-style lead.

Including response information for the consumer is critical. If you don't write it into the release, the editor may leave it out of the story, dramatically decreasing inquiries generated as a result of the media placement.

To let editors know that they've reached the end of your story, simply type **END** or **###** or **-30-**.

Putting News in Your News Releases

Editors get hundreds of press releases weekly, all typed in the correct format, and they throw out 99 percent of them. A professionally prepared release is important — the editor probably won't read one that is handwritten on a scrap of grocery bag — but *content* is what makes your release the one in a hundred that actually gets read and used.

The following factors can help your release stand out from the crowd and actually make it into the publication or program:

- ✔ **Make sure that the subject of your release is important to the publication's readers.** If you were the editor and you had dozens of releases but could publish only a few, would you select your own release? Are the information and story in your release really important — not to your business, but to the publication's readers? If not, forget it and look for a new angle.

- ✔ **Make sure that your release is really news and not just an advertisement in disguise.** Editors aren't in the business of publishing advertising. Almost all will immediately discard publicity that is really advertising in disguise. Of course, most publicity has some advertising value or purpose, but write your publicity to give news or helpful information only.

- ✔ **Write your release so that the publication's readers benefit from it.** Your publicity will get published more often if it contains important news that will benefit the publication's readers. This could be new technology that the readers will be interested in, helpful information, or an emerging trend.

- ✔ **Keep it short and to the point.** Editorial space is very limited, and busy editors don't have the time to sort through irrelevant copy and cut it down to the main points. Write clear and crisp sentences using only the important, relevant information. Tighten the writing. Keep paragraphs and sentences concise. Avoid jargon and repetition. Use strong verbs. Create lively, but accurate, text.

- ✔ **Include what the editor wants in your press release.** That is, does it have facts to back up your statements? Include the *who, what, when, where, how,* and *why* details.

✔ **Use subheads in longer stories, at least one per page.** A *subhead* is a smaller head that divides documents into sections, as do the smaller subheads throughout this book. Subheads in a press release help the editor grasp the entire story at a glance.

✔ **Consider adding a tip sheet for details that would otherwise clutter your release.** For example, a new restaurant, when sending out a press release announcing its grand opening, included a separate tip sheet listing five specialty dishes along with the ingredients and recipes.

✔ **Make the release stand on its own.** Don't include a cover letter. If you feel a cover letter is needed to explain why are you sending the release or why an editor should be interested in using it, then your press release isn't strong enough. Go back and rewrite your press release until it's irresistible to editors.

✔ **Get all the facts and establish perspective before starting to write.** Adding and rewriting later costs time and money.

✔ **Keep the news up front, not behind the interpretation or buried in paragraphs of analysis.**

✔ **Cut out puffery; stick to newsworthy information.**

✔ **Put opinion and interpretation in an executive's quotation.** For example: "Within a decade, file transfer between different computer platforms will be seamless and device-independent," says Bill Blathers, CEO, MicroExchange Software.

Operating under pressure to be objective and neutral in reporting, editors won't run subjective opinion statements unless they can attribute such statements to a source. To solve this problem and get editors to run all your material, put controversial statements and claims in quotations and attribute them to an executive from your organization.

For example, if you write in a press release, "AML is currently the only logistics company specializing in the shipment of medical products and materials," the editor may say, "To print this statement, I have to check every business directory in the country to make sure that, indeed, there is no other firm offering such a shipping service." If she didn't, and it turns out there were other firms providing the medical shipping service, she'd be printing inaccurate information. Because the editor cannot conclusively prove through research that AML has no competitors, her most likely move would be not to print the statement.

But when we phrase the same information as an attributed statement — for example, "'As far as we know, AML is the only logistics company currently specializing in the shipment of medical products and materials,' says Norman Freeman, company president" — the editor will readily print it, because she is on safe ground. By printing it as an attributed quotation, she is not claiming that AML is in fact offering a one-of-a-kind service. She is merely reporting that the company president claims his service is one-of-a-kind — and the fact that Mr. Freeman has made such a claim is beyond dispute, because it's right there in his press release.

- ✔ **Use straightforward headlines.** Forget the cute headline that forces an editor to dig through a paragraph or two to discover the *who, what, when, where,* and *why.* The headline should summarize the release so that an editor quickly understands your point.

- ✔ **Leave plenty of *white space* (blank space).** Doing so is especially important at the top of page 1 because editors like room to edit. Double-space and leave wide margins. Never use the back of a page.

- ✔ **Write for a specific editorial department: news, lifestyles, real estate, financial, new products.** Similarly, provide separate story slants (in separate releases) for different categories of magazines. To publicize a directory of free information, for example, press releases could highlight the free information resources of interest to different editors. A press release featuring free information on gardening, real estate, and do-it-yourself tips could be aimed at home magazines. A different release featuring free information on starting your own business could target business editors.

- ✔ **Create separate, shorter releases for radio and, at minimum, color slides and scripts for television.**

- ✔ **End releases with a boilerplate paragraph that explains the organization or division.** Many press releases include, before the closing paragraph containing the response information, a standard description of the company and its products. This information is helpful for editors who are unfamiliar with you or want to give their readers a little more description of who you are and what you do.

- ✔ **Consider editing the news release copy for product bulletins, internal publications, and other uses.**

- ✔ **Write to gain respect for your organization and your next release.** Be accurate and honest. Present clear and useful organization. Deliver value to the reader. Avoid hype and blatant self-promotion.

- ✔ **Streamline the clearance process so that only two or three executives approve each release.** Doing so saves time and minimizes the chance to muddy the text.

Using a Press Release Checklist

There are many elements that make up an effective press release. Be sure to use this checklist so you don't forget anything:

- ✔ Did you include the release date?

- ✔ Did you include the website address?

- ✔ Did you list the contact person?

- ✔ Is the contact person readily accessible seven days a week?

✔ Who will be available to be interviewed?

✔ Did you include all e-mail addresses?

✔ Did you include whether product samples are available upon request?

✔ Does the headline make you want to read the document? (Be sure to get a second opinion.)

✔ Is the text of the release written appropriately for the market that it is targeting? (Consumer releases must be written in layman's terms. Business-to-business releases can use jargon and technical terms.)

✔ Has the document been edited, re-edited, and re-edited again?

✔ Is additional background information that will be disseminated with the release written in the same tone? Did you check to make sure it doesn't conflict with what's in the release?

Deciding How to Send Press Releases

The polls change everywhere because people change constantly about how they prefer to receive information. That's why what's most important is to know your journalists and how they prefer to receive info and know that it can and will change. You should use all three distribution methods (mail, fax and e-mail) and keep meticulous notes on who prefers what so you can cater your distribution to each.

Journalists' preferences change continually. The greatest reason is that the technology is changing so quickly. When I wrote the first edition of this book, a significantly smaller percentage of journalists wanted information delivered via e-mail. Today, many more want it that way. What's essential is keeping track of each journalist's preference in a database and send each according to that journalist's preference. But RSS is coming up fast (see Chapter 17).

A number of editors I've talked with tell me that they don't open all their e-mails, and sending releases via snail mail is too slow. For this reason, we send most of our press releases via fax broadcast. Doing so gives you speed and immediacy nearly equal to e-mail but without the two big e-mail problems: fear of opening an e-mail because of virus concerns and difficulty opening an e-mail because of file format incompatibility.

For materials that can't be sent via fax, such as press kits, we send them via regular first-class mail. The cost, including postage, envelope, and paper, is less than $1 apiece for each publication to which we send the kit.

When an editor lets us know that he's willing to accept releases via e-mail, or that he even prefers it, we change our database so that any future releases sent to him are transmitted via e-mail. Keep a separate mailing group on your address book of editors and publishers who prefer receiving press releases over the Internet, and e-mail your releases to this group separately.

E-mailing press releases works best when you want to follow up a press release mailing (sent via regular mail) with a phone call. Then when the editor expresses interest but says that he doesn't remember getting or didn't save the original release, you can e-mail him a copy instantly and then follow up later that day to confirm receipt of the e-mail.

Don't send an attachment. If the editor has the least bit of trouble opening your attachment, she'll click Delete faster than you can say, "Not interested." Further, most television stations won't open an attachment unless they know you. Send e-mail press releases as pasted-in text messages. So paste your release into the body of your e-mail message if you want it read.

Chapter 9

Writing and Placing Feature Articles

*P*lacing feature articles with appropriate trade, consumer, or business publications is one of the most powerful and effective of all marketing techniques.

Unlike a news article, which gives a straightforward report of recent events, a feature article is a longer piece that explores its subject in greater depth. Feature articles often present a detailed case study, explanation of technology, or guidance on how to do something, whether it's how to write a business plan or pick a telephone carrier.

Many people naturally assume that all the feature articles they read are written by freelance writers or reporters employed by the newspaper or magazine. Sure, some of the articles are written by "feature" writers. But every day, thousands of articles appear that have been written by — PR professionals, self-employed professionals, business executives, and technical specialists — as a means to promote themselves, their businesses, or their products or services.

In this chapter, we explore two time-tested methods of getting feature articles written about your company or service: proposing and writing the article yourself, and sending a pitch letter to editors to encourage them to write their own article about you.

Getting Exposure in Feature Articles

A company seeking publicity and exposure submits an article in hopes that a publication will spotlight or feature the company, its ideas, or products or services. A *planted,* or *placed, feature story* is an article written and submitted to a publication by a corporation, entrepreneur, or business professional — either directly by the business or on its behalf by its PR firm or consultant.

You can get one, two, or more pages devoted to your product or service without paying for the space. (A paid advertisement of that length could run $3,000 to $20,000 or more.) Your message has far more credibility as "editorial" material than as a sponsored advertisement. The publication of the article results in prestige for the author and recognition for the company. And reprints make excellent, low-cost sales literature.

Just one article in a magazine can generate hundreds of leads and thousands of dollars in sales for a company. And with more than 6,000 magazines and trade journals from which to choose, you can safely bet that at least one is interested in a story from your company.

Getting an article published in a trade journal or local business magazine isn't difficult — if you know how. Trade-journal editors are quick to reject inferior material or "puff" pieces, but they're hungry for good, solid news and information to offer their readers. And, unlike newspaper reporters who are investigative and frequently antagonistic and adversarial toward businesses, trade-journal reporters are a friendlier audience and are more willing to work with you to get information to their readers.

Avoiding beginners' mistakes

Common mistakes that novices make when writing and placing articles include the following:

- **Not querying the publication** first to find out whether it has an interest in running an article on the topic you propose.
- **Addressing the query letter "Dear Editor"** rather than finding out the name of the editor and addressing your communications directly to him.

- ✔ **Offering the editor a bribe** to run the article ("We'll buy a big ad if you run our article") or making a threat ("We won't buy ad space unless you run our article").

- ✔ **Handing in a sloppy, incomplete article** and saying, "I'm not a writer. Here's the information — you fix the grammar and make it read right." (The editor doesn't have time to do your work and expects articles that are well written and edited.)

- ✔ **Not being able to submit the article as a computer file** in Microsoft Word or another common format.

- ✔ **Missing the deadline after being given the go-ahead** to write an article for submission. Even worse is missing the deadline and not notifying the editor that the manuscript will be late.

- ✔ **Not reading the magazine** and being totally unfamiliar with its readership, style, content, and editorial requirements.

Coming up with ideas for articles

Your chances of getting your article published increase dramatically when you offer editors an article of the type they regularly publish. For instance, don't send an article of recipes to a magazine that doesn't run recipes.

A handful of standard article types account for 90 percent of the articles published today. These include the following:

- ✔ **Case histories:** Product success stories, focusing on companies that had a problem and how those companies used a particular product, service, or method to solve the problem

- ✔ **How-tos:** Instructional advice (for example, "How to Size Lighting for Industrial Facilities")

- ✔ **New products:** Explanations of how a new technology works (for example, "New Mounted Chip Technology Doubles Processing Speed")

- ✔ **Developments and trends:** Analysis to help business readers plan their strategy ("Plastics Industry Moves to Global Supply Chain Business Model")

The *case history* or *application story* is one of the most popular types of articles that trade and business magazines publish. This type of story tells how a specific company solved a problem or addressed a need, and usually highlights the product or service the company used to solve its problem. The PR department of the company whose product or service was used to solve the problem sends a query letter (see the "Writing a Query Letter" section, later in this chapter) suggesting case histories to editors. Getting case histories published is an effective marketing tool, because it shows readers how to apply your product and demonstrates its proven success.

Aside from case histories, most planted feature articles are of the how-to variety, aimed at executives, managers, professionals, or technicians in a given field. Editors are also interested in stories on new products, developments, or trends in their industry.

One way to come up with article ideas is to make a list of the ads you would run (and the magazines in which you would run them) if you had an unlimited ad budget, write articles based on topics related to those ads, and place them in those magazines.

For example, if you wanted to advertise your new wood-chip stacking system in *Pulp & Paper* magazine but didn't have the budget for it, you might consider writing an article titled, "A New Way to Stack and Inventory Wood Chips More Efficiently" for that magazine. Writing and placing articles in magazines and for secondary markets in which print advertising is unprofitable or beyond your budget is cost-effective.

Many trade journals will send a sample issue and set of editorial guidelines to prospective authors upon request. These guidelines can provide valuable clues as to style, format, and appropriate topics. The guidelines often tell you how to contact the magazine, give hints on writing an article, describe the manuscript review process, and discuss any payment or reprint arrangements.

The quickest way to turn off an editor is to offer an idea that has nothing to do with her magazine. Every magazine is a little different in some way from other magazines. To increase your chances of getting a placement, you must study tone, style, content, and the quality of a journal's writing and graphics.

Mum's the word

Although as a businessperson you're writing an article for self-serving promotional objectives, and editors know it, keep it to yourself. Editors are interested in serving their readers, not you. Keep the self-promotion in your article to a minimum — for instance, don't mention your company name 50 times — and give the editor an article that will be of real value to her readers. That serves your purpose, too, because the more useful the article, the more readers will contact the author for additional information — which can often lead to purchase of your products.

Tying in with special issues

You can increase your chances for coverage by requesting a magazine's editorial calendar and scanning the list of "special" issues to see whether there is a possible tie-in between your products and services and any articles to be featured in these issues. Call the magazine's advertising department, say that you're a potential advertiser, request a free media kit, and ask for an editorial calendar of special issues along with a sample issue. These items will be sent without charge to potential advertisers.

Go over the editorial calendar to see which topics would be most appropriate for your subject matter and articles. Fitting into what they already have planned gives you a leg up on getting into the magazine. But don't be pushy about it. Simply suggest that your material might fit in nicely with a particular theme. Then let them decide how and where.

However, if you spot a new trend in, say, packaging food in recyclable cardboard containers instead of plastic, and you can provide statistics and information to back up your claim that this trend is important, contact the editors at the appropriate packaging magazine. They'll probably appreciate your interest and effort.

Offer an editor the type of article that his magazine seems to prefer, and your odds of placing the story increase. If a magazine contains all short articles of one or two pages, don't send a 6,000-word thesis. If it doesn't run case histories, don't propose one.

Study issues of magazines to see which topics they cover. The key to success is not to send an idea for an article on something never covered, but to offer an article that presents a new slant or angle on one of a magazine's frequent topics.

Selecting the Right Magazine

The best magazines to target are the ones you are now getting. This is because you read them, are familiar with their editorial slant and style, and are aware of what articles related to your topic they have run recently. If you don't subscribe to many magazines in your industry or you aren't familiar with those publications, some good resources you can turn to are *Bacon's Media Directories* or *Writer's Market*. Or simply spend some time in the magazine section of your local bookstore and pick the top ten for your material.

Contact each publication you choose and ask for a sample issue and editorial guidelines. When the sample issue comes, study it and become familiar with the publication.

Here's another way to target magazines for article placement. You probably have a wish list of five to ten publications in which you would love to advertise — if you had the budget. Advertising is an expensive way to get exposure in these magazines, but you can hit all of them affordably through feature article placement. The result: You can get pages of coverage without paying for them!

Writer's Market, although not traditionally used for PR purposes, is in fact especially good for getting a sense of a magazine — its slant, topics, appropriate editors to pitch stories to, and editorial requirements. *Writer's Market* lists more than 4,000 consumer, general, business, and trade publications that accept articles from outside sources. Listings give detailed descriptions of what editors are looking for, along with names, addresses, phone numbers, and other contact information.

Timing is important. For a monthly magazine, an article that you want to appear in a special issue should probably be proposed to the editor three to six months in advance of that issue's publication date.

Finding the best target for articles

The editor most likely to be receptive to your queries is one that you've written for successfully in the past. When you sell one article to an editor, it makes sense to fire off a second letter immediately if you have another good idea that might be right for him. Figure 9-1 shows a sample of such a follow-up query letter.

In a P.S. to the follow-up query (refer to Figure 9-1), Bob could add a thumbnail sketch of his professional background. What is the point of that postscript when the editor has already done business with him? ***Remember:*** She has accepted only one previous article and doesn't know Bob all that well, so it could be beneficial to remind her of why he is exceptionally well qualified to write this article for her.

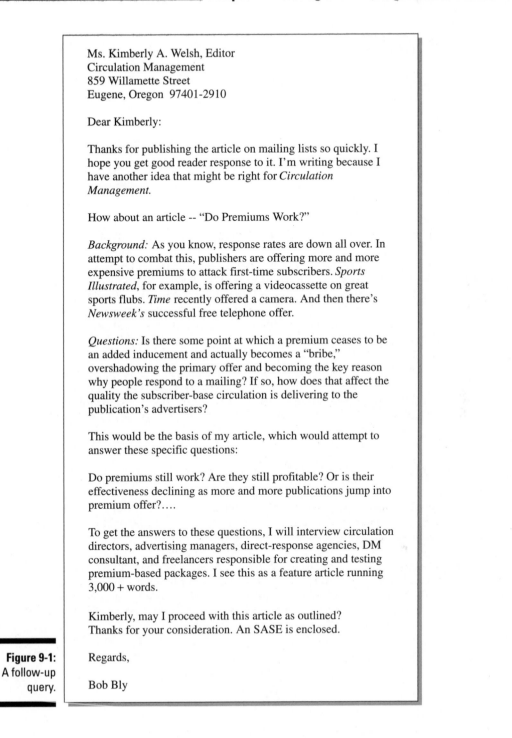

Ms. Kimberly A. Welsh, Editor
Circulation Management
859 Willamette Street
Eugene, Oregon 97401-2910

Dear Kimberly:

Thanks for publishing the article on mailing lists so quickly. I
hope you get good reader response to it. I'm writing because I
have another idea that might be right for *Circulation
Management.*

How about an article -- "Do Premiums Work?"

Background: As you know, response rates are down all over. In
attempt to combat this, publishers are offering more and more
expensive premiums to attack first-time subscribers. *Sports
Illustrated*, for example, is offering a videocassette on great
sports flubs. *Time* recently offered a camera. And then there's
Newsweek's successful free telephone offer.

Questions: Is there some point at which a premium ceases to be
an added inducement and actually becomes a "bribe,"
overshadowing the primary offer and becoming the key reason
why people respond to a mailing? If so, how does that affect the
quality the subscriber-base circulation is delivering to the
publication's advertisers?

This would be the basis of my article, which would attempt to
answer these specific questions:

Do premiums still work? Are they still profitable? Or is their
effectiveness declining as more and more publications jump into
premium offer?....

To get the answers to these questions, I will interview circulation
directors, advertising managers, direct-response agencies, DM
consultant, and freelancers responsible for creating and testing
premium-based packages. I see this as a feature article running
3,000 + words.

Kimberly, may I proceed with this article as outlined?
Thanks for your consideration. An SASE is enclosed.

Regards,

Bob Bly

Figure 9-1:
A follow-up
query.

Avoiding puffery

Impartiality is a must with many editors. They're not there to praise your company's products.

To make sure your articles are run, they have to be as objective as possible. Be sure your articles aren't one sided and only highlight the positive. The media need to spell out advantages as well as disadvantages. So, for example, an article about storage methods needs to include as many as possible, not just the methods used by the company sending the material.

Approaching editors one at a time

Many potential home buyers avoid a "cookie-cutter" home, and editors are no different when it comes to printing articles. After all, what value does a story add to a publication if its competitor has the same one? Emphasize *exclusivity* by never submitting the same idea or story to more than one competing magazine at a time. Approach another editor only if the first publication rejects your idea. Most editors want exclusive material, especially for feature articles.

If a story is particularly timely or newsworthy and has run in a magazine not directly competing with the one you're approaching, however, you may be able to get around this problem by working with the editor to rewrite the piece. But be upfront about it or you'll risk losing the editor's confidence and goodwill.

Making the Initial Contact

Should you call or write the editor? Most editors don't object to either method of pitching an idea, but they usually prefer one or the other. It's simply a matter of personal choice and time constraints.

If you don't know how a particular editor feels on the subject, call and ask. An appropriate opening might be: "This is Joe Jones from XYZ Corporation, and I have a story idea you might be interested in. Do you have time to spend a few minutes over the phone discussing it, or would you prefer that I send you an outline?"

Editors who prefer to get the story in writing will tell you so. Editors who prefer a quick description over the phone appreciate your respect for their time, whether they listen to your pitch on the spot or ask you to phone back later.

But even those editors who listen to your idea over the phone also want something in writing. If your idea is on the right track, the editor may request a detailed outline describing the proposed article. Also, some editors may not be able to make an editorial decision until they see the query letter.

All letters should be addressed to a specific editor by name. A letter that begins "Dear Editor" may not reach the right person; plus, it indicates you were too lazy to find out that person's name.

Writing a Query Letter

The best way to communicate an article idea in writing is to send a *query letter.* A query letter is a miniproposal in which you propose to the editor that you write an article on a particular topic for his magazine (and that it be published).

A query letter is, in essence, a sales letter. The "prospect" is the editor. The "product" you want to sell is the article you want to write for the magazine.

Querying the editor

Many businesspeople ask me, "Why bother with a query? It seems to slow things down and creates an extra step and more work. Why not just write and send the full article?"

In my opinion, you should always query. Ninety-five percent of editors prefer a query and will not look at a full manuscript that they didn't request.

Why do editors prefer queries to completed manuscripts? Two reasons:

- ✔ **It takes less time to read a one-page query and make a decision than to read the entire article.**

- ✔ **The query is a proposal — if the editor wants a different article than is proposed, he can go to the writer and request it.** Editors perceive that authors are more willing to change direction in the query stage than they would be if they have already submitted a completed article. So queries give the editor a greater degree of editorial control, enabling them to tailor articles to their readership.

Querying also saves you, the publicist, the time and trouble of researching and writing an article that may never get accepted anywhere.

Even if you've already written the article, it's better to condense and summarize it in a query, and send the query first — acting as if you haven't yet written the article. You should send the story only when the editor reads the query and says, "Let me see the article."

Getting the query letter written

Follow these guidelines for writing query letters:

- **No typos or misspellings.** Editors look for professionalism in query letters. Address the letter to a specific editor by name and spell her name right.

- **Write the first paragraph or two of your query so it can be used, as is, as the lead for your article.** This shows the editor that you know how to begin a piece and get the reader's attention.

- **Get the facts straight.** Editors hate lazy writers — those who want to see their byline in a publication but refuse to do research or get their facts straight. Put a lot of hard, nuts-and-bolts information in your letter — facts, figures, statistics — to show that you know your subject. Most query letters (and articles) are too light on content.

- **Use your credentials to impress editors.** State why they should trust you to write the article. If you're an expert in the subject, say so. If not, describe your sources. Tell which experts you'll interview, which studies you'll cite, and which references you'll consult. Highlight the breakthrough research your company has done to become a leader in its field.

- **Develop the idea fully.** Editors hate to take risks. The more fully developed your idea, the better. If you spell out everything — your topic, your approach, an outline, and your sources — editors know what they'll get when they give you the go-ahead to write the piece. The more complete your query, the better your chance for a sale.

- **Write the highest quality letter you can.** Editors have high standards for article acceptance, no matter who writes the articles. Don't think you can get away with a poorly written query because the editor realizes you're not a freelance writer and you're just trying to get some PR. The editor's readers don't expect PR-placed articles to be inferior, less objective, or less interesting than the other material in the magazine, and neither does the editor.

- **Never state in your query letter "And best of all, you don't have to pay me for this article, because I'm doing it to publicize my firm."** Even though editors know this, it's a breach of etiquette for you to come out and say it. (Why this is, I have no idea.)

Following are some typical query letters you can refer to for style and format. In Figure 9-2, note that the article proposal is in two parts: a letter selling the basic idea and an outline listing the details. The author used this format simply because it fit the material; the outline can be separate from the "sales pitch," if you want, but usually it isn't.

Ms. Jane Doe, Associate Editor
Chemical Engineering
1234 Main Street
Anytown, USA 12345

Dear Ms. Doe:

When a chemical engineer can't write a coherent report, the true value of his investigation or study may be distorted or unrecognized. His productivity vanishes. And his chances for career advancement diminish.

As an associate editor of *Chemical Engineering*, you know that many chemical engineers could use some help in improving their technical skills. I'd like to provide that help by writing an article that gives your readers "Ten Tips for Better Business Writing." An outline of the article is attached. This 2,000-word piece would provide 10 helpful hints—each less than 200 words—to help chemical engineering write better letters, reports, proposals, and articles.

Tip number 3, for example, instructs writers to be more concise. Too many engineers would write about an "accumulation of particulate matter about the peripheral interior surface of the vessel" when they're describing solids buildup. And how many managers would use the phrase "until such time as" when they simply mean "until"?

My book, *Technical Writing, Structure, Standards, and Style,* will be published by the McGraw-Hill Book Company in November. While the book speaks to a wide range of technical disciplines, my article will draw its examples from the chemical engineering literature....

I'd like to write "Ten Tips for Better Technical Writing" for your "You and Your Job" section. How does this sound? An SASE is enclosed for your reply.

Sincerely,
Bob Bly

Figure 9-2a: This query and outline (see Figure 9-2b) got an immediate go-ahead to write the article, which was accepted and published.

Article Outline

TEN TIPS FOR BETTER TECHNICAL WRITING
by Robert Bly

Know your readers. Are you writing for engineers? managers? laymen? Write in a clear, conversational style. Write to express-not impress.

Be concise. Avoid wordiness. Omit words that do not add to your meaning.

Be consistent... Especially in the use of numbers, symbols, and abbreviations.

Use jargon sparingly. Use technical terms only when there are no simpler words that can be better communicate your thoughts.

Avoiding big words. Do not write "utilize" when "use" will do just as well.

Prefer the specific to the general. Technical readers are interested in solid technical information and *not* in generalities. Be specific.

Break the writing up into short sections. Short sections, paragraphs, and sentences are easier to read than long ones, photos, and drawings can help get your message across.

Use the active voice. Write "John performed the experiment," to "The experiment was performed by John." The active voice adds vigor to writing.

Figure 9-2b:
Outline that accompanied the query letter in Figure 9-2a.

The first paragraph of the query letter in Figure 9-2 became the lead paragraph of the published article. This is no accident. A catchy lead in the query — one that could logically be used to begin the article — helps grab editors' attention and convince them that you have something interesting.

Figure 9-3 shows a query letter pitching a case history application story. An application story shows the reader how a particular product or system was used in the workplace or home to solve a specific problem. This letter and two follow-up calls gained acceptance from the publication's editor.

Joe Smith, Editor
Engineering Trade Journal
Anytown, USA 12345

Dear Mr. Smith:

Attached is a promotional brochure describing our client XYZ
INDUSTRIES' High-Flow Lifting System.

I have sent this to you as initial reference concerning High-Flow
use in an industrial situation. The application involves the
specialized handling and absolute precision positioning and
insertion of TV picture tubes into a console lined with a quick-
drying adhesive, thus permitting NO removal or replacement.
This custom-designed unit presently operating at an RCA plant
in Pennsylvania.

Because of the unique safety, economic features, and functions
of the High-Flow System, I believe you might want to treat the
above a feature article.

I will call within a few days to ascertain your interest. Please
know we will cooperate with you or your staff to develop any
editorial detail including up to submission of a complete
manuscript.

I look forward to talking with you.

Sincerely,
[signature]

Figure 9-3:
Sample
query letter
for a
product
story.

Also, note that the query letters shown are detailed, not superficial. You may
object, "But that's a lot of work to do with no show of interest or commitment
from an editor." Yes, it is. But that's what it takes to get published, and there's
no way around it.

Using illustrations or photos

Depending on the publication, you may or may not need to offer photos or drawings to get your article published. Most newspapers and magazines require only text for the article and will design graphics in-house to go with it.

Other magazines do not require, but certainly prefer to get, good photos or illustrations to run with articles. The availability of such material can sometimes be the deciding factor in choosing one story over another. Even though the larger journals have illustrators on staff to produce high-quality finished drawings, they often work from materials supplied by the article contributor.

You can get a good idea of how important visuals are to a particular magazine by scanning a couple issues. Consider the following:

- Is there no, little, moderate, or heavy use of photos and drawings to accompany articles?
- If photos are used, are they black and white or color?
- How many visuals appear per magazine page?

Prepare and supply the quantity and quality of visual material the editor desires. Otherwise, your article may have a lesser chance of publication.

Professional photographs, though nice, aren't necessary for most trade journals. Straightforward, good-quality 35mm color slides are good enough for most trade editors. Some magazines also take black-and-white glossies or color prints. An editor will be happy to tell you what's acceptable.

Today, digital cameras can capture images that are of high enough quality for many publications. You can submit digital images on a CD or even e-mail them to the editor. And be sure to ask what file size and resolution the editor wants before submitting your images.

Following up on your query

One of three things will happen after you send your query letter:

- **The editor will accept your article *on spec* (on speculation).** This means the editor is interested and wants to see the completed manuscript but is not making a firm commitment to publish. This response is the most positive one you're likely to get, and unless the article you write is terrible, there is better than a 50 percent chance it will get published.
- **The editor will reject your query.** The next step is to send the query to the next editor and magazine on your list.

✔ **You won't receive a response either way.** This alternative is the most likely one to happen because

- The editor may not have gotten around to your query.

- She may have read it but has not yet made a decision.

- She didn't receive it, or she lost it.

Your follow-up should be a polite note or phone call asking the editor (a) whether she received the article proposal, (b) whether she had a chance to look at it yet, and (c) whether she's interested.

If you send a letter, you can enclose a reply card, as shown in Figure 9-4, that editors can use to check off their response. The reply card should be stamped and self-addressed. It includes a space for you to write the article title, so when it comes back from the editor, you know what article she's responding to.

---

*Article:*_____

*Author:*_____

____ YES, we're interested. Please submit manuscript (on spec, of course).

____ NOT for us. Sorry.

____ MAYBE. We haven't made a decision but will let you know shortly.

____ DIDN'T receive your query. Send another copy.

Figure 9-4:
Optional
reply card to
include with
query letter.

Many professional writers use such reply cards to make it easy for editors to respond. Others don't supply a reply card but enclose a self-addressed stamped envelope (SASE) so that editors can jot replies on their letter and mail it back in the envelope.

If you don't get a reply to your query after four weeks, send a follow-up letter asking whether the editor received the original query (a copy of which should be enclosed), and whether he's interested. A quick phone call or e-mail message can also be used to prod the editor's memory.

Call again if you don't get a reply to your query after another four weeks. You can also send a follow-up note asking whether editors received the original query (a copy of which should be enclosed) and whether he's interested.

If you don't receive a reply to the follow-up letter, make *another* phone call. If you don't get through after three or four calls, move on and submit the proposal to the next magazine on your list.

You may be thinking, "If it takes four to six weeks to get an answer from each publication, it may take many months to get my story into print." The answer is to have multiple press releases and query letters in the mail simultaneously. Doing so ensures a steady stream of media pickups and makes the results of any individual query much less critical in terms of your overall PR success.

This is referred to as "multiple submissions" and you should do this even if the publications say they don't accept multiple submissions; just don't advertise that fact. Then if your article is accepted by one publication, you simply drop a note to all the other ones to let them know it's no longer available. Use the opportunity to pitch another article instead.

Build a personal editorial Rolodex. Whenever editors respond to a press release or query or they call to interview someone in your company, put them on your media list to ensure that they receive all future news you issue.

Writing a Pitch Letter

An alternate method of getting feature story placement is to get stories written *about* you and your product rather than place stories written *by* you.

How do you get the press to write about you? Sending press releases, as described in Chapter 8, is one method. If an editor receives a release to an article he is planning, he may contact you to interview people in your company even if the material in the release isn't exactly what he needs.

Another way to get articles written about you — or at least get your company mentioned in articles — is to send a pitch letter. Unlike the query letter, which proposes that you write a specific article, the *pitch letter* simply offers your company as an expert source for interviewing purposes. Figure 9-5 shows a pitch letter that my PR firm did for one of our clients — the home furnishings company IKEA.

Dear Editor:

Anxiety, indecision, intimidation and agony are common feelings that surface whenever you begin the process of decorating your home. Do you tackle a big room in the house — the kitchen — or start with something smaller like reorganizing the closets? What simple home accessories can you use to brighten up the look of your living room? What type of storage do you have to keep your space from looking cluttered?

IKEA has quick and simple decoration solutions to all of these questions that are frequently asked when taking on the daunting task of decorating your home.

Enclosed, please find examples of before and after visuals with easy and affordable tips on how to reorganize a closet as well as redo a kitchen. Also included is an anxiety fact sheet and an IKEA 2000 Catalog.

An IKEA spokesperson is available to demonstrate simple and quick makeover steps for the kitchen, living room, bathroom, closets, and any other room in the home. We will literally create these rooms on your set with "before" and "after" displays that are simple, fun, creative and affordable — and most importantly — will not cause anxiety and fear about decorating a room.

I will follow up with you later this week. In the meantime, if you have any questions or need more information, please feel free to contact me at 212-645-6900 x128.

Regards,

Jeanette Chin

Figure 9-5:
Pitch letter
for IKEA.

Figure 9-6 shows another sample pitch letter. This time, the lead contains a news angle, based on an industry trend.

Dear Robert:

Compact disc (CD) sales are booming. In fact, some music industry executives are projecting disc sales will surpass album sales by the end of the year:

The first "compact disc only" retail store, Compact Disc Warehouse, in Huntington Beach, California, opened in November, 20XX. It grossed nearly $1 million in sales in just 18 months operating out of a 1,200 square foot store.

Now Compact Disc Warehouse, Inc. is launching the first CD franchise offering to meet the national demand for the hottest home entertainer product in the music industry today.

Edward Dempsey, president of CD Warehouse, is an expert on why CDs are changing an industry that has been dominated by record albums for decades and how the retail world is gearing up to meet the CD demand.

If you would like to arrange an interview, please call our offices.

Sincerely,

Mitch Robinson, Account Executive
S&S Public Relations, Inc.

Figure 9-6:
Another pitch letter, based on an industry trend.

Sending pitch letters is effective because editors and reporters are constantly on the lookout for accessible sources of expert information whom they can call to get a quote or fill in a missing fact for a story when they're on a tight deadline.

Always follow up the pitch letter. The first follow-up is to confirm receipt and to make clear the availability of the expert to be interviewed on these issues. Then whenever a big news story breaks that your expert could appropriately speak about or shed some light on, call the journalist again. Remind him of your expert and the link between his expertise and the story the journalist is probably following. If the expert can contribute to a particular aspect of the story or provide new information, say so.

One tactic that pays off is to include a Rolodex card with your query letter that reporters or editors can file under the appropriate category. That way, when a reporter is working on a story on CDs, she turns to her card file, finds Edward Dempsey's name, calls him for a quote, and quotes him in her story.

Edward Dempsey, then, and not his competition, becomes known as the industry leader because he's constantly quoted in the press.

I'm sure you've noticed that, within your own industry, the same spokespeople are quoted again and again. Well, it's not by accident. Diligent public relations efforts — not fate — ensure that one person or company is publicized while others wallow in obscurity.

Getting the Editor's Go-Ahead

An editor is interested. Hurrah! You've passed the first step in getting your article published. Now the real work begins.

After your idea is accepted, you need to know the requirements for story length and deadlines. If the editor doesn't volunteer this information, ask. The answers may prevent misunderstanding later on.

As a rule, be generous with length. Include everything you think is relevant, and don't skimp on examples. Editors would rather delete material than request more. But avoid exceeding the promised length by more than 20 percent. For example, if you promised 2,000 words, you're better off sending 2,400 words than 1,600 words. Removing 400 words is easier than creating 400 new words to bring it up to length.

Although a few magazines are flexible on length, most editors give authors specific *word lengths* (or *word counts*) to shoot for. To measure word count, you can manually count the words or, if you use Microsoft Word, choose Tools⇨Word Count. The software will display an exact word count for the document you have open.

Ask how long your article should be. To translate word lengths to typed pages, every 500 words is equivalent to two, double-spaced, typewritten manuscript pages. In its final printed form, a "solid" page of magazine copy (no headlines, photos, or white space) is an average of 800 to 1,000 words for a magazine with a standard 7-x-10-inch page size. The first page, which has to leave room for a headline and byline, is approximately 700 words. By comparison, a double-spaced manuscript page from your computer is approximately 200 words. Therefore, three manuscript pages equal one published page in the magazine.

Table 9-1 can help you translate word length and magazine page length to typed manuscript pages.

Table 9-1	Guide to Article Length	
Number of Words	**Number of Magazine Pages**	**Number of Manuscript Pages**
800–1,000	1	3–4
1,500	2	6
2,000	2–2½	8
2,500	3	10
3,000	3½–4	12

Deadlines also can vary considerably among journals. Some don't like to impose any deadlines at all, especially if they work far enough in advance that they aren't pressed for material. But if the article is intended for publication in a special issue, the editor will probably want the finished manuscript at least two months before the publication date. This deadline allows time for revisions, assembling photos or illustrations, and production.

Don't put an editor's patience to the test. Missing a deadline may result in automatic rejection and waste the effort you spent making the placement and writing the article. Submit every article on the deadline date, or sooner. If you can't make the deadline, let the editor know well in advance and request a reasonable extension. Editors don't like late copy, but they *hate* surprises.

Placing Articles Online

For the most part, placing articles online is a different animal than placing them in traditional offline publications. Many Web sites are so hungry for content that they don't have time to go through the querying process, so they'll often accept a full-blown article when the offline publications won't. Offering a few well-written articles at article databases — Web sites that compile articles and make them available to publications that are looking for content — can increase your exposure quickly. Do a simple search for "article database" and then submit your articles to the ones you fine.

Here are a few of the best techniques to try:

✔ **Submit your articles to industry sites.** Make sure your articles appear on the Web sites of the industries you specialize in, the ones your prospects and clients are visiting.

✔ **Become a regular columnist at an online publication where your prospects go to get help.** Tons of publications are out there, including the online versions of offline traditional publications, as well as strictly online publications.

✔ **Submit your article to individual e-mail newsletters.** Search directories (such as www.ezinearticles.com) for publications in your area of expertise. Then find out if the publisher accepts article submissions and what the guidelines are. If he does, send a personal e-mail message along with your article, asking him to consider including it. Don't do this unless their audience is your ideal target market.

Here's a sample message:

Hi, John.

Are you willing to accept articles for XYZPublication.com? My articles tend to focus on Internet marketing topics, such as viral marketing, building opt-in lists, and so on. I'll look forward to hearing from you.

Best,

Mary Smith

✔ **Create a partnership with an author or writer in your area of expertise.** This strategy is an effective and uncomplicated one for affiliating your name with content that relates to your topic. Authors are willing to co-brand articles in exchange for advertising revenue or promotion on your Web site. Simple adding a "sponsored by" and a mention in the bio is all you need.

Chapter 10

Promoting Yourself through Public Speaking

Speaking in public is one of the most effective marketing tools for your business in terms of reaching qualified prospects because your audience is very likely to be people interested in what you have to say. It's a very unique opportunity and needs to be handled differently from other PR tools.

In this chapter, I show you how to reach your key audiences and find the right venues, how to decide what to speak about, and how to make sure you get enough promotional bang for the effort you put in.

Reaching Key Audiences through Public Speaking

As a promoter of your organization, you're likely to speak to people other than those in the media. Public speaking — giving lectures, talks, papers, and presentations at public events, industry meetings, conventions, and conferences — is a PR technique that businesses use widely to promote their products or services.

Why is public speaking so effective as a promotional tool? When you speak, you're perceived as the expert. If your talk is good, you immediately establish your credibility with the audience so that members want you and your company to work with them and solve their problems.

Unlike an article, which is somewhat impersonal, a speech or talk puts you within handshaking distance of your audience. And because in today's fast-paced world, more and more activities are taking place remotely via fax, the Web, and videoconferencing, your personal presence firmly plants your image in their minds. If that meeting takes place in an environment where you're singled out as an expert, as is the case when you speak in public, the impression is that much more powerful.

Speaking is not ideal for every product or marketing situation. If you're trying to mass-market a new soft drink on a nationwide basis, television and print PR will be much more effective than speaking, which limits the number of people you reach per contact. On the other hand, a wedding consultant whose market is Manhattan would probably profit immensely from a talk on wedding preparation given to even a small group of engaged couples at a local church.

Speaking is an effective PR tactic when

- Confidential matters are to be discussed.
- Warmth and personal qualities are called for.
- An atmosphere of openness is desired.
- Strengthening of feelings, attitudes, and beliefs is needed.
- Exactitude and precision are *not* required.
- Decisions must be communicated quickly or important deadlines must be met rapidly.
- Crucial situations dictate maximum understanding.
- Added impact is needed to sustain the audience's attention and interest or get them to focus on a topic or issue.
- Personal authentication of a claim or concept is needed.

Speaking is also the promotional tool of choice when you're targeting your PR efforts to a narrow vertical market in which many of your best prospects are members of one or more of the major associations or societies in that market. For example, in the household appliances business, you might consider getting on the roster to give a presentation at the annual housewares show in Chicago.

Finding speaking opportunities

Unless you're sponsoring your own seminar or other event, you need to find appropriate forums to which your company personnel can be invited to speak. How do you go about that?

Check your mail and the trade publications you read for announcements of industry meetings and conventions. For example, if you sell furnaces for steel mills and you want to promote a new process, you may want to give a paper on your technique at the annual Iron and Steel Exposition.

Trade journals generally run preview articles and announcements of major shows, expos, and meetings months before the events. Many trade publications also have columns that announce such meetings on both a national and a local level. Make sure to scan these columns in the publications aimed at your target market industries.

You should also receive preview announcements in the mail. If you're a marketing manager or the owner of a small business, professional societies and trade associations will send you direct-mail packages inviting your firm to exhibit at their shows. That's fine, but you have another purpose: to find out whether papers, talks, or seminars are being given at the show, and, if so, to get your people on the panels or signed up as speakers. If the show's mail promotion doesn't discuss papers or seminars, call the organizers and ask.

Propose some topics with your company personnel as the speakers. Most conference managers welcome such proposals because they need speakers. The conference manager or another association executive in charge of the *breakout sessions* (the usual name for the presentation of papers or talks) will request an abstract or short 100- to 200-word outline of your talk. If others in your company will be giving the talks, work with them to come up with an outline that is enticing so as to generate maximum attendance but that also reflects accurately what the speaker wants to talk about.

Because many companies will pitch speakers and presentations to the conference manager, the earlier you do it, the better. Generally, annual meetings and conventions of major associations begin planning 8 to 12 months in advance; local groups or local chapters of national organizations generally book speakers 3 to 4 months in advance. The earlier you approach them, the more receptive they'll be to your proposal.

Choosing the right talk

You can recycle your talks and give them to different groups in the same year or different years, tailoring them slightly to fit current market conditions, the theme of the meeting, or the group's special interests. When you create a description, outline, or proposal for a talk, keep it as a file on your computer.

Then when other speaking opportunities come your way, you can quickly edit the file and e-mail a customized proposal or abstract to the person in charge of that meeting. I have a basic talk on PR that I've given half a dozen times over the past year at association meetings ranging from the American Pet Products Manufacturers Convention to the Hotel and Motel Association. I get at least one major new client every time I give the talk.

Get on the mailing list

If you're not on the mailing list to receive advance notification of meetings and conventions of your industry associations, write to request that the associations place you on such a list. Their names and addresses are listed in the *Encyclopedia of Associations* (Gale Research), available at your local library.

Because your goal is to sell your product or service, not educate the audience or become a professional speaker, you want to pick a topic that relates to and helps promote your business but is also of great interest to the group's audience. The presentation does not sell you directly, but sells you by positioning you and your company as the expert source of information on the problem your product or service addresses. As such, it must be objective and present how-to advice or useful information; it can't be a sales or product presentation.

For example, if you sell computer automated telemarketing systems, your talk can't be a sales pitch for your system. Instead, you could do something such as "How to Choose the Right Computer-Automated Telemarketing Software" or "Computer Automated versus Traditional Telemarketing Systems: Which Is Right for Your Business?" Although you want people to choose your system, your talk should be (mostly) objective and not too obviously slanted in favor of your product; otherwise, you will offend and turn off your audience.

I once spoke at a marketing meeting at which one of the other presenters, a manufacturer of such computerized telemarketing systems, was giving a talk. Although he was supposed to talk about how to improve telemarketing results with software, he proceeded to haul in his system and give a sales pitch. The comments from attendees were openly hostile and negative. I'm sure he didn't get any business — and this talk didn't enhance his reputation either.

Screening speaking invitations

On occasion, meeting planners and conference executives may call you and ask you (or a representative from your firm) to speak at their event, instead of your having to seek them out and ask them.

Being approached is flattering, but beware: Not every opportunity to speak is worthwhile. Meeting planners and committee executives are primarily concerned with getting someone to stand at the podium, and they don't care whether your speaker or your firm will benefit in any way from the exposure. So before you accept an opportunity to speak, ask the meeting planner (or the conference organizer, if you're seeking them out yourself) the following questions:

- What is the nature of the group?

- Who are the members? What are their job titles and responsibilities? What companies do they work for?

- What is the average attendance of such meetings? How many people does the meeting planner expect will attend your session?

- Does the group pay an honorarium or at least cover expenses?

- What other speakers have presented recently, and what firms do these speakers represent?

- Did the group pay those other speakers? If so, why not you, too?

If the answers indicate that the meeting is not right or worthwhile for your company, or if the meeting planner seems unable or unwilling to provide answers, politely thank the person and decline the invitation.

Negotiating your promotional deal

If you're asked to speak either for free or for a small honorarium and you're not offered a multi-thousand-dollar fee like a professional speaker would get, you can use the group's lack of payment for your talk as leverage to negotiate for concessions. What kinds of things can you ask for? Anything that can help maximize the promotional value of your talk for your firm.

Tell the meeting chairperson that you'd be happy to speak at no charge, provided that you receive a list of the members with their contact information. You can use this list to promote your company via e-mail and/or direct mail before and after your presentation. A pre-talk mailing can let people know about your upcoming talk and be a personal invitation from you to them. A post-talk mailing can offer a reprint or audio recording of your presentation to those who missed it.

At larger conferences and conventions, the conference manager provides attendees with show kits that include a variety of materials, such as a seminar schedule, passes to luncheons and dinners, maps, and sites of interest to out-of-town visitors. These kits are either mailed in advance or distributed at the show.

You can tell the conference manager, "I'll give the presentation at no charge, but in exchange, we'd like to have you include our company literature in the conference kits mailed to attendees. Is that possible? We'll supply as many copies of our literature as you need, of course." If the conference manager agrees, you get your promo pieces mailed to hundreds, even thousands, of potential clients *at zero mailing cost.*

Turning one speech into an extended campaign

A speech is an effective way of making yourself known to a particular audience (the members of the organization and, more specifically, those members who attend your presentation). But as you know, making a permanent impression on a market segment requires a series of contacts, not a single communication.

You can easily transform a one-shot speaking engagement into an ongoing PR campaign targeted to the membership of this particular group. One way, already discussed, is to get the mailing list and do your own mailings, plus have the sponsor include your literature in the mail-out kit. Another is to get one or more PR placements in the organization's newsletter or magazine. For example, tell the meeting planner that you'll supply a series of articles (your current press releases and feature articles, recycled for this particular audience) to run in the organization's newsletter before the talk. This makes you known to the audience, which is good PR for your firm and also helps build interest in attending your program.

After your talk, give the editor of the organization's newsletter the notes or text of your speech, and encourage her to run all or part of it (or a summary) as a post-talk article so that those who could not attend can benefit from the information. Additional articles can also run as follow-ups after the talk to reinforce your message and provide additional detail to those who want to find out more, or to answer questions or cover issues you didn't have time to cover.

If the editor will not run a resource box with your phone number with the articles, talk to the meeting planner about getting free ads for your product or service. For a national organization that charges for ads in its magazine, the value of your free ad space should be approximately twice what your fee would be if you were charging for your talk.

The organization will do a program or mailing (or both) with a nice article about you and your talk. Usually, it prints more than it ends up using and throws out the extras. Mention that you'd be glad to take those extra copies off its hands. Inserting those flyers in press kits and inquiry fulfillment packages is a nice touch.

Exchanging your "fee" for a videotape of your talk

A professionally done audiotape or video of you giving a seminar can be a great promotional tool and an attention-getting supplement to printed brochures, direct mail, and other sales literature. But recording such presentations in a studio can be expensive.

One way to get an audio or video produced at low cost is to have someone else foot the bill for the taping. If an organization wants you to speak but can't pay you, and especially if its audience is not a prime market for you, say, "I'll tell you what. Normally, I charge $X for such a program. I'll do it for you at no charge, provided that you can arrange to have it professionally videotaped (or audio-recorded, or both) and give me a copy of the master."

If the organization objects to the expense, say, "In exchange, you can copy and distribute the video or audio of my speech to your members, or even sell it to those who attend the meeting or belong to your group or both, and I won't ask for a percentage of the profits. All I want is the tape master when you're through with it."

Bargaining for ownership of the audiotape

At many major meetings, it's standard practice for sponsoring organizations to audiotape all presentations and offer them for sale at the conference and for one year thereafter in promotional mailings. If you're being taped, tell the sponsor that you normally don't allow it but will as long as you get the master. (Also make clear that, although you will allow the sponsor to sell it and will waive any percentage of the profits, the copyright is to be in your name.)

If you use overheads or PowerPoint slides, offer to provide them in PDF format (for which you'll need the full version of Adobe Acrobat, not just the free Acrobat Reader). Organizations are now starting to post speaker handouts on their Web sites. You instantly expand the audience for your talk from dozens to perhaps thousands with this Web exposure.

If the group is a local chapter of a national organization, ask the meeting chairperson for a list of the other state or local chapters, along with the names, addresses, and phone numbers of the meeting organizers for each chapter. Then contact the chapters and offer to give the talk to their members.

Preparing and Delivering Your Presentation

Of course, your objective is to sell. But be careful. People attending a luncheon or dinner meeting aren't there to be sold. They want to be entertained, informed, educated, made to laugh or smile. Selling your product, service, or company may be your goal, but in public speaking, it has to be secondary to giving a good presentation. A "soft-sell" approach works best.

Organizing your presentation

Say that your talk is primarily informational. You can organize it along the following lines:

1. **An introduction that presents an overview of the topic**

2. **The body of the talk, which presents the facts in detail**

3. **A conclusion that sums up for the audience what they've heard**

This repetition is beneficial because, unlike readers of an article, listeners of a spoken presentation can't flip back to a previous page or paragraph to refresh their memory or study your material in more detail. For this reason, you must repeat your main point at least three times to make sure that it's understood and remembered.

The talk should always be about the issue your product addresses, not about the product itself. For instance, when I had "The Juice Man," Jay Kordich, giving talks nationwide to promote juicing, he talked about the nutritional benefits of drinking freshly made fruit and vegetable juices, not about the features of his machine or how to buy one.

Many other organizational methods are available to speakers. For example, if you're describing a *process,* you can organize your talk along the natural flow of the process or the sequence of steps involved in completing it. This would be ideal for a talk entitled "How to Promote Your Chiropractic Practice" or "How to Start a Fad or Trend."

If you're talking about expanding a communications network worldwide, you might start with the United States, and then move on to Asia, and then cover Europe. If your topic is vitamins, covering them in alphabetical order from vitamin A to zinc seems a sensible approach.

Mastering the three parts of a talk

A talk has three parts: beginning, middle, and end. All are important. But the beginning and ending are more important than the middle. Most people can manage to discuss a topic for 15 minutes, give a list of facts, or read from a prepared statement. And that's what it takes to deliver the middle part.

The beginning and ending are more difficult. In the beginning, you must engage the audience's attention *and* establish rapport. Not only must members be made to feel that your topic is interesting, but also they must be drawn to you, or at least not find fault with your personality.

Canned presentations

The trick to reducing preparation time is to have two or three *canned* (standard) talks that you can offer to various audiences. Even with a canned presentation, you need at least several hours to analyze the audience, customize your talk to better address that particular group, and rehearse once or twice.

To test this theory, a well-known speaker put aside his usual opening and instead spoke for five minutes about himself — how successful he was, how much money he made, how in demand he was as a speaker, and why he was the right choice to address the group. After his talk, he casually asked a member, "What were you thinking when I said that?" The man politely replied, "I was thinking what a blowhard you are."

How do you begin a talk? One easy and proven technique is to get the audience involved by asking questions. For example, if you're addressing telecommunications engineers, ask, "How many of you manage a T1 network? How many of you are using 56K DDS but are thinking about T1? And how many of you use fractional T1?" If you're speaking on a health topic, you might ask, "How many of you exercised today before coming here? How many of you plan to exercise after the meeting tonight? How many of you exercise three or more times a week?"

Asking questions like these has two benefits:

- ✔ It provides a quick survey of audience concerns, interests, and levels of involvement, allowing you to tailor your talk to their needs on the spot.
- ✔ It forces the audience to become immediately involved. After all, when you're in the audience and the speaker asks a question, you do one of two things: You either raise your hand or don't raise it. Either way, you're thinking, responding, and getting involved.

Look for ways to engage the audience on an intellectual or emotional level. I often begin my talks on PR by reading the openings of the day's front-page stories in major media such as *USA Today* and the *Wall Street Journal.* Then to the audience's amazement, I tell them which PR firms placed the stories and the key message points in each. Starting this way dramatically demonstrates the wide reaching influence of PR, even into the uppermost levels of the major media.

Although the beginning is important, don't neglect a strong closing, especially if you're there not just for the pleasure of speaking but also to help promote your company or its products.

Action doesn't have to be literal. If you simply want the people in your audience to mull over your ideas, tell them that this is what you want them to do.

Although you want a great opening that builds rapport and gets people to listen and an ending that helps "close the sale," don't neglect the body, or middle, of your talk. It's the "meat"; it's what your audience came to hear. If your talk is primarily informational, be sure to give inside information on the latest trends, techniques, and product developments. If it's motivational, be enthusiastic and convince your listeners that they *can* lose weight, make money investing in real estate, or stop smoking.

If your talk is a how-to presentation, make sure that you've written it so that your audience walks away with lots of practical ideas and suggestions.

When speaking, tailor the content to listeners' expertise. Being too complex can bore people. But being too simplistic or basic can be even more offensive to an audience of knowledgeable industry experts.

Timing it right

Talks can vary from a ten-minute workplace presentation to a two-day intensive seminar. How long should yours be? The meeting planner, and the event itself, often dictate length.

- ✔ Luncheon and after-dinner talks to local groups and local chapters of professional societies and business clubs usually last 20 to 30 minutes, with an additional 5 to 10 minutes allotted for questions and answers.

- ✔ For breakout sessions at major conferences and national expositions, speakers generally get 45 to 75 minutes. For a one-hour talk, prepare a 45-minute talk. You'll probably start five minutes late to allow for late arrivals, and the last ten minutes can be a more informal question-and-answer session.

- ✔ The luckiest speakers are those who get invited to participate in panels. If you're on a panel consisting of three or four experts plus a moderator, you'll likely be asked to respond to questions from the moderator or the audience, eliminating the need to prepare a talk.

- ✔ Most executive speeches are about 20 minutes in length. A typed, double-spaced page of manuscript should take the speaker two and a half minutes to deliver. This means that an eight-page, double-spaced manuscript, which is about 2,000 words, will take 20 minutes to deliver as a speech. That's about 100 words a minute. Some speakers are faster, talking at 120 to 150 words a minute or more. So the 20-minute talk can really be anywhere from eight to ten typed pages.

Keeper of the time

Because most people can't concentrate on two things at once — giving a talk and watching a clock — try this trick: Ask someone in the audience to be the timekeeper and keep you on track. For example, if you're giving a 45-minute talk, ask him to shout out "Time!" every 15 minutes. The first two interruptions tell you where you are and how closely you're on track; the last tells you to stop and shut up.

Incidentally, instead of finding this shouting of the word *time* annoying, audiences like it. Make it fun, telling the timekeeper, "You must shout out 'time' in a loud, obnoxious voice!" Then when he does and the audience laughs, ask them to rate, in a tongue-in-cheek way, whether the timekeeper was indeed loud and obnoxious enough. It gets a laugh every time.

The most important thing about a talk is to not exceed the allotted time. If you're given 20 minutes with an additional 10 minutes for questions and answers, stop after 20 minutes. People won't mind if you finish a bit early, but they will become fidgety and start looking at their watches if your time limit is up and you don't seem even near finished.

Here are some other tips for adding punch to your presentations:

✔ Write your own introduction and send it to the sponsoring organization in advance of your appearance. (Also bring a copy with you for the master of ceremonies in case she loses your original.)

✔ Self-effacing humor works best. Poke gentle fun at yourself, not at the audience or the sponsor.

✔ Ask the audience questions.

✔ Don't give a talk; have a conversation.

✔ The presentation doesn't have to be the best one they've ever heard. Tell your audience that if they get one good idea out of your talk, it will have been worthwhile for them. Create a realistic expectation in the beginning, and the audience will be satisfied at the end.

✔ To announce a break, say, "We'll take a five-minute break now, so I'll expect you back in ten minutes." It always gets a laugh.

✔ To get the audience back in the room, go out into the hall and shout, "He's starting, he's starting."

✔ If panic strikes, just give the talk and keep your mouth moving. The fear will subside in a minute or two.

✔ Tell touching stories. If the stories are about you, be the goat, not the hero. People like speakers who are humble; audiences hate braggarts.

✔ Asking people to perform a simple exercise (stretching, Simon Says, and so on) as an activity during a break can increase their energy level and overcome lethargy.

✔ At the conclusion of your talk, tell your audience that they were a great audience, even if they weren't: "You've been a wonderful audience. [pause] Thank you very much."

The most important tip? Be yourself. Talk to the audience. Don't worry about being smooth, polished, funny, clever, dynamic, or dramatic. Because you aren't expected to be a professional speaker, coming off as a bit amateurish and inexperienced can even endear you to the crowd and get them on your side.

Using Visual Aids

In the 1970s, slides were all the rage in the corporate world. Nearly every presentation was an audiovisual presentation. Two managers could not get together for an informal chat without one pulling out a slide projector and dimming the lights.

Slides are still popular today, mostly in the form of PowerPoint presentations, but audiovisual aids are not necessary for most presentations. Most corporate presentations depend on PowerPoint (and some still on overheads), and they're boring. Handouts, however, can be very helpful to your audience, not to mention the fact that they provide a takeaway with your contact information and details about your company.

Thinking twice about audiovisual aids

Most professional speakers who earn thousands for a brief talk do *not* use audiovisual aids. I feel that businesspeople, especially in the corporate world, become dependent on the visuals and lose the spontaneity and relaxed manner that come with "having a conversation" rather than "making a presentation."

The problem with the corporate approach to visuals is that the audiovisual aid is seen as something that must run continuously and concurrently with the talk. So, although only 10 percent of the presentation requires visuals, the slide projector runs for 100 percent of the time, and the speaker fills in with word slides that are wasteful and silly. For example, if the speaker is going to talk for three or four minutes on branding, she hits a button, and the word *branding* appears on the screen in white against a black background. Such a visual adds nothing to the talk and is, in fact, ridiculous.

A better approach is to have visuals that you can use when appropriate, and then deliver the rest of your talk unaided. For a small audience, you can give an unrehearsed, interactive feel to your talk by using flip charts and markers. The key: Don't prepare them in advance. Rather, draw as you speak, which adds excitement and motion. It also creates anticipation: The audience becomes curious about what you're creating before their eyes.

Always arrive at least one hour before your speech is scheduled and request access to the room where you're speaking. Run through your slides or other audiovisuals once, quickly, to make sure that everything is working properly and that the materials are in the right order.

I've seen speakers who, interrupted by an error, lose their train of thought and never fully recover. Errors or mishaps with audiovisual support can be extremely disconcerting, especially when making a good impression is important or the presenter is uncomfortable with public speaking in the first place.

At times, however, high-quality visuals are needed to demonstrate how a product works, explain a process, show the components or parts of a system, or graphically depict performance. For instance, if you're trying to promote your landscape design practice by giving a talk entitled "How to Design a Beautiful Front Yard," you want to show pictures of attractive front yards that you've designed. If your speech is entitled "Advancing Science Using Supercomputer-Generated Images," people will want to see color slides of those images.

Also, consider your audience and how they best take in information. If you're speaking to a group of graphic designers, for example, who are visually oriented, they may respond better to information presented visually. In such cases, I suggest that you prepare visuals that you can show briefly and then put away. If you use slides or PowerPoint, turn off the projector and turn on the lights when the visuals are not in use.

If you do use slides, make them bold, bright, colorful, and easy to read. Use them to show, demonstrate, and create excitement. Don't use them to transmit complex detail. Too much detail in a slide or overhead makes it unclear. To test the readability of a slide, hold it at arm's length. If you can't read the text, your audience won't be able to, either.

Giving your audience a handout

A handout can take one of several formats: hard copy of the presentation or slides, brochures, article reprints, or reprints of the narration (with visuals incorporated, if possible). It can be the full text of your talk, an outline, just the visuals, or a report or article on a topic that is either related to the presentation topic or expands on one of the subtopics you touched on briefly in the talk.

Every handout should contain your company name, address, phone, fax, and, if possible, a full resource box with a brief summary of who you are and what you do — as should *every* marketing document you produce.

If the handout is the full text of your talk or a set of fairly comprehensive notes, tell the audience before you start, "There's no need to take notes. We have hard copies of this presentation for you to take home." This relieves listeners of the burden of note taking, freeing them to concentrate on your talk.

Handouts such as transcripts of a speech, articles, reports, or other materials with lots of copy should be handed out *after* the talk, not before. If you hand them out before you step to the podium, the audience will read the printed materials and ignore you. You can hand out reproductions of visuals or pages with just a few bullet points in advance so that attendees can write notes directly on them.

Why do you need handouts? They enhance learning. But the main reason to give handouts is to ensure that every attendee (most of whom are potential customers, or you wouldn't be addressing the group) walks away with a piece of paper containing information about what you offer and how to contact you. That way, when the person goes to work the next morning and thinks, "That was an interesting talk; maybe I should contact them to talk about how they can help us," he has your phone number in hand. Without it, response to your talk will be zero or near zero; most people are too busy, lazy, or indifferent to track you down if they don't have immediate access to your contact information.

Using the "green sheet" method

Giving a useful, interesting, information-packed talk that convinces prospects you know what you're talking about and makes them want to talk with you about doing work for them is vital. But without the contact information immediately in hand, the prospect's interest and curiosity will quickly evaporate. Because you can't tell in advance who in the audience will want to follow up with you and who won't, your goal is to get everybody — or as many people as possible — to pick up and take home your handout material.

There are several ways to distribute handouts at your talk. The most common is to leave the materials on a table, either in the back of the room or at the registration table where people sign in for the meeting or your session. But this technique is not effective. Most people will walk right by the table without picking up the material. Many won't even notice the table or stack of handouts. Even if you point out the table and say that reprints are available, many people won't take one. And you may feel embarrassed at the silence that follows your announcement; it makes you seem less authoritative, more of a promoter.

Another technique is to put a copy of your handout on each seat in the room about a half-hour before the start of your presentation. Most people will pick it up and look at it; about one-quarter to one-half will take it with them when they leave; and half or more will leave it on the chair. Disadvantages? People may read the handout and not pay attention to your presentation. Also, some people resent this approach, seeing it as too pushy and salesy.

The most effective method of distributing handouts is the "green sheet" method. It maximizes the number of attendees who take handouts, increases their desire to have the material, and, most important, eliminates any hint of self-promotion or salesmanship. Make the handout an essential supplement.

Here's how it works: Prepare a handout that expands on one of the points in your talk, covering it in more detail than you can in a short presentation. Or make the handout a supplement, covering additional points not discussed but related to the topic.

Another option is to do a handout that's a resource guide — for example, a bibliography of reference books on your topic, tables of technical data, a glossary of key terms, or a series of equations or examples of calculations. The important point is that the handout relates to *but does not merely repeat* information covered in your talk; instead, it *expands* on it.

When you get to that topic in your talk, which should be about halfway or three-quarters through the talk, discuss the point and then say something similar to the following (adapting it to your topic and handout, of course): "I really can't cover in this short talk all the techniques related to this, so I've prepared a checklist of 25 points to consider when planning this type of project and reprinted it on this green sheet." Pause, hold up the sheet for everyone to see, and then continue: "I have plenty of copies, so if you want one, come up to me after the talk."

After your talk, you will be surrounded at the podium by a large crowd of people with their hands out to get the free green sheet. Try it — it works. Oh, and why a green sheet rather than plain white paper? Doing it on colored paper and calling it a green sheet seems to make it more special; also, instead of having to remember what's actually on the sheet (many people would not and, therefore, would hesitate to ask for it), people can just come up and say, "May I have a green sheet, please?"

Capturing Attendee Names for Your Prospect Database

Say the conference organizer won't release a list of attendees or the people who go to your specific session, but you want to capture as many of those names as possible for marketing follow-up. In that case, offer your handout as a bait piece instead of giving it out at the session.

At the conclusion of your talk, discuss your handout and what it covers and say, "So if you'd like a free copy of our free telecom security checklist, just write *TSC* on the back of your business card and hand it to me. I'll mail a free copy of the checklist to you as soon as I get back to the office." The more enticing and relevant your bait piece, the more business cards you'll collect. A really strong bait-piece offer can get you the business cards of 25 to 75 percent of attendees or more.

My variation is to offer a free issue of my company's newsletter to everyone who gives me his or her business card. At the end of the talk, I get flooded with people handing me their cards to receive the free newsletter.

We send the newsletter and add the names to our database. They then get the newsletter mailed quarterly. Our database has grown, largely through this method, to 10,000 names. We now get one new client with every quarterly mailing of the 10,000 newsletters. The entire cost of the newsletter, including production, printing, and mailing, is paid for by the first month's fee from this new client. (Refer to Chapter 3 for details on PR firm compensation.)

Part IV

Choosing the Right Medium for Your Message

The 5th Wave   By Rich Tennant

"For three generations the Clegman family has been into megaphones, and now you're telling me if we have something to shout about I should write a blog?!"

In this part . . .

To turn your clever PR ideas into action, you have to establish a good working relationship with the media, which is what I show you how to do in Chapters 11 and 12. The remainder of Part IV gives specific tips for increasing your PR coverage in specific media — radio (Chapter 13), TV (Chapter 14), print (Chapter 15), and the Web (Chapter 16) — and using the newest PR tools: blogs, RSS, webcasting, podcasting, and whatever is next (Chapter 17).

Chapter 11

Getting Your Message Out

. . . .

In This Chapter

▶ Establishing your media contacts and database

▶ Delivering your message to the media

▶ Matching media with your marketing message and objectives

▶ Looking at ways to break through the PR clutter

▶ Mastering the follow-up technique

. . . .

*E*ven the most brilliant campaigns and clever PR materials don't get results if they never leave your in-basket or hard drive. A vital step to generating PR is getting your PR documents into the hands of the right audience — the editors and producers who can make the decision to run them in their publications and on their programs.

Fortunately, you don't have to hire an expensive PR firm to "buy" your way into these media contacts. They're readily available, as well as quick and easy to assemble. This chapter shows you everything from how to develop and cultivate media contacts to the most appropriate ways to talk to them, plus, how to break through the clutter so that your story gets in tomorrow's morning paper. And if you have a product that's sold around the world, we offer some of the nuances of doing PR on a global level.

Compiling a Personal Contact List

I require many of my employees to compile what I call a *personal contact list,* also known as a *call list.* It contains the names, publication or program, and contact information of both the editors and producers they know personally, as well as the media outlets they've found out about through experience or research. My employees should have at least 100 names on their personal contact list. When they're doing a PR program, they start calling the people on this list first to see whether they're interested in running the story we're pitching for our client. They call the people on their personal contact list even before they mail to media directory lists (which I cover in the following section).

Think of your personal contact list as your "house file." Just as you have a customer list from which you get great results whenever you send direct mail to them, you have a personal contact list of media outlets that are more likely to run your press releases than other editors and producers.

Start compiling your own personal contact list now. Does your local chamber of commerce publish a business magazine for the region, and are you a member? Put the magazine and its editor on your list. Are you a member of an industry association? Its newsletter should go on your personal contact list. Other media to add to the list include your alumni magazine and your hometown newspaper.

Any time you're featured in or on any media, get the name of the writer or producer, and add it to your personal contact list. The journalist who has interviewed or written about you in the past knows your name and is, therefore, more likely to pay attention to future items from you. As an analogy, think of her as a customer who has bought something from a direct-mail piece you sent out. She's more likely to buy from you again than is a stranger on a mailing list who has never purchased from you before.

Developing a Mass Media List

Just as marketers mail to rented mailing lists to augment their customer mailings, you should mail to other media outlets beyond those on your own personal contact list.

Although these mass media lists will not generate quite as high a percentage of pickups (a *pickup* means that a publication used your press release or ran your story as a result) as your personal contact list, you can still get very significant publicity results. Don't be surprised if your press release is not picked up verbatim. Unless it's a weekly or community publication, it's much more likely that the press release will get you an interview with a journalist. From there, he will either write his own story or include you in a story he's working on. And the cost to mail to a few hundred or even a thousand media outlets on these lists is fairly nominal. Here are a few suggestions about how to build a database of appropriate names, followed by some options to distribute your materials when they're ready:

✔ **You can buy major media directories, such as *Bacon's Media Directories*.** Many of these media directories will send you updates every six months or more to ensure that you're working with up-to-date information.

✔ **You can order mailing labels from the media directories and affix them to your envelopes when you want to mail a press release or tip sheet.** Ordering labels saves labor and ensures that you have the most recent address and correct editor or producer.

✔ **You can send your press release to media services that can fax, mail, or e-mail the press release to the media you select.** Most of the major media directories have mail, e-mail, or fax distribution services or some combination of these. This is the easiest, fastest distribution method.

Distributing Materials to the Media

You can distribute materials to the media in several different formats:

✔ **Mail:** The old standby — mailing your press releases in a #10 business envelope to the media — still works. In fact, you'd be hard pressed to find an editor or producer who *objects* to this method of distribution. The drawback, of course, is that it's slower than electronic distribution and somewhat more difficult to time the delivery this way. Mailing is fine for feature pieces — but news and other time-sensitive releases (especially those tied to an event) are better delivered by another method.

✔ **Express delivery or messenger:** When the press kit consists of more than a text-only document and you want it to have maximum impact, send it by overnight courier or — for local media — messenger, although this method is obviously expensive. We sometimes messenger videos for local broadcast media, although as we discuss in Chapter 14 on television PR, a faster and better alternative to hand-delivering videos is satellite uplink services. If you have a particularly handsome or impressive press kit, mail it via the post office if timeliness is not critical; messenger or express the kit if timeliness is of the essence.

✔ **Fax:** Fax broadcast is an extremely popular way to send press materials. With *fax broadcast* (also known as fax distribution), a single press release is simultaneously sent to anywhere from one to a thousand media outlets via fax. Almost all the broadcast media accept media alerts via fax, and most of the print media seem okay with it, too. Many major media distribution services recommend fax broadcast as the preferred medium of distribution for press releases.

✔ **E-mail:** Some editors love e-mail, and others hate it. So a mass mailing of a press release over the Internet to editors you don't personally know is risky. Ask editors which distribution method they prefer and whether they like e-mail. Note their preferences on your personal contact list.

Getting to Know Global PR

A decade ago, if a crisis originated in another country on a Friday, we had until Monday morning to prepare. Today, news is so instantaneous and global that we have no time. That's how much things have changed.

Deliver us from e-mail

One of my staff members pitched a story to an editor at the *Dallas Morning News* via e-mail with an attachment. He got back a stern e-mail telling him never to send an attachment for a number of reasons: They take up bandwidth. They cause e-mail to download much slower, wasting the busy editor's time. And in this case, the editor couldn't read the document. In my experience, cutting and pasting documents into the body of an e-mail is the only way that your information will be read electronically by a journalist. Yes, you lose formatting, but you also dramatically increase the number of journalists who will read your message. In fact, an attachment is often a red flag for spam filters and will often cause your message to be filtered out.

Taking cultural differences into account

When doing PR on a global level, you must consider cultural differences when putting your message together. You can't standardize campaigns globally. You have to take a basic message and make adjustments for each culture that will hear it. A press release will have some basic information that can be distributed globally, but the rest of the release will need to be tweaked for each culture.

Messages you develop for your U.S. audiences are likely to be very different from those you develop in other countries. For example, in general, people in Sweden are very humble and find bragging distasteful, while most Americans have no problem with it. How do you get around a cultural difference like that? One alternative is to make a campaign more factual or more fun for Sweden.

Even that, however, doesn't guarantee that the right message gets distributed. One international newswire could get hold of your release and end up spreading the wrong message all over the world. We once did a global survey for a client and the results were picked up in Europe before in the United States. When we opened the morning paper, we read the European message, which wasn't ideal but which also meant that we could no longer release it in the United States — people here had already seen it.

Keeping up with different media

One other aspect to keep in mind is that not all media are like the U.S. media. In the United States, there are thousands of news shows and talk shows, while in many small countries, there is only one (often state-owned) TV station. If your entire database of media is one state-owned television, you'll write a media plan to pitch that station. However, if you're dealing with the United States, where there are literally thousands of shows, you'll write your plan with the objective of attracting as many of those shows as possible.

Selecting PR Media

Selecting media means choosing, from among your personal contact list and mass media database (directories or distribution services), the media outlets to which you want to send your press releases and other PR materials.

Because of the incredibly low cost per media contact of PR versus advertising, the winnowing down process is somewhat different. In advertising, running an ad or commercial can cost thousands of dollars — even tens or hundreds of thousands of dollars — per insertion. So although you may want to run your ad in many publications, budget forces you to select only those few media whose subscriber or viewer demographics are the closest match with your potential audience. You think restrictively based on the finite budget you have to work with.

In PR, the cost per media contact is literally only the cost of mailing or faxing or e-mailing another copy of your press release to another media outlet: about a dollar or less per publication or program. The physical distribution is a minor cost component, and because the media don't charge you a fee to run your PR materials, you don't have to pay a pickup cost.

Therefore, in PR media selection, think expansively rather than restrictively, as in advertising. As you study the media directories and scan the marketplace to see what's out there, add to your list any media outlet that seems to reach your target market in some way, even if these media are peripheral to your marketplace or industry rather than central to it. Remember all those publications you wanted to advertise in but couldn't because of your limited budget? All of them should be on the media distribution list to get your PR materials. PR is a great way of getting coverage in the media that you want to target but can't afford to target through advertising.

For instance, suppose that 5 magazines cover the aquarium industry and 100 magazines cover pets in some fashion. An aquarium manufacturer may be able to afford advertising in the one or two best-read aquarium magazines. But aquarium people also read pet magazines. A press release announcing a new aquarium filter could be sent, easily and inexpensively, to all 5 aquarium magazines and all 100 pet magazines, gaining broader coverage than can be affordably acquired with paid advertising.

In PR media selection, the general rule is, "When in doubt, *don't* throw it out." If you think, "Maybe some of the people watching this program *might* be interested in my product," add it to the distribution list. When in doubt, *send* it out. Even if one person watching the show becomes a customer, it's worth the first-class stamp it took to mail the release, right?

Reaching Reporters the Right Way

Before you pick up the phone to call a reporter, you need to consider a few things. First, what is the editor's preference when it comes to being contacted? Based on your particular experience with that reporter, or clues that can be found in Bacon's and other reporter databases, you should have a sense how each reporter wants to be reached.

Most reporters prefer e-mail because they're often on the phone conducting interviews, but if you have an immediate source to offer and it's close to the reporter's deadline, the phone is usually the best option.

Another question to consider is what format works best for the information you want to convey? If you're offering a third-party source for a breaking news story, a phone call is most appropriate. If, however, you have a long pitch for a feature story, use a combination of e-mail, fax, snail mail, and a follow-up phone call.

To follow up an initial contact, do the opposite of what you did first: If you e-mailed a pitch, follow up with a call, and vice versa.

Don't call a reporter if the reporter is on deadline unless you have something you know he can use at that moment. "Are you working on deadline?" is the first question you ask when you call anyone in the media.

Here are some general rules of thumb about deadlines: if it's a daily print publication, don't call after 3 p.m. If it's a weekly or monthly magazine, don't call late in the week or late in the month. For example, the deadline at *People Magazine* for Monday's issue is the Thursday before at 5 p.m.

If you call a TV program the hour before they go on the air and you don't have breathtaking, breaking news, you will not only get hung up on, you'll probably be remembered as the person who called at the worst possible time.

Turning the Press into a Client

A common misconception is that an adversarial relationship exists between PR and the press. There is a small element of truth in this: Some journalists really do dislike PR people and prefer not to work with them — but they are in the minority. Most journalists view PR people as resources who can provide both story ideas and access to sources (their clients) for stories they're working on. If you're a good resource, your relationship with the media will be a win-win situation.

As a PR agency partner, I see many PR firms that are advocates for their clients. That's fine. But I take a different approach. I see my role as not only helping my clients but also helping the media do their jobs. Treat the media as customers — consumers of your information — and then tailor information that they actually want and can use.

How do you do this? Much the same way you meet the needs of your customers. For instance, when a customer isn't happy, you ask what would make her happy? When an editor says that he isn't interested in running one of my stories, I don't hang up the phone in rage. Instead, I ask him, "What type of stories are you interested in? What you are looking for?" Then I can note his preferences in my personal contact list and pitch my next idea in terms that will be attractive to him. For instance, if I'm promoting a product launch and the producer rejects a story because it doesn't have a local angle, I might find a retailer that carries the product or a customer who uses it in her town before my next call. As a result, the producer may want to send a camera crew to the local store for a short piece on the product, giving the story local color.

When a publication writes a story about you, send a note to the writer saying how much you like the article and what response you've received to the piece. Not only does your personal note flatter the writer, but also writers like hearing about responses — it tells them that people are reading their stuff.

Breaking through the PR Clutter

In Chapter 6, I give you my "bag of tricks" for coming up with creative PR campaigns. Now I'm going to dip into the bag again and look at some of my favorite techniques for breaking through the PR clutter in your media relations.

Using the surround strategy

Some PR professionals and businesspeople have a misguided belief that the only way to reach a CEO is by getting a story on the front page of the *Wall Street Journal,* or that a chemical engineer will notice your product announcement only if it appears in *Chemical Engineering* magazine.

But are those assumptions really true? Do you read only magazines and newspapers focusing on your business or industry interests? Of course not. You read the sports page — or the comics. You probably don't limit your television viewing to shows about your business, either. You watch the news, ESPN, or the *Biography* series on A&E.

I naturally target my PR campaign to cover all the publications central to a market or audience, but then I spread out to cover all the other print or broadcast media that that target may read, hear, or see. I call this the *surround strategy* because, by taking this approach, I can surround the prospect with my story and message in multiple media. The message not only gets through, but it also reaches its audience through multiple exposures, thereby increasing credibility and making more impressions.

The lesson of the surround strategy hit home for me on a flight where I sat next to the CEO of a big company. When the flight attendant handed out reading matter, I silently guessed whether he would pick *Forbes* or *Business Week*. Instead, he chose *USA Today* and began reading Section D, the Life section. When I asked him about it, he told me that was the first thing he read every day, at home or at the office.

Having a go-to guy

In Chapter 9, I talk about using pitch letters to establish someone in your company (an in-house employee or a hired spokesperson) as an expert in your particular industry or subject. I call this person the "go-to guy" because he becomes the source the media goes to first for commentary on that particular topic.

Donald Trump is currently the go-to guy in real estate. Dr. Ruth Westheimer (author of *Sex For Dummies,* published by Wiley) is the go-to expert on sex. Richard Kirshenbaum and Jon Bond have become the go-to guys in advertising. Alan Dershowitz is the go-to guy for the law. And Warren Buffett is the go-to guy on stocks (or at least on value investing).

Positioning someone in your company as a media go-to guy is a great way to break through the clutter, because if you're the source the media goes to first, you — and not your competitors — are the one constantly quoted in stories on your topic. In addition to multiplying your media exposure, this advantage will drive your competition crazy.

Have you noticed that someone else in your industry is constantly being quoted? Have you ever complained, "Why does the media keep featuring this guy? He doesn't know a thing! I'm much more expert than he is!" When you're the go-to guy, you're the one the media calls, not the one complaining that the media called someone else.

Offering an exclusive

If I want to place my story in a specific publication or program, I offer that publication or program an *exclusive*. That means this media contact has first crack at running the story. If this media contact accepts, I won't release the story to any other media until the story runs first as an exclusive with that publication or program.

The benefits are twofold:

> ✔ Offering the exclusive increases the likelihood that my first-choice media outlet will run the story, because the media love exclusives.
>
> ✔ If I get into a prestigious print publication through an exclusive, I make copies of the story and include it when I send the release or media kit to other publications after it has run.

When the other media, especially broadcast, see the reprint, they too become more likely to run the story. Reason: Pickup in a big national publication serves as a media "endorsement" of the story to the other media. Editors and producers see the reprint and think, "If the *New York Times* ran it, this must be legitimate." Just as testimonials from your customers help sell other customers on your products, endorsements from the media help sell other media on running your release or covering your event.

Tying in to an existing story

Just after my last book, *"Leadership Secrets of the World's Successful CEOs,"* was released, lots of CEOs were getting in trouble for excessive pay and other improprieties. So I used that current news issue and pitched myself and my book — with interviews of 100 successful leaders — as "the answer" for great leadership, and as a result, got a lot of press.

As I mention elsewhere in this book, our campaign for Domino's Pizza received major TV coverage when Domino's sent pizzas to taxpayers standing in line at the main post office in Manhattan to file last-minute returns on the evening of April 15.

The technique we used in that campaign, "Go Where the Cameras Are," is based on the fact that it's easier to piggyback on a story or event that the media are already covering in force than to entice them out for the sole purpose of covering your story. If cameras are already shooting and you walk in with something they can't help but notice — in Domino's case, fresh, hot pizza — it's as easy as moving a few inches to the right for those cameras to turn on you for a few seconds. And really, that's all you need.

Using timing in your favor

In Chapter 6, I discuss the idea of creating a PR campaign that ties in with a holiday, special event, or other calendar date. Even if that's not the central hook of your campaign, see whether you can work an element of timeliness into it. For instance, if you're doing a campaign to promote a nutritional supplement that lowers stress, why not give free samples in front of Macy's or another giant department store December 23, the last full shopping day before Christmas? Or at a college dorm during finals week? You get the idea.

Following Up: The Media Blitz

I tell my clients you need two ingredients to PR success, and that having media contacts is not one of them.

The two ingredients of PR success are creativity and hard work. I cover creativity in other chapters on creating PR campaigns, especially Chapters 4 through 6. The hard work comes in the media follow-up.

Many businesses send out press releases with no follow-up; others call only the one or two most important publications in their industry to see whether the press release was received and will be used. At our agency, we call more than one or two publications.

Specifically, we call every media outlet to which we sent the press materials — and we call them several times. Why? It's my experience that if you make a thousand phone calls, you can't help but get some media placements. So we make the thousand phone calls — for every press release we mail. And doing so pays off. The more you follow up, the more pickups you get.

"Did you get the materials I sent you?"

When you call an editor or producer, your first question should be, "Did you get the materials I sent you?" Approximately 50 percent will say they don't have it. They don't remember getting the release or they misplaced it. Send it again by fax or e-mail (asking which the editor or producer prefers) and then follow up later that day or the next day.

Working Your ABC Lists

I have a cold-calling technique for selling stories to the media. It's literally as simple as ABC. If you have a list of, say, 1,000 prospects to call, break it up into three segments — A, B, and C — as follows:

- ✔ **A — the prime prospects:** These are your most desirable targets — television networks, the *Los Angeles Times,* the *Wall Street Journal, Time,* and *Newsweek.* Include the major national media that would bring prestige and credibility to your firm if they used your piece. This list should probably include about 50 to 100 names.

- ✔ **B — the smaller publications:** These are the small media that you don't view as essential to your PR campaign. They are the least critical and desirable media outlets, like your local *penny saver* (the free weekly newspaper every resident of your town gets). You should have about 25 to 50 names on this list.

- ✔ **C — the remaining 900-plus names:** This list includes everybody else.

First, call the Bs to practice your pitch. Use feedback to refine your script and improve response to your next list, the As. For instance, if the Bs won't take the story because it's been done before, can you think of a fresh angle or twist to overcome that objection?

Next, call the As. Do everything in your power (short of bribery, of course) to convince at least one of these media outlets to run the story.

Now, call the Cs and let them know about the prestigious new pickups you have from the A list. The Cs are influenced by big names and are more likely to run your campaign because of the endorsement of the A media.

Separating Advertising and Editorial

In one case, a PR client was approached by the leading trade journal in his industry, which said it would write and publish a feature article about him in exchange for a big order of ad space. What's more, the publisher said, the client could get an even larger article and be featured on the front cover, if he paid a sum of several thousand dollars *in addition* to the cost of the ads. And this was from a highly respected industry publication that readers valued for its editorial excellence, reporting, and objectivity. If only they knew!

Another colleague reports that a local business magazine, published by the chamber of commerce, offered to run a large, positive feature article about his business — an article that he could write and submit, and that would be run as written — if he joined the chamber. In fact, the chamber makes this offer to all potential members.

The smaller the publication, the less of a separation there will be between advertising and editorial. For example, if you live in a small town, take a look at the local weekly "shopper" newspapers distributed free to all residents. Such newspapers are not reporting *hard* news per se — they're really in the business of disseminating news about people and organizations in the community, including businesses. Send them a press release, and they'll publish it. Take an ad, and you get featured in editorial roundups highlighting local businesses and their services.

Because many publications do give editorial favors in exchange for your ad dollars, should you ever take the initiative in suggesting such an arrangement to the media? You should not — at least not when communicating with staff writers and editors.

Never say to an editor, "Please run my article; I advertise in your publication" or, "I may place a lot of ads in your publication if you run my press releases and cover my grand opening." Such requests are likely to infuriate the editor. They demean the profession of journalism, insult the editor personally, and kill any chance that the editor will use your material now or in the future.

If the media outlet is one that allows advertising sales to influence editorial decisions, you'll find out when someone makes such a suggestion to you. It may come from the editor, but typically it comes from the publisher or advertising rep who says, "Run an ad with me, and I'll get your press release published" or makes the lesser promise of "Run an ad with me, and I'll personally place your press release on top of the editor's desk and try to get him to run it."

If you do decide to broach the subject of getting press coverage in exchange for placing your ad with the publication, bring it up with the publisher or advertising rep, not the editor. Say something like, "If I run these ads with you, what can you do for me editorially?" You'll quickly find out whether and to what degree the advertising department can influence the editor in favor of running the PR story of a particular advertiser.

Chapter 12

Handling the Media

. . . .

In This Chapter

▶ Taking advantage of opportunities to deliver your key messages in person

▶ Handling media interviews like a pro

▶ Turning bad press into favorable coverage

▶ Coping with hostile interviewers

▶ Preparing for on-air interviews

. . . .

*W*riting is a big part of how you communicate your PR message, but don't discount the spoken word. The more effectively you speak with the press, local government agencies, regulatory boards, and other audiences, the better your chances of getting the results you want. What you should say to the media — and where and when you should say it — is the topic of this chapter. I also cover how to handle face-to-face meetings with a variety of audiences, including the press and analysts, as well as the different formats those meetings may take.

Meeting the Press

The number-one rule in dealing with the media is "Be available." When a reporter is doing a story, needs information for a deadline, and calls with a question, take the call. If you're doing something else, drop it. A journalist on deadline for today's broadcast or tomorrow's edition can't wait for you and won't accommodate your schedule. If you're immediately available, you have a good chance of being quoted or covered in the story. If not, the reporter will move on to the next source. That's true whether you're the mailroom clerk or the CEO.

When a company president tells me that he's too busy to talk to a media outlet he's been trying to get into without success (and calls him at last because of a tie-in with a current story), I tell him, "You don't understand. You are only important to this publication or program *right now*. Tomorrow, they won't even return your call." Journalism is a *now* business. You either play by their rules or lose before you start. The one exception is highly sought-after celebrities — generally speaking, they're the one group whose time frame the press will accommodate.

Whatever your story, *it is not as important to the media as it is to you.* Media people are under deadline, and if you aren't available right now, they'll do the story without you — or skip the story and do another.

Suppose the press is not banging down your door for an interview or a quote, but you still have a message that you want to get out to your market. You can reach the press in person through analyst meetings, media tours, expert interviews, and deskside briefings.

Analyst meetings

A company seeking market share or planning an initial public offering (IPO) must submit to the scrutiny of at least a few industry analysts. But a poorly planned visit to an industry analyst can be damaging. Analysts ask tough questions about every facet of a company's business — technical and financial — so it's paramount that the company be prepared.

The first thing to do is identify who all the key analysts are in your industry. If your company is publicly held and you don't know who they are, you'll find out quickly the hard way. (They will be talking about you and they won't be as informed as you want them to be.) One easy way to identify the five to ten top analysts is through trade publications where you see them quoted often.

After you've identified the key analysts, you have to make it very convenient for them to receive your information in the most positive, truthful, and accurate light. They will want to be briefed regularly, probably when you release quarterly earnings, have a new product introduction, or a change in senior management. Make sure they get any and all information from you first. Give them the opportunity to ask probing questions so they can understand the significance of what is being covered.

In terms of format, these meetings with analysts generally take place via conference call, with the CEO or CFO and a PR practitioner on the line. These calls are usually recorded so that key analysts can listen at a later time in case they weren't available for the live call. Podcasting is the newest trend for disseminating this information, as well as the Internet (see Chapter 17 for more on these online tools). And don't forget about in-person meetings with analysts, which are still done for industry leaders.

To prepare for these meetings, it is the job of the PR practitioner to rehearse the CEO or CFO by asking the tough questions that are likely to be asked by the analysts. For example, if your company makes a food product and the issue is a food-borne illness, you must be ready for a question like, "How can you guarantee that this will never happen again?" For a drug company, it could be "How do you ensure the safety of XYZ drug so we don't have another situation like the recent recall of ABC?" Or "What is your personal opinion of the policy that your insurance company just changed and how does it affect your own family?" You must have answers ready to all the worst questions that could possibly be asked.

Although analysts write lengthy reports, and investors do sometimes read them, a lot of stocks are sold by brokers who describe the company to their clients over the phone in about 30 seconds. Therefore, you need to create a sound-byte description of your firm. For example, a company that designs search engine software used by major Internet portals described itself as the "toll takers of the Internet," because every time somebody accessed the Internet through a popular search engine running on their software, they got a royalty.

Media tours

A media tour involves sending a company or product spokesperson on the road to talk about or demonstrate a product to local media in different cities. For example, my PR agency has a literary division, and we frequently arrange book tours for the major authors we handle. We arrange for the author to do book signings at bookstores in major cities across the country. Up to eight weeks in advance before the author is scheduled to arrive, we fax media alerts (see Chapter 15) to local TV and radio stations and print publications letting them know the author is available for interviews.

How can you use the book-tour technique to publicize your business? Substitute *product* for *book* and *author* for *company owner* or *product expert*. Set up demonstrations, seminars, or other events in cities in key target markets. Alert the media via advanced notices. Call to follow up before your appearance to remind them that you're coming and tell them why your topic will be of interest to their audience.

Press conferences

For a press conference, you invite print and broadcast journalists from various media outlets to a central location to announce an important story. The story should be major news; reporters and on-air personalities don't want to be dragged away for a trivial announcement. If it's not a breaking news story, there's no need for a press conference. This is tool you use only when you want to give a large number of reporters who are eager to cover a story equal access in the most time-efficient manner.

A sad example is the recent mining accident in West Virginia. A small company had to deal with national news media and press conferences were the only way. The situation dictated it, as it always will. The only other possible situation that warrants a press conference is if you have a major celebrity that the press wants to cover.

Deskside briefings

In deskside briefings, you (or your expert or spokesperson) visit journalists individually at their offices for conversations or interviews. Instead of the journalist going to a press conference, you take the press conference to the journalist. And you do it one-on-one rather than in a group.

Every day, reporters seek expert commentary on all kinds of breaking stories, many of them about technology. How often do you see articles in which your company's product or service has a direct or peripheral relationship to the subject being written about? Every one of those instances represents an opportunity for your company to have a spokesperson give a professional opinion that reflects positively on the entire organization.

In Chapter 11, I discuss strategies to get the press to call on you rather than your competition as an expert. I call this the "go-to guy" strategy because the goal is to become the person the media goes to for interviews on your particular topic. A well-written pitch letter (see Chapter 9) can help you get the press to ask for your opinion.

Print journalists are easier to speak with because they often interview you over the phone. Radio producers may want you to be a guest on their show, which you can often do on the telephone while sitting in your office. (Rarely does a radio show require you to come to the studio.) A TV interview, of course, requires you to go to the studio and appear on television, the rules for which I cover later in this chapter. Chapter 13 covers the ins and outs of radio interviews.

Becoming Savvy with Media Interviews

Here's what's most important to know about the press. They represent a very unique audience that needs to be treated in a special way. Rule #1: People in the press are not your friends. They're journalists who are doing a job. And the job is to do a story in a fair, accurate, and balanced way. If you keep that in mind, it's a fabulous starting point, especially for a media interview.

Handling media interviews like a pro

I've spent a good part of the last two decades training businesspeople on how to speak with the media. Follow these same guidelines that I give my clients:

- **Start with a goal.** Approach all media interviews with a game plan and key messages in mind. Planning ahead — being prepared — is the key to a successful interview. In preparing for a media interview, first develop communications objectives — the key points or messages that you should convey to the audience. Select one or two core messages to convey during the interview. One way to measure the effectiveness of your PR campaign is to count how many of your key message points make it into the articles and broadcasts in which you receive coverage.

✔ **Take control of the interview.** *Control* is a key word in planning for a successful interview. Don't sit back and hope that the interviewer will ask the right questions — take control. Work your key message points into the interview early. Answer questions, but always steer the conversation back to what you want to get across. Don't wait, or it will be over before you know it, and you'll kick yourself for not getting to what you wanted to cover.

✔ **Preview the media outlet.** Educate yourself in advance about the print or broadcast outlet that will be conducting the interview. For *print* interviews, read the paper or magazine to get a feel for its editorial position and reader demographics. For *broadcast* interviews, preview the program before the interview and have a brief conversation with the show's producer or host. Will the interview be taped or live? How long will the interview last? Sometimes you can ask what the focus of the interview will be, but not many will actually supply the questions in advance, unless you're Bill Gates and they really want your answers. If you're Bill Smith, it's not likely. The bigger the publication or show, the less likely they'll comply. One small exception is television. Some will do a preinterview for two reasons: (1) to see if you're any good on camera and (2) to get a sense of the direction of the interview.

✔ Here is another difference from one country to another. In Europe, they will often give you the questions in advance and they may even let you see the piece before it runs. That doesn't happen in the United States.

Be cautious when asking questions of media people. Some will answer them happily, but others may resent having the interview subject turn the tables and interview *them!* If you sense resistance or annoyance, stop asking questions and let it go.

✔ **Anticipate questions and prepare answers in advance.** The next step in interview preparation is anticipating the interviewer's questions and planning how to answer them. Compile a list of questions that are likely to surface during the interview and prepare the answers.

I recommend preparing a list of relevant questions you want to answer and giving this list, sometimes called a *tip sheet,* to radio and TV producers prior to the broadcast or taping. Show hosts usually do not have the time to read your press kit or do much preparation, so a tip sheet saves them effort and is a much-appreciated shortcut. Your benefit is that you make sure the questions you want to answer are asked.

Prior to the interview, ask the reporter what topics are going to be covered. Find out what other sources the reporter has contacted and what those sources may have divulged.

✔ **Be a credible spokesperson.** Always stick to your knitting — your area of expertise. Talk about things you've experienced firsthand, things you believe in. Give facts that prove what you're saying. It's essential to support a statement, especially a controversial one, with proof. In advance of the interview, gather all relevant facts so that you have them ready to use when appropriate. But don't overwhelm the listeners with information. Be clear and concise. Avoid reams of statistics, dates, or numbers that might confuse the audience. Summarize your proof in one or two pithy statements.

How you handle questions that you don't understand or can't answer for lack of information also affects your believability. If you don't understand, ask for clarification before responding. If you don't know the answer, offer to get information. Then do so at once and get back to the person who asked. Admitting that you don't know the answer is not a mistake, but failing to follow up is.

✔ **Find out the reporter's first name.** Using the interviewer's first name positions you as a warm, caring, courteous individual. In contrast, addressing the interviewer by his surname may suggest coldness or stiffness. By maintaining this formality, you create an artificial barrier in the minds of the audience, which is not what you want.

✔ **Be conversational.** Keep the tone conversational and informal, especially during a broadcast interview. Use short words and simple sentences to create an air of informality, and avoid industry jargon. Strive to make the interview a conversation with the reporter rather than a scripted performance. By doing so, you increase your believability and make a more favorable impression on the audience.

Framing your story

An effective technique for communicating with any audience is to frame your story within the listener's experience. Framing helps you organize your thoughts and present them clearly, and also helps the audience absorb key messages quickly and easily. Frames help reporters and editors structure the story — without having to analyze or interpret the information provided.

Depending on your audience and your message, you can use framing in several ways. The *frame of definition,* for example, helps you introduce a new product, service, or concept by answering these four key questions:

✔ What is it?

✔ How does it work?

✔ Who benefits?

✔ Why should anybody care?

By addressing these four questions, you give the reporter and the audience a concise, well-structured presentation. You also ensure that the story communicates the key points you want to convey.

Another useful frame is the *frame of perspective*. The answers to these questions quickly communicate your organization's mission and goals to those unfamiliar with you:

✔ Where were we?

✔ Where are we?

✔ Where are we going?

✔ Why are we going there?

The *frame of scope* is appropriate when your product, service, or organization deals with a cause, illness, condition, or need, whether it's protecting the environment or improving worker safety. The media is probably passingly familiar with the problem but unaware of its scope. In your press conference, you should answer the following questions, whether they're asked or not:

✔ What is the problem?

✔ How bad is it?

✔ Who has been affected?

✔ What measures are being taken to prevent reoccurrence?

You use the *frame of clarification* to correct misconceptions. State the misconception, identify it as such, and then give the correction, as follows:

(Myth):	It's been suggested that XYZ is what happened.
(Fact):	In fact, what really happened is ABC.

Turning bad press into favorable coverage: The 15-10-15 formula

What if you've been getting negative coverage and you fear that the media is planning more of the same? You need to do some planning of your own to seize opportunities to convey the messages you want to get across (for example, that your company is friendly to the environment or your pretzel is made without chemicals). With advance planning, you can use negative questions as bridges to communication objectives. You accomplish this transition — from negative to positive — by responding directly to the interviewer's questions and then continuing the answer by developing a positive statement or the key message that you want to emphasize the most.

When planning such responses, use the 15-10-15 formula to ensure conciseness. Time the direct response to about 15 seconds, the transition statement to 5 or 10 seconds, and the positive conclusion to about 15 seconds. That way, the response will not exceed the 40- or 45-second period that is usually most effective in a news interview.

Simple transition statements include the following:

✔ You should also know . . .

✔ One other related topic that we should discuss . . .

✔ What's important to remember, however . . .

✔ Let me also add . . .

When the list of questions and responses is as complete as possible, rehearse the answers — out loud — until you're confident with them.

Handling hostile interviewers

Some interviewers like to heighten the entertainment value of their programs or interviews by baiting their guests or trying to get them emotionally involved. The types of interviewers described in this section are the exception and not the rule. Usually, interviewers are very accommodating and are interested in what their guests have to say. However, being prepared for all types of interviewers is important.

Never say anything to a reporter that you wouldn't be comfortable seeing in print, hearing on the radio, or seeing on TV. Reporters will not always honor an "off the record" request. If you say it — even if you *say* it's off the record — it's on the record. The media's job is to report and gather news, not promote your product or business. If you give them something juicy, they'll use it whether you like it or not.

✔ **The Interrupter:** The Interrupter constantly interrupts your thoughts with controlled questions or comments that throw you off the main point. When dealing with an interrupter, you can do one of two things:

- Stop, listen to the question, suggest that you'll address that topic in a moment, and then continue your thought with, "As I was saying. . . ."

- Ignore the interruption, complete your thought, and then address the interviewer, "Now, Sally, you asked me something else. What was it again?"

✔ **The Machine Gunner:** The Machine Gunner fires several questions in rapid succession. Suggest to the interviewer that he is posing several questions and ask, "Which one do you prefer that I address first?"

✔ **The Paraphraser:** The Paraphraser is an antagonistic interviewer who incorrectly (and unfairly) restates everything you say. Respond by restating your position: "I guess I didn't make myself very clear. What I said was. . . ."

✔ **The Personalizer:** The Personalizer tries to separate personal views from professional ones in order to solicit a more controversial response. Don't get trapped into contradicting yourself or expressing inconsistent ideas.

✔ **The Dart Thrower:** Probably the most dangerous type of hostile interviewer, the Dart Thrower attempts to convict you, your company, or your industry by innuendo. Never answer a Dart Thrower's question without first addressing the innuendo. If you don't respond, you've tacitly admitted the truth of the implication.

✔ **The Repeater:** The Repeater's technique is to ask the same question over and over with slight modifications each time. Concentrate on what is being asked. When the same question resurfaces in a different form, point out to the reporter that you've already answered that question.

✔ **The News Relater:** This interviewer makes a special point of scanning the day's headlines and looking for stories that may relate to your company's interests. The day's news then forms the basis of the News Relater's line of questioning. This can be frustrating when they want to pursue the issue, and you don't feel it has the slightest relation to what you're doing.

✔ **The Hypothetical Questioner:** This interviewer loves to ask questions that begin, "Suppose. . . ." (For instance, "Suppose you discovered an employee had harassed a customer when delivering to her home?") Avoid answering hypothetical questions unless you've anticipated the made-up scenario and are comfortable in dealing with it.

✔ **The Pauser:** The Pauser's interviews are filled with silences, especially as you complete a thought. This tactic is meant to throw you. Instead, seize the moment as a chance to deliver your key message points. As you complete the first thought and meet the Pauser's empty look, smoothly transition into another thought.

✔ **The Gossip Monger:** The Gossip Monger brings up rumors about other companies and asks you to comment on them. Resist the temptation to respond. Don't comment on what others are doing or saying unless you're being interviewed to supply expert commentary on a given event.

✔ **The Limiter:** The Limiter hurls negative questions about a very specific topic and tries to keep you from bridging to a positive message — even after responding directly to the questions. When being interviewed by a Limiter, insist on bridging into more positive waters. Steer the discussion toward what you've done to resolve the problem and what you're doing to prevent it from happening again.

✔ **The Presumptive Negative:** The media is invariably skeptical, adopting what may sound like a negative stance when questioning the people behind institutions. Respond by challenging the form in which the question is asked and launch into a positive statement.

In any media interview, total and complete concentration is essential; you need a sharp antenna. Total concentration becomes imperative when you're dealing with antagonistic, hostile interviewers. So maintain a polite, distant, and measured stance.

Bettering your broadcast interviews

People who are cool and collected in almost any situation may get anxious when facing the prospect of a TV interview. Being a little nervous is healthy and positive. That nervousness creates a heightened sense of awareness — it sharpens your antenna. So let yourself be a little nervous — not to the point of being immobilized, but just sensitized. Plus, by following the basics, you can calm the butterflies in your stomach and deliver a credible performance that interests viewers and gets them on your side.

You're the expert! You know more about your company — its history, its philosophy, its people, its products, and the issues it faces — than the reporter who is interviewing you or the audience. You're being interviewed because you're the expert. Your knowledge is your strength. Speak from that strength and succeed as an effective company spokesperson.

Mastering your look

How to sit is very important. Here are some pointers for perfect TV interview posture:

- ✔ Cross your legs at the knee, not the ankle.
- ✔ Fold your hands one over the other (not clasped) on your lap.
- ✔ Lean forward slightly in your chair. This "attack" position helps keep you alert and concentrated.

What you wear is important as well; your wardrobe can speak volumes about you. And if you don't dress appropriately, your audience will focus on your clothes rather than your message.

Men should follow these wardrobe guidelines:

- ✔ Choose a dark suit in a solid color; avoid patterns or stripes, which appear too busy on the screen.
- ✔ Choose a tie in muted tones.
- ✔ Don't wear a white shirt. Light blue is a better choice.

Women can use these general rules for on-camera dress:

✔ If you like pastels, wear them; they work wonderfully on television.

✔ Avoid wearing very bright or flashy jewelry; it doesn't televise well.

✔ Don't wear large or dangling earrings.

Whether you're male or female, choose comfortable, nonconstraining clothes so that you can focus on your message and not have to worry about your garments.

Preparing before the interview

Here is a list of ideas that anyone can do at absolutely no cost to prepare for an interview:

✔ Arrive early to familiarize yourself with the studio — at least a half-hour before your appearance. After the interview begins, you don't want to be distracted or intimidated by unfamiliar sights and sounds.

✔ Watch the program to determine the format, interviewer's personality, length of interviews, and attitude toward the industry audience.

✔ Read newspapers and watch television to catch late-breaking news.

✔ Prepare. Rehearse key messages and "gee-whiz" information — little-known facts that you can release to support your point.

Focusing at the studio

After you arrive and before you go on air, is a key time to get yourself in the proper frame of mind. Following are some suggestions to make sure you don't spend your first 30 seconds on air getting yourself to that stage.

✔ Make friends. That's the bottom line. You want the media to believe you and write favorably about your company.

✔ Introduce yourself to the producer, host, or other contact person. Review the agreed-upon format and subject areas of the interview.

✔ Ask to see the studio for the set arrangements. Sit in the chairs to check comfort levels and lighting. Ask for changes if appropriate.

✔ Prepare your props.

✔ Allow studio personnel to put makeup on you. It will make you look better.

✔ Drink water or warm tea with lemon to loosen up your throat. Avoid milk products and powdered donuts.

✔ Take a few minutes to relax and refresh yourself.

✔ Remind yourself of the two or three messages you want to communicate.

✔ Remember posture, eye contact, and gesture rules.

✔ Give a full mic check.

✔ Stay positive. Remember that you're trying to reach the audience, not the interviewer.

Nailing the interview

The most important thing to remember to get your interview right: This is fun and a terrific opportunity. Following are some tips so you don't overthink when you're actually on the air.

✔ Stay focused and keep talking. Look the interviewer in the eye, even if she isn't looking at you. Unless otherwise instructed, focus on the person you're speaking to. If you look your best and maintain an alert, attractive presence, you'll come across as the kind of person who cares about yourself, your company, and your audience.

✔ Look into the camera lens as if you're looking directly at the person asking the question, and talk directly into it.

✔ Part your lips slightly when listening; your expression will be less stern.

✔ Sit up straight.

✔ If the subject is light, show your sense of humor. If it's serious, let your feelings show on your face. Anger is much trickier — generally, it's best to show dignity and calmness instead of going full-throttle on those feelings.

✔ Even if you think you've said something inaccurate, keep talking, perhaps correcting yourself in the next few sentences. But don't stop and say, "Can we do it over?" unless you've asked ahead of time if that is a possibility.

✔ Have fun! The interview will turn out best if you relax and enjoy yourself. Being enthusiastic about the subject will make the interview a pleasure for the host and the viewers.

Chapter 13

Tuning In to Radio

. . . .

. . . .

*M*any people live with the radio — in their homes, in their cars, and on the go. Many consider it their primary method of gathering information because they can multitask while listening — they can get ready for work, make dinner, and commute. In fact, 82 percent of adults age 18 or older listen to the radio while they drive. This high percentage might also be attributed to the fact that radio is a medium built on habit. With preset stations on the car radio, the clock radio, and even streaming audio, people's radio tendencies tend to vary little day to day. Data gathered over the last five years reveal little change in where people listen to the radio. The lone shift here has been a steady climb in car listening over the past five years.

The newest evolution of radio is the advent of satellite networks, like Sirius Satellite Radio and XM Satellite Radio, which enable radio listeners to have more and more control over what they listen to, whether on their radio or over the Internet. Some analysts estimate that subscribers to satellite radio will reach 74 million by 2015.

The selective quality of radio has produced loyal listeners. This loyalty assures advertisers of a consistent audience of the type of listener that the radio campaign is designed to attract. And most large manufacturers have co-op advertising programs for radio through which the manufacturer reimburses the local advertiser — a supermarket, retailer, or other distributor — for a portion of the advertising expenditures.

Opportunities to get on radio talk shows are plentiful. In North America, there are 459 national radio talk shows, 251 syndicated radio talk shows, and 5,102 local talk shows. About a third of these shows are general interest; the others cover specialized topics ranging from agriculture and business to sports, health, personal finance, and travel.

All this to say that radio is a very important part of the strategic PR mix, one that often gets overlooked. It's perceived as not as "sexy" as TV or as "permanent" as print. However, it's a very effective and influential form of communication and should definitely be part of your media outreach — this chapter explains how.

Getting the Facts about Radio

If you've every thought radio wasn't worth your effort, check out these facts about radio and radio advertising from the Radio Advertising Bureau in New York:

✓ Radio reaches 77 percent of consumers daily and 95 percent of consumers weekly.

✓ The average consumer spends almost five hours a day reading, listening to, and watching media. Forty-four percent of this time is spent listening to radio versus 41 percent watching TV and 15 percent reading newspapers and magazines.

✓ Radio, more so than other media, generates immediate purchases. More consumers buy products within one hour of hearing a radio commercial than within one hour of seeing a TV commercial or reading a newspaper or magazine ad.

✓ Consumers spend 85 percent of their time with ear-oriented media such as radio and TV, but only 15 percent of their time with such eye-oriented media as newspapers and magazines.

Radio is everywhere. It goes places other media can't. The time lapse between exposure to the promotional message and the retail reaction (that is, the time between when the buyer hears the commercial and goes to the store to shop for the product) is the fastest with radio: 2 hours for a radio commercial compared to 3½ hours for television, 3¾ hours for newspapers, and 4 hours for magazines. Radio has the fastest rate of return.

Looking at the Advantages of Radio over Other Media

PR novices tend to focus on print media to the exclusion of radio and TV. As a result, the more seasoned PR professionals may be able to get broadcast coverage for their company or product that their competitors can't.

Actually, overlooking radio producers in your PR campaign makes no sense, because radio offers a number of advantages other media do not:

- ✔ **Economy:** Radio commercials are inexpensive to produce because the listener's imagination — and not a costly photographer or video production house — provides the picture. And radio time has a lower cost per thousand than newspapers, magazines, and television. Of course, in this chapter, I show you how, through PR, you can get all the radio time you want, absolutely free. So the cost is virtually zero.

- ✔ **Selectivity:** Radio offers a wide selection of program formats, each catering to a specific segment of the population. (I list various formats later in this chapter.)

- ✔ **Penetration:** Radio reaches nearly 99 percent of the consumer market.

- ✔ **Mobility:** Radio can reach customers just about everywhere, even at the point of sale.

- ✔ **Immediacy:** Advertisers can change their message quickly and easily. They can get new commercials on the air rapidly. A commercial can be written and taped or read live literally the same day, if necessary.

- ✔ **Flexibility:** Radio enables advertisers to talk to customers during the time of day and in an environment that's likely to induce a selling response.

- ✔ **Intrusiveness:** Radio can pervade a listener's mind, even when interest doesn't exist. Radio can and often does invade the mind of a preoccupied listener, forcefully delivering a message. Have you ever found a Top 40 sound running through your head? Constant exposure on the radio is the reason.

- ✔ **Audience:** Radio can reach virtually any segment of the consumer market, including people who don't frequently read newspapers (teens, for example). It reaches newspaper readers who don't read retailer ads because they aren't regular customers. It reaches prospects for your business whose names are not on the mailing lists you rent or who don't read unsolicited mail. And radio enables you to pinpoint your target audience by demographics, psychographics, and geography. A *psychographic* is a psychological characteristic of a target market. For example, market research shows that baby boomers are nostalgia oriented, so using spokespeople and images from their youth appeals to them when you're marketing products.

We live in an age of electronic information, with people reading less and watching and listening more. Therefore, getting on radio and TV enables you to reach additional prospects who may not read the newspaper or magazines.

Another advantage is that radio doesn't require intense concentration on the part of the listener. You can listen to the radio while doing other things, making radio especially appealing as a medium in today's time-pressured society.

Taking Advantage of Satellite Radio

AM radio reinvented itself when FM became the dominant form for music. Now, AM is thriving, thanks to talk format. Broadcast television survived cable TV. Likewise, as satellite technologies move into the radio space, traditional radio (which is now being called *terrestrial radio*) will also find its own place.

But for PR practitioners, satellite radio is a godsend. Across the United States, as of the end of 2005, Sirius Satellite Radio has 120 channels and XM Satellite Radio has 150. That means you now have hours and hours of more opportunities to promote your company, your product, anything. So the faster you hop on the satellite radio bandwagon, the greater the reward.

Pitching to satellite radio is no different from pitching to terrestrial radio, although the demographics of satellite radio are broader and more national. You can actually segment out the audience and focus on strong demographic profiles. So, for example, with terrestrial radio, you can target country music listeners in a specific geographic area. But with satellite, you target country music listeners across the country or the world, for that matter.

With so much new space available on satellite radio, becoming the host of an Internet radio show is a simple way to not only attract the media and great PR, but also to become the media itself. It also instantly positions you as an authority, whatever the topic you'd like to be covered on.

One drawback, however, is that because satellite is so new, you can throw your measurement techniques out the window. There's no way yet to know how many people are actually listening. But that will change. It's a bit like the Wild West. It will be fluid and changing and you'll have to change with it. But it's definitely here to stay.

Don't discount traditional radio, however. Although these new national satellite services promise listeners more choice, consistent niche programming and less commercial distraction, they don't offer local news, weather, and sports. So the future of traditional radio will focus on being "live and local" and interacting with listeners in a positive way.

Getting on the Radio

You don't have to be a celebrity to be a guest on a radio show. Hundreds of radio shows are in need of interesting, informative guests. Celebrities do get lots of airtime, but at least as much airtime goes to people who, like you, have knowledge of a specialized subject of interest to a particular audience and can communicate this knowledge in an interesting, enjoyable, and clear way.

Radio talk shows are a great way to get your message to the world because they are always looking for interesting guests. Approximately 30 percent of radio and TV producers surveyed say that they're interested in booking guests who speak on topical issues; 16 percent are interested in having people speak about new products; and 12 percent like to book authors.

This book's appendix lists several directories of radio talk shows and their personnel, including the producers, receptionists, program managers, and hosts. To get on a radio show, you begin by contacting the producer, because the producer usually decides who the show's guests will be, especially at larger radio stations. At many smaller stations, the hosts are often their own producers and are therefore the ones you should contact.

Making a pitch for yourself

How do you go about pitching yourself as a potential guest? Here are some guidelines:

✔ **Be brief.** As in any sales call, you immediately say who you are and why you're calling and give reasons why the person should listen to you — why she should consider having you as a guest on the show. The most effective way to convince a producer that you are a good fit with her show is to be familiar with the program. Turn on your radio and listen to the program a few times before calling to pitch your story. A radio producer is more likely to book you if, in addition to having a good story and being a good guest, you're a listener or even a fan. For more tips on pitching your story to producers, refer to Chapter 14 (the techniques are very similar).

✔ **Don't pretend to be a publicist.** If you're calling for yourself, say so. Don't try to overimpress or exaggerate, and don't lie. Producers can tell a phony immediately.

✔ **If the producer isn't interested, thank her for her time, get off the phone, and call the producer of the next show you want to get onto.** Don't argue with a producer who turns you down, and don't try to prove that you're a good potential guest; producers know what they're looking for in a guest. Don't ask producers who turn you down for a referral or recommendation to another show, either; they're not in business to be your publicists.

✔ **Have a media kit ready to send out.** You're unlikely to get booked for a show over the phone. Producers who are interested will ask you to send a package of information about yourself and your topic. That media kit can include such items as press releases, a personal biography, testimonials or endorsements, reprints of articles written by or about you, a sample of your product, and a *tip sheet* (a list of 10 to 15 suggested questions the host may ask you about your topic). In addition, if you have made prior appearances on radio or TV, you can include a list of them (with program names, stations, dates, and topics). I also recommend including an audiotape or videotape of a recent media appearance if it's impressive.

Persistent follow-up helps increase your success rate. Media people are busy. If you want to be on the show, persist. Follow up your initial contact with a phone call, a second phone call, and a note. If this follow-up still doesn't work, send another letter saying that you're going to stay in touch because the topic is important. Then stay in touch. Send clippings from print media featuring you, media releases, and articles you've written. *Remember:* One show can easily get you the attention of millions of people who can buy what you're selling. What you're seeking — publicity — is valuable. And you have to work to get it.

Being an accessible expert

A key ingredient of getting publicity in any medium, but especially on radio, is to be accessible, flexible, and accommodating. When the producer calls and says, "We got your material and are interested in having you on *The Bob Smith Show;* how does 10 a.m. on Thursday sound?" say yes. Give the media first priority, and accept the first suggested time or date unless you absolutely can't do so. If you're difficult, hard to schedule, and have a conflict with every date that producers suggest, they're going to get impatient, say, "Thanks anyway," and call the next candidate from the pile of hundreds of media kits they have received.

Although producers generally treat guests nicely, I recommend that you behave as if producers were customers of your business: You exist to serve their needs, not the other way around. This attitude gets results.

Preparing for Airtime

TIP

You've been invited to be a guest on a talk radio show. Now what? Don't go in cold. Do the following preparation, and your appearance will go more smoothly and be more successful for you:

- **Familiarize yourself with the show on which you're going to appear.** Know the host's name and manner of interviewing, the format of the show, and what is expected of you. Get to know the host's idiosyncrasies so that you can avoid surprise and potential embarrassment (for example, if you've written a book on liberal politics and didn't know that the host is ultraconservative).

- **Know the audience — who listens to the show?** Ask the producer or contact the advertising sales department and ask for a media kit. Media kits, which are designed for potential advertisers, usually give details on the audience demographics such as age, income, family, and economic status.

- **Take advantage of every opportunity to promote your appearance.** For example, if you're going to be on a popular radio show broadcast in the Washington, D.C., area, call your Washington-based clients and let them know.

- **Rehearse answering all possible questions that may be asked of you — not just the ones on your tip sheet.** (Refer to the section "Putting together a tip sheet," later in this chapter.)

- **Know in advance the major points you want to make and the messages you want to get across.** Practice saying them in short phrases that you can slip into the conversation in case the host doesn't ask questions whose answers help make your point.

- **If you're on a call-in show, arrange for two or three friends to call in with prepared questions.** These calls can get things going, save you the embarrassment of a quiet phone line (if people aren't calling), and ensure that you get to answer the two or three questions you most want to talk about.

- **Have your toll-free number or local telephone number and mailing address ready.**

- **Take with you any materials you may need to refer to.** If you're an author doing a call-in radio show, for example, have a copy of your book with you. If you want to support your opinions with facts and statistics but your memory is not great, jot down the key facts on index cards and have them handy.

✔ **Have a free tip sheet, special report, booklet, or reprint that you can offer callers or viewers as a giveaway.** This bait piece contains information that expands on one or more of the topics you discuss on the show. Having such a bait piece can make the difference between tremendous versus minimal lead generation from a radio appearance.

✔ **Work on a definition of what you do and boil it down to a single brief sentence that you can say.** For example, you might say, "My company, CTC, helps businesspeople improve their writing skills."

✔ **For in-studio radio shows, leave for the interview early.** This is one interview for which you absolutely can't be late. A client or recruiter can always wait, but an 11 a.m. show must start at 11:00 whether you're there or not. If the show starts at 11:00, you were told to be there at 10:00, and it takes an hour to drive in normal traffic, you may think that you should leave at 9:00. I recommend that you leave at 8:00 or 8:15 at the latest . . . just in case. Nothing is as uncomfortable as being stuck in traffic at 10:45 for an 11:00 radio appearance. Trust me. I know from experience.

Boning up on your topic

Spend some time boning up on your topic before you go on the show. A radio appearance is the ultimate think-on-your-feet challenge. No matter how well you prepare, callers and hosts will ask questions on specific situations that require you to work out an answer instantly, on the spot, and present it in a clear manner, without hesitation, in 30 to 60 seconds.

Spend an evening reading through your press releases, press kit, book, article clippings, brochure, annual report, or whatever source material is the basis for your topic. Take notes on interesting highlights and jot these key facts and figures on a few index cards or a sheet of paper. Take this material with you. You can study it while you wait to go on the air and refer to it while on the air without the audience knowing that you're using a crib sheet.

Putting together a tip sheet

Radio program directors and show hosts are busy, and they often don't have time to read your material, study your press kit, do their homework, and prepare questions to ask you. Therefore, they appreciate it if you prepare the questions for them and submit them before your interview. A sheet of prepared questions is sometimes called a *tip sheet* because it tips the interviewer off about what he should discuss.

Although putting together a tip sheet sounds like extra work, it's to your advantage to send one with your press kit in advance. By creating the questions, you can shape the interview — ensuring that the topics you want to cover are discussed during your appearance.

Being interviewed at home

For call-in radio shows that interview you by phone from your home or office, arrange for absolute silence and no interruptions during the interview. Being interrupted is unprofessional, is annoying to the host and listeners, ensures that you will never be invited back, and can make you lose your composure and throw you off track. Put a DO NOT DISTURB sign on your door — a big one, in large, bold letters. Let others know that you will be doing a radio show via phone and can't be disturbed for any reason.

Do you have call waiting? Use the call-blocking feature to shut it off, or have someone call you to tie up your second line and prevent your phone interview from being interrupted by the annoying call-waiting signal. If other phones in your home or office can ring within earshot, take them off the hook until after your interview.

Turn off your radio, too. You can't talk on the phone to a radio show and listen to it at the same time.

Finally, make sure that you have a glass of water handy and that the air conditioner or heat is not turned up too high. You want to be comfortable before you begin, because you won't be able to get up and change the thermostat after the interview starts.

Making a Good Impression during the Interview

Talking on radio is not the same as making a sales presentation to a prospect in your showroom or during a sales call. The key differences:

- ✔ Your time on radio is strictly limited by the segment length defined by the producer.
- ✔ Listeners prefer crisp, concise answers, and lose attention if you're windy.

Keeping all that in mind, here are some general tips for making your radio appearance a success:

- ✔ When asked a question, restate the question before giving your answer.
- ✔ Be brief. After 20 to 30 seconds, you're probably overanswering. If an answer goes longer than that, summarize.
- ✔ Use humor, but don't tell jokes. Short anecdotes are effective.
- ✔ Demonstrate that you're an authority by using facts to enumerate your points.
- ✔ Use dramatic statistics and findings to grab your audience's attention.
- ✔ Elaborate beyond yes or no responses. Make specific points, using examples to bring home each point.
- ✔ Don't come off like a stiff. Be relaxed and let your personality shine through during the interview.
- ✔ Use names — the person interviewing you and the people calling into the show. Later in the show, refer by name to people who have called in.
- ✔ Be positive and show enthusiasm and conviction.
- ✔ Don't repeat or paraphrase a caller's damaging question. It's okay to interrupt a question based on a false fact or premise.
- ✔ End each segment with an upbeat, summarizing benefit of following your advice or using the product you're selling.

Handling surprise gracefully

Being a guest on a radio talk show is not always a winning situation. Getting yourself on the show, preparing, and doing the interview take a lot of effort and time. For small-business people, time is money — you don't do publicity for the fun or glory; you do it for the sole purpose of publicizing your product or service, generating leads, enhancing your visibility and reputation, and making more sales and profits. (At least that's my motivation.)

So when you go to all this trouble and the media appearance doesn't work out, you tend to get upset. But don't let it show. Instead, handle the situation gracefully: Never yell or complain, and always leave people thinking well of you. This positive behavior increases your chances of getting more and better media opportunities. Negative behavior will give you a reputation as a difficult person and make media people want to avoid you.

Most media appearances go well, but horror stories do exist. One friend recalls driving two hours in torrential rains to keep an appointment to appear on a radio show. When he arrived, another guest was sitting in the inter- viewee's chair. "Whoops," the assistant program manager said. "I must have forgotten to make a note after we talked, and I guess I forgot to schedule you. Can you come back next week?"

Don't make product pitches on the air

Some experts tell you to plug your product or service when on the air. I dis- agree. People don't want to hear about your book, video, or accounting firm; they want to get solutions to pressing problems. So rather than talk about yourself, your product, or your service, focus on the listeners — what they need, what they want, and what their problems and concerns are.

For example, Bob Bly, my co-author, was recently a guest on a number of call- in radio shows to promote his book *Selling Your Services: Proven Strategies for Getting Clients to Hire You (or Your Firm)* (Henry Holt). Repeatedly, the hosts would say, "Tell us about your book, Bob."

He answered, "I'd be happy to talk about the book, Mr. Host. But what I'd really like to do is help your listeners overcome their fear of making cold calls, overcome the objections they're getting from prospects, feel more con- fident about selling, and get better results. So, those of you listening out there, when you call, we'll go through your particular selling situation and solve the problem right over the phone!"

The hosts were delighted with this approach, as were the listeners. Bob cre- ated a much more interesting, useful show by working with the listeners as if they were clients, rather than saying, "my book this" and "my book that," as 99 percent of authors do. And what about promoting the book? No problem: The host did that for him, because he was enthusiastic about the information and wanted to help listeners get more of it.

The benefits were twofold. First, Bob came across as a credible, respectable expert, not a self-interested author trying to get the listeners to buy a book. Second, the host promoting the book is more effective than the author pro- moting it because it amounts to a third-party endorsement: the host saying that the book is great and telling his listeners that they should order it.

Radio is warm and intimate. You must personalize what you know, reach out and talk directly to your prospects as friends, entirely honestly, as if you're having a conversation. The fact that you can't see the people you're talking to is irrelevant. Those listeners must feel the force of your personality.

Chapter 14

Getting PR on the Tube

PR is the most inexpensive TV commercial of them all, overcoming television advertising's cost constraints. For the same dirt-cheap dollar or so that it takes to send a media kit to your local paper, you can send the same media kit to CBS and reach millions of viewers that same evening. This chapter takes a look at how to do a PR campaign aimed at the broadcast media and get results from it.

This chapter outlines the differences between television and the other media that we hope you'll be pitching as part of your overall PR plan. It also shows a variety of tactics to get your story on television and how to get the most out of it.

Understanding How TV PR Differs from Print

The same public relations campaign that you design for newspapers, magazines, and radio can work in TV, too, provided that you *add a visual element* to the campaign.

The most engaging visuals are dynamic, showing lots of action — for example, hot air balloons with the client's logo launching into the skies over a local park while a fair sponsored by the client is going on below.

The more unusual the visual, the more it will catch a producer's eye and engage the viewer. The chairman of Empire Kosher Chickens talking about food safety is okay. Having him talk about food safety as he walks through a poultry processing plant is better. Having him give the same talk while standing in the middle of a football field with a thousand chickens strutting around him — something I actually did — is engaging video.

How, for example, would you get local television stations to feature Fred DeLuca, chairman of Subway (the sandwich-store chain), if you sent him on a media tour across the country, as we did? By adding a visual element. We had Mr. DeLuca traveling to various cities, where he was available to go on the air and demonstrate to viewers how to build a perfect sub sandwich. Every time he traveled, we would send a media alert or press release to local television stations and get him on — at the very least — one TV station.

TV is a visual medium, so campaigns with an inherent visual element work better on TV than those that don't have a visual component. An event that has lots of action can make a good short segment for a feature spot on the TV news, for example.

My PR agency's "World's Fastest Pizza Maker" contest for Domino's Pizza, with its pizza-twirling contestants and winner, was a natural for TV (although it worked well in print, too).

Another campaign with a strong visual element to appeal to television was our "Smelly Socks" contest for sneaker maker British Knights. Consumers were invited to send in their smelly socks, which would be judged in a contest, and the winner would get free British Knights sneakers. The visual gimmick was that one of the judges was a dog (actually, my dog).

We sent media alerts (covered later in this chapter) to the New York AP Day Book (also discussed later in this chapter) and all local TV stations. The news cameras ate up the video of me, the British Knights chairman and marketing director, and my dog sniffing the socks as we judged which were the foulest. The story aired on both Fox and WABC (the New York City affiliate of ABC TV).

The most boring visuals are "talking heads" — people being interviewed on camera. Some people have the ability to be engaging on the air; even more do not. Unless you're a totally dynamic personality, do not go on and on with video of yourself chatting. Find something you can show or demonstrate, like how to make the perfect sub sandwich or inspect your furnace or build a compost heap in your backyard.

Are there exceptions to the rule of needing a powerful visual element? Just one. You can get away with straight video only with a personality who has strong charm, charisma, or appeal on camera. TV producers will have you on — and ask you back — if you're one of those rare individuals who is a great guest.

Author Matthew Lesko, whom we once handled, was a "great guest." His personality was so dynamic, his enthusiasm so contagious, that he lit up the screen, even though he was basically a "talking head" without a strong visual element. If you've seen Matthew on TV as a guest or in his infomercial, you know that he is super-animated — and almost hypnotic to watch.

I'll never forget when we got Matthew on the *Late Show with David Letterman.* As Matthew grew more and more excited discussing his topic (which is the seemingly mundane subject of how to get free information from the government), Letterman laughed louder and louder, finally commenting, "Matthew, could I suggest decaffeinated coffee?" Similarly, Matthew was talking excitedly on *Larry King Live* when Mr. King, grinning, interrupted him and pointed out, "Matthew, I haven't even asked you the question yet!"

If you're a great guest — photogenic, enthusiastic, appealing, and maybe a bit unusual — you may be a natural for television, able to get by just on your own appeal. But that's rare. For most clients, I advise improving the odds with a clever campaign built around an engaging visual element.

For a publishing client, I promoted the book *The OJ Legal Pad* by having a Judge Lance Ito lookalike give out copies of the books on the courthouse steps during the O.J. Simpson trial. When O.J. accepted a copy of the book from our lookalike on those steps, the video made the evening news.

Did we plan or prearrange with O.J. to accept a copy of the book? That would have been impossible. Rather, it was a case of, as scientist Louis Pasteur once said, chance favoring the prepared mind. I am a media hound, and a public relations professional, so of course I watched the trial every day. I knew camera crews were on the courthouse steps every day. So although I couldn't guarantee my client that O.J. would take the book, the odds were in our favor.

Sorting Out the TV Shows

Not all TV shows are the same. By recognizing the different kinds of shows and their programming, you can increase your chances of getting coverage by offering them a story that fits in with their format. Here are some of the types of shows you can pitch stories to:

- ✔ **News programs,** such as the local and national TV news, whether on major networks or cable. Look for short feature segments of interest. Local news programs obviously prefer a local angle.

- ✔ **News shows,** such as *60 Minutes, 20/20,* and *Dateline NBC,* do longer feature segments, often focusing on an important issue, a trend, or a family's or individual's story.

> ✔ **Talk shows** range from local cable TV to *Good Morning America, Oprah,* and *Late Night with David Letterman.* Stories they look for vary from host to host and show to show. For example, Oprah Winfrey likes heartwarming stories, self-help, and fun; Jay Leno looks strictly for funny stories.

In Chapter 11, I talk about how I see my role as a public relations professional to be not only an advocate and partner for my client — the business seeking exposure — but also for the media in getting them stuff they can use. I practice this philosophy especially in TV PR. When a TV show is considering doing a segment on you, think of the show as your customer. Provide whatever assistance they need to make the segment come off.

Recently, my firm worked with the *Oprah Winfrey Show* on behalf of our client, IKEA, on a segment. Viewers wrote in to tell Oprah their home decorating horror stories. The show picked two viewers, and IKEA experts redecorated and refurnished their homes. Managing the entire process from start to finish took four months, but to get on *Oprah,* it was worth it.

Targeting a Specific Show for Your PR Campaign

How do you go about targeting shows for your PR campaign? Here's the step-by-step:

1. **Watch TV.**

   You will quickly be able to figure out which programs are a good fit for your PR efforts, and which your target audience is watching.

2. **After you've found a program you think you may want to get featured on, watch it a number of times, paying attention to the format and the types of segments it runs.**

3. **Think of a way to fit your message into the show's format and, even better, one of its regular segments.**

4. **Prepare a press kit to mail to the show.**

   What should be in it? The two documents discussed later in this chapter — a pitch letter and a media alert — are essential. You might also include a press backgrounder, your bio, articles published about your company — anything that might help sell your story to the producer.

5. **Send the press kit.**

6. **Follow up with a phone call to the producer.**

   Ask whether he would be interested in running the story. If not, why not? How does it not meet his needs? If he isn't interested in this story, what kind of stories is he looking for? Elicit information on why you're being rejected so that you have a better chance of getting a positive response to your next story idea.

7. **If you're rejected, be gracious and end the call pleasantly.**

   Don't sacrifice what could be a valuable long-term relationship with an important media outlet in a fruitless attempt to badger the producer into running your story. It probably won't work, and it may very well alienate the producer for life.

Many PR novices tell me that calling the producer is the step that causes them the most anxiety. "How can I call a TV producer whom I don't even know?" they ask me. "After all, I'm nobody to them." The secret is that the person who makes the call may get on the show, but the person who never gets up the courage to make the call is *definitely* not going to be on the show!

When I started doing PR for Matthew Lesko, I was a kid in my 20s fresh out of college and with zero public relations experience. Because I didn't know any better, my first day on the job, I picked up the phone, called the *Larry King Live* show, and asked if they would like to have Matthew — who was then largely unknown — on the show. And guess what? They booked him! When people asked Matthew back then how he got on *Larry King,* his answer was, "A 20-year-old who does not know that 'no' is a possibility."

Don't accept no as a possibility. Or, at least consider that no means "no, not now" — it doesn't mean "no forever." I always keep calling. As a PR pro seeking placement for my client's products and services, I always strive to turn a *no* into a *maybe,* and a maybe into a *yes.*

Preparing Your TV Media Kit

You can use the same press releases and media kits that you prepare for other media (refer to Chapter 9) when pitching PR to TV, without modifying or customizing them for television. In addition to your standard media kit, a few other formats are especially effective. You can use them as stand-alone pieces or add them to media kits going to TV producers.

Article reprints

Whenever you get coverage in major print media, such as the *Wall Street Journal* or the *New York Times,* make reprints (with the paper's nameplate at the top of the page). Include the article reprints with all media kits mailed to broadcast media. A TV producer will be more likely to run a segment on your story if a national and well-respected print publication has already covered it. Producers figure that if *Time* or *USA Today* ran the story, it must be legitimate.

A lot of cross-pollination exists between print and broadcast media. Pay attention to the media. You'll soon notice that stories you read in *USA Today* in the morning you then hear on the radio driving home from work at night. During the first season of the TV show *Survivor,* we conducted a campaign to promote a PR firm by asking CEOs what they would do if stranded on an island. CNBC picked up the story directly from the *Washington Post* article about our survey.

Those in the TV world see an article reprint from a major paper as a legitimate media endorsement of the story. Always try to get one big print placement in the beginning so that you have an article reprint to include with your outgoing media kits.

Articles that appear in a magazine or newspaper are the copyrighted property of the publisher, as is the publication's nameplate. Be sure to get permission before photocopying either piece.

Media alerts

A *media alert* is a short, one-page notice that looks like a cross between a standard press release and a wedding invitation. It quickly hits the highlights, using a graphic format that makes it easy to scan, and sticks to the facts without puff or elaboration. As you can see in Figure 14-1, media alerts focus on the basic five *W*s and one *H* of journalism — *who, what, when, where, why,* and *how.*

Figure 14-1 shows a media alert used to announce a promotional event. Notice that the times for photo opportunities are given. TV crews don't want to waste their time standing around or fighting to get the star or celebrity on camera. You should set aside a specific time when camera operators can shoot video of the featured attraction and specify this time in your alert.

If the media wants to do a live remote, cooperate fully. For a live remote at an IKEA store featuring IKEA's chairman, we were inside the store at 4:30 a.m. helping the TV crew set up for a 7:00 a.m. spot on a morning show. Why is this important? When we got to the store, we found that there was an automatic AC timer that had turned on the air conditioning, the noise from which would have made the live remote inaudible. Because we were there to handle it personally, the problem was fixed, the show went on, and IKEA got the PR coverage.

<u>MEDIA ALERT:</u>

****

WORLD SERIES CHAMPION

Orlando "El Duque" Hernandez

SMOKES A VICTORY CIGAR FOR CHARITY

****

Yankee Pitching Sensation "Teams" Up With Club Macanudo and Hoyo de Monterrey at an Auction To Benefit The Institute of International Education

WHO: Orlando "El Duque" Hernandez, Club Macanudo and Hoyo de Monterrey
***Other notable attendees include: Oscar de la Hoya, Montel Williams and Star Jones*

WHAT: "The First Annual **Club Macanudo** Charity Auction,"
benefiting The Institute for International Education, will feature "El Duque." The auction, conducted by Christie's, will offer a number of exclusive items including: pre-Castro Cuban cigars, autographed Yankee paraphernalia, and signed boxes of the new Hoyo de Monterrey Seleccion Royale "Duque."

WHERE: 26 East 63rd Street (Between Park & Madison) New York, NY

WHEN: TODAY -- 7:00 p.m. to 10:00 p.m.

                            <u>7:00 - 7:30 PM Photo Opportunity</u>
Orlando Hernandez puffs on a victory cigar as he is bestowed his own personal "El Duque" humidor presented by General Cigar CEO, Edgar Cullman, Jr.

                            <u>7:30 - 10:00 PM</u>
Orlando Hernandez meet and greet. Auction of autographed items for charity.

CONTACT: Jessica Wolff
Jericho Communications -- (212) 645-6900 ext. 123

Figure 14-1:
Sample media alert announcing an event for television.

There's an old saying: "God is in the details." Well, TV is a detail-oriented medium. The TV crews that show up expect your site to be "TV-ready" — no odd noises, no lighting problems, no logistics hassles. If things aren't just right, the shoot won't come off.

For events, you can use either a pitch letter or a media alert. Figure 14-2 shows a pitch letter that my firm did inviting TV producers to a fun event featuring TV personalities of yesteryear. The event got coverage on national network TV.

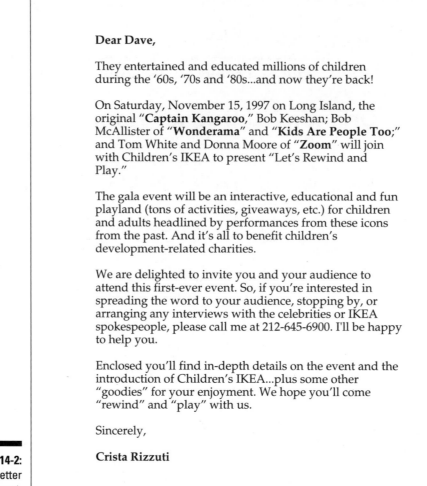

Dear Dave,

They entertained and educated millions of children during the '60s, '70s and '80s...and now they're back!

On Saturday, November 15, 1997 on Long Island, the original "**Captain Kangaroo**," Bob Keeshan; Bob McAllister of "**Wonderama**" and "**Kids Are People Too**;" and Tom White and Donna Moore of "**Zoom**" will join with Children's IKEA to present "Let's Rewind and Play."

The gala event will be an interactive, educational and fun playland (tons of activities, giveaways, etc.) for children and adults headlined by performances from these icons from the past. And it's all to benefit children's development-related charities.

We are delighted to invite you and your audience to attend this first-ever event. So, if you're interested in spreading the word to your audience, stopping by, or arranging any interviews with the celebrities or IKEA spokespeople, please call me at 212-645-6900. I'll be happy to help you.

Enclosed you'll find in-depth details on the event and the introduction of Children's IKEA...plus some other "goodies" for your enjoyment. We hope you'll come "rewind" and "play" with us.

Sincerely,

Crista Rizzuti

Figure 14-2:
Pitch letter for an event.

Prepared footage

So far in this chapter, I've talked about sending written documents with the goal of getting TV placement. But because TV is a visual medium, should you create video PR materials and send them to TV producers? Yes. Will they use them? Yes.

Producers have limited crews and limited budgets. Much as they'd like to, they can't always send a crew to cover your event or story. Without video, they're less likely to use the story (although on-air personalities doing the news mention many stories that aren't accompanied by video clips).

Typically, I hire a video production company to shoot the event. The company sends a crew — usually a camera operator and a producer or director — to take footage. The result is what we call *prepared footage* or *b-roll:* a quick video compilation designed to give a TV producer footage of a story that he can use to create a feature segment on the event or product.

B-roll is best produced by professional, video-production companies, using professional-quality video. TV producers generally won't use home video unless it's a news event of extraordinary value or extremely rare footage, like a hurricane, earthquake, or the Rodney King beating.

Time is of the essence when it comes to b-roll. The footage should be shot on the day of the event, preferably early in the day. The production company will edit the video to contain several different segments on the event, ranging from 30 seconds to a few minutes. Some of these segments may be question-and-answer interviews, and others are merely sound bites — snippets showing people making brief comments. The video should also contain action shots, such as kids throwing pies or riding roller coasters.

Immediately after completion of editing, send the b-roll to the appropriate TV producers. If you're targeting local TV shows, make quick duplicates of the b-roll and deliver the tapes via messenger for possible airing that day.

What will it cost? Production for one b-roll will run $2,000 to $5,000. Add satellite uplink service to distribute your video to TV producers (refer to the next section), and you're looking at a package price of around $15,000 to $22,000.

Satellite feed services

What if you're targeting national media or other media not in your town? Overnight shipping won't work in most cases, because an event held today will only be covered today; by tomorrow, it's old news. In such cases, the solution is to use a satellite feed service. These services take your b-roll video footage and uplink it to a satellite. (I'm not sure of the exact technical method, but for our purposes here, it really doesn't matter.)

TV producers are then given the coordinates of the satellite. They can download the video from the satellite and use it on their shows that day. With a satellite feed service, you can distribute your b-roll to TV stations throughout the entire country on the same day you shoot and edit it.

Video news releases

A video news release (VNR) is a more elaborately produced video than pre-pared footage (otherwise known as *b-roll*). Instead of a series of short clips, a VNR consists of one entire feature story, usually running 30 seconds to 3 min-utes. It's meant to be run in its entirety, although many producers use only a portion of the video. B-roll is the current format of choice when you have a current event, a hot announcement, or another story for which immediacy is paramount. VNRs are more complete pieces used for feature stories rather than hard news. The trend today in PR is away from VNRs in preference of b-rolls. Reason: B-rolls are cheaper to produce than VNRs, and TV stations like them just as much.

Creating a good VNR is very expensive — production costs run $10,000 to $20,000, plus satellite uplink distribution for a total package price of $20,000 to $30,000. Yes, that's a lot more than a press release, but a high-quality VNR is the only one that has a chance of getting used. Plus, it's a lot less expensive than most TV commercials.

Pitching Your Story to Producers

How do you approach a TV producer? In much the same way that you approach a magazine or newspaper editor (refer to Chapter 9), with just a few differences.

- ✔ If you're trying to impress a producer with whom you have no prior rela-tionship, a nicely packaged media kit sometimes helps.

- ✔ If you want to increase your chances of getting coverage on a particular TV show, offer the producer an exclusive on your story — give the show first crack at running it. If the producer accepts, she gets to run the story first; then you're free to give the story to other shows and stations.

Offer an exclusive only if the story is breaking news or something else important enough to warrant it. When my agency did PR for best-selling author Peter Golenbock's book on a college basketball scandal, *Personal Fouls,* the media considered it a big story. We got continual coverage by offering a new exclusive angle on the story to a different media outlet each day.

- ✔ When time is of the essence — and this is frequently the case for TV producers, who produce segments daily and often focus on the day's news — fax press releases and media alerts. The best way to make sure that a producer knows about your event is to fax a media alert and then follow up with a phone call. The first thing you want to know is whether the producer got your media alert. If he received it, ask whether he needs additional information or wants to interview anyone.

✔ Don't push too hard to sell your story to the media. Yes, you'd like to get it on the air. But you're also building a relationship with that producer. Being too aggressive can turn him off and ruin your chances for future placements.

Look to target TV segments that others aren't pitching. I already gave the example of remote shots for TV weather. Another underpitched segment is monologues on talk shows. Here's an idea: Call shows like the *Tonight Show with Jay Leno* and ask who's in charge of writing the monologues. Then send feature material to that person. These shows can always use good jokes, and if what you send fits, you just might hear it on the show that day.

Once, we did a humorous campaign for Domino's Pizza in which we gave free pizza to college seniors who came in with rejection letters from potential employers. Johnny Carson talked about it on his monologue on the *Tonight Show,* and pizza sales for Domino's soared the next day.

Many TV shows plan their shoots for the day by consulting the *AP Day Book.* Each day, the *AP Day Book* wires stories and events to TV producers around the country. I recommend that you send all your TV media alerts to the *AP Day Book;* doing so can increase TV coverage of your events and campaigns. The Associated Press (AP) has bureaus in major markets throughout the United States, and each bureau has its own daybook covering its region. AP bureaus are listed in major media directories, such as *Bacon's Publicity Checker.*

Doing TV PR on a Shoestring

What if you don't have $10,000 to $30,000 to spend on a b-roll or VNR? Relax. There are many less expensive, yet just as effective, ways to use TV PR to make you and your product famous.

Finding the right angle

For one campaign, my firm's job was to publicize a tool called RotoZip, which you use to smooth small dents in your car. Media interest was mild. But when I had the wife of the company owner demonstrate the tool, the story began to get TV coverage. The idea of a woman fixing her own car instead of relying on a man to do it seemed to be the angle that producers were looking for.

Here are a couple techniques I have used with success:

✔ **Come up with an angle that appeals to a TV audience.** If you have an interesting angle, the producer will have you come to the studio and be interviewed — or, better yet, have you do some kind of demonstration on her set. For Jeff Stein, cofounder of Camp Beverly Hills Clothing, we got major TV coverage by positioning Jeff as the "Clothing Psychologist." On the air, he would look at someone and then recommend a wardrobe based on the person's personality.

✔ **Pay attention to the media.** Certain segments on TV repeat every year; in the trade, we call them *evergreens*. For instance, you can bet that next Thanksgiving, hundreds of local stations across the country will have a chef visit the set to show how to make Thanksgiving dinner. If you run a food company, you could send a pitch letter offering to have your chef do the segment with some unique recipes featuring your company's products. If the producer is looking for a new chef for this year's segment — and that's often the case — your chef may just become the station's new holiday gourmet.

Getting a Tape of Your Guest Appearance

Whenever possible, get a tape of each TV (and radio) appearance you make. These tapes have a number of uses:

✔ You can use them to convince producers of other radio and TV shows that you're a good guest — entertaining, pleasant, bright, and informative, with information relevant to their audience. Producers are somewhat reluctant to book guests who are experts but have no or little experience in broadcast media. An audiotape of a good performance can eliminate that reluctance.

✔ Listening to the tapes can help you improve your performance so that you're better the next time.

✔ You can use the tapes as marketing communications tools. For example, if you're a consultant who specializes in quality and you were on a radio show to discuss quality, you can make copies of the tape and send it to clients and prospects.

✔ You can give copies of the tapes to your parents. They'll be thrilled. (The extra copies are for mailing to Uncle Ned and Grandma Nellie.)

How do you get a tape? Before your scheduled interview, call the producer and say, "May I ask a favor? I would love to get a tape of the broadcast. If I send you payment, would you be willing to tape the show and mail the tape to me? If not, no problem, of course." Most will agree and, further, will not charge you for the tape (but you should always offer to pay). Others may ask for a nominal sum to cover the cost of duplication and mailing, usually just a few dollars.

Although getting an original tape from the studio is best (because originals give the best-quality duplications), you can always arrange to tape your appearance yourself.

Chapter 15

Getting More Ink (Print Isn't Dead Yet)

In This Chapter

▶ Avoiding dead-end news releases

▶ Understanding the trick to creative press releases

▶ Offering a free booklet as a hook

▶ Tying your news to a special event, fad, or news

▶ Promoting telephone hotlines or trade-ins

▶ Using a new product, survey, or call to action as an angle

*T*he Internet has changed the way business is done in the United States, and it's now transforming the way we live. Rumors of the Internet's demise in the early '90s were greatly exaggerated.

But print media such as newspapers and magazines are viewed differently by many people. Some say that print is not only "not hot" but also in danger of disappearing entirely. A few of these skeptics predict that printing words on paper will become as rare as carving commandments on stone tablets.

I disagree. Print is still alive and well. More than 8,000 magazines and 6,900 daily and weekly newspapers are published in the United States. Nearly 60 million newspapers are sold every day!

So, to promote your business interests, you still want to reach print journalists and get your business covered in their publications. This chapter tells you more about how to do that successfully.

Cracking the Journalists' Secret

Journalists, like all of us, have too much to do and not enough time to do it. If you give them a good story idea, you automatically improve the odds of getting into print. If you give the story to them written, packaged, and ready to

go, your chances of getting ink increase dramatically. The best way to deliver such a story is in the standard PR document called a *press release.*

Chapter 8 covers the structure and style of a press release. In this chapter, I focus on how to fill your release with content that gets editors to print it and publicize your product, service, organization, or offer.

Knowing What Not to Do

Many PR practitioners waste an enormous amount of time churning out routine, standardized press releases that, almost invariably, land in the editor's wastebasket. Figure 15-1 shows a typical example.

> **FROM: XYZ Company, Anytown USA**
> **CONTACT: Paul Paterson at 555-5555**
>
> *For immediate release*
>
> ### JOE JONES PROMOTED TO EXECUTIVE VICE PRESIDENT AT XYZ COMPANY
>
> ANYTOWN, USA- Joe Jones has been promoted from vice president to executive vice president at XYZ Company. In his new position, he will be responsible for managing U.S. operations as well as long-range strategic planning for all business units.
>
> Before being promoted to executive vice president, Mr. Jones had served for 5 years as vice president for the ABC Division of XYZ Company.
>
> Prior to joining XYZ, he had been a program manager for Another Bigco in Sometown, USA, and had also worked as staff analyst at SmallCo in Another-town, USA.
>
> Mr. Jones holds a B.S. in systems engineering from Nice College and an M.BA. in finance from NightSchool U. He is a member of Tau Beta Beta Rho and the Society for Systems Engineering.
>
> Mr. Jones currently resides in Anytown with his wife, Janet, and his three children, John, Jamie and Jack.
> --

Figure 15-1:
A ho-hum, dead-end press release.

Most publications receiving a press release like the one shown in Figure 15-1 will ignore it. Oh, sure — one or two industry publications will run a one-line mention of Joe's promotion, as will his alumni magazine. And if he lives in a small town, the weekly newspaper may run a short feature article with his picture and the text of the release. But except for some warm fuzzies around Joe's house, the result is minimal visibility for Joe's company — zero leads, inquiries, or new business. In short, the time and money invested in preparing and distributing the release yields virtually no return.

Perhaps 90 percent of all press releases are similar to this fictional example, generating a similar lack of interest, media coverage, and benefit. Press releases of this type, despite their popularity, are ineffective for a number of reasons:

- ✔ **The topic is a nonevent.** Hundreds of people get hired or promoted every day. So there is nothing to differentiate the announcement from the other dozen or hundred or more the editor receives that week.

- ✔ **The topic is not meaningful.** The promotion is important to Joe Jones and his family — but that's about it. The release contains nothing to interest an editor or a reader.

- ✔ **The announcement does not help promote Joe's firm or sell the firm's products, other than by mentioning the company name.** (Journalists, of course, have no interest in promoting your product, but in your role as your company's PR person, you should.)

- ✔ **The reader has no reason or incentive to pay attention — the information presented offers no benefit or usefulness.**

- ✔ **There is no call to action, no response for readers to take if they want to do business with Joe or his firm.**

Despite this lack of effectiveness, the "Joe Jones Promoted" press release is the most commonly used and most popular; approximately 80 percent of releases are structured just like it. (Other common company themes are expanded facilities, new hires, awards won, other honors, corporate reorganizations, openings of new facilities, and company anniversaries.)

Such press releases remain popular with publicists for two reasons. The first is that they're easy to write and can be prepared quickly without much effort, research, or creative thought. The second reason has to do with the way PR firms and professionals traditionally have earned their keep.

Many PR firms work on retainer: In exchange for a fixed monthly fee, they produce a set number of releases and articles. Or they devote a certain number of hours per month to developing and disseminating PR materials on behalf of their clients. To fulfill this obligation, the outside PR firm (and often, the inside PR manager) looks around the company, asks, "What's new?" and writes and distributes releases on these topics.

If a lot is going on during a particular month, the releases have substance and will work. If nothing noteworthy is happening, the PR person still has to produce *x* number of press releases. That's when bland releases are hatched on nonevents such as Joe Jones's promotion or Sam Smith's election as treasurer of the fraternal club.

Think twice about sending press releases on new hires or promotions. Such releases offer little benefit to your company, and their publication can cause headhunters to call the employees featured and lure them with job offers.

There are only two situations in which I think sending out new-hire or promotion press releases is to your advantage:

- ✔ **When you hire a big gun for a top executive position:** Having the big shot on your team makes the company sound better, especially to investors.

- ✔ **When your business is in the dot-com sector:** Venture capitalists buy résumés, and if you announce to the press that you've just hired the former founder of Big Dot-com as CEO of your Little Dot-com, that can help get the venture capital cash flowing into your coffers.

Catching an Editor's Eye with a "Creative" Press Release

A *routine* press release is an almost mandatory write-up of an event, usually important to the organization issuing the release but mundane to the media and the general public. In routine press releases, the facts drive the release — something happens or exists, and the publicist, searching for a topic, finds it and writes about it.

"Creative" press releases are more effective than routine press releases. A *creative* press release differs from a routine press release because:

- ✔ **It has a "hook."** A creative press release has an angle or slant designed to get the attention of the media (so they will publish the story) and the public (so they will read it). I use the term *creative* because the publicist, instead of just working with the facts as they exist, either creates or helps shape the story hook, with an idea that is not obvious from the story itself.

    But the creative release is always built around a genuine story, a real event, important information, or other "meat." If it's just an angle with nothing behind it, the release will get attention but be rejected as a publishable story.

✓ **Its story is built around something that would interest prospects — the readers of the publication or listeners of the program.** An effective release doesn't begin with the product or the point the publicist cares about.

Too many people write press releases from the product marketer's point of view. They put out story after story about things that are of interest only to the company and its managers.

You do this either in the mistaken belief that others care about you and your company as much as you do (which isn't true) or to stroke someone's ego. Often, an executive orders the PR department or agency to put out a release on a person or his or her accomplishments as a way to recognize and honor that person. It may flatter the subject of the release, but editors don't care . . . and neither do your prospects.

As with any effective marketing effort, good public relations focuses on the prospect, not the product. As far as PR goes, don't think about what is important to you; concentrate on what is important to your prospects. What are their problems, their needs, and their most pressing concerns? What information, advice, products, services, tips, or guidance do they require to improve their lives, do their jobs better, or save time and money? What information do you have that they would want to know and read about in a magazine, hear on the radio, or see on TV?

A press release should not be created merely to stroke the client's ego or serve some internal requirements to have certain topics covered in releases. Press releases succeed when they're focused on what appeals to media people and interests their audiences the most.

Using a "Hook" to Snare Attention

You can choose from numerous ways to make a press release more creative. The "hooks" I discuss in this section you can attach to your release — these hooks have proven successful time and time again in luring attention from the mass media. (I cover other tactics in Chapters 4, 5, and 6. Adapt these formulas to your own PR campaign, or come up with your own ideas.)

When writing your own release, you can closely copy the format and style of the example releases in this book, substituting details specific to your topic. For example, I've used the format for a free-booklet press release to promote numerous products and services — always with substantial results.

Free-booklet press release

The free-booklet press release works as follows: You write a booklet, report, or tip sheet on a topic relating to your product or service, and then you send out a release about your free booklet. For example, if you're selling seeds by mail, write some gardening instructions and offer them as a free reprint. If you sell spices, offer a booklet of free recipes.

Preparing the release

After you write your booklet, report, or tip sheet, you then send out a release that

- ✔ **Announces the publication of your new booklet or report.** Editors are primarily interested in what's new, so if you're offering a new booklet on a topic, your headline should always begin with "New Free Booklet," followed by a description of the topic, contents, or issue the information addresses.

- ✔ **Describes some of the useful information it contains.** Your press release should repeat (either word for word or edited) some key points highlighted in the booklet or report. This technique makes it easy for the editor to run your release as a "mini-feature article" on the topic.

Just saying that you have a booklet available may get you a small mention. But if you allow editors to reprint some of its contents, by putting such material in the release you send, they're more likely to run longer, more in-depth pieces featuring all the useful information you've provided.

"But if all the information in my booklet is revealed in the article, then people will have no reason to send for my booklet!" you might protest. That sounds like a logical objection. But experience proves the opposite is true: The more the articles describe the contents of your booklet, the more people will read the article and send for the booklet. "The more you tell, the more you sell." That's an old saying favored by mail-order ad copywriters, but it also applies to free-booklet press releases.

Experience has shown that even if the entire text of a booklet is reprinted in an article (or an ad), people still want to get that text in booklet form. Why? Perhaps people don't like to tear out an ad or article, and they find that booklets and reports are a more permanent medium.

Do not assume that the editor will read your booklet and pull out pertinent material for an article. The press release should be a self-contained mini-article ready to use as is so that the editor doesn't have to refer to any enclosures or other materials.

✔ **Offers the booklet free.** Your free-booklet release must call for action. In the last paragraph, you say, "For a free copy of [title of booklet], call or write [your company name, address, and phone number]."

Many editors include that contact information and a call to action when running your releases, and if they do you'll get many requests. Some editors, however, won't print such contact information. You have no control over that. However, if you don't include contact information and a call to action, *no* editors can tell their readers how or where they can request your booklet, and without such information, no one will contact you. So, always close with the call to action.

Including a copy of the booklet with your release

Including a sample of the booklet may be desirable, but it isn't necessary. I have had great success mailing press releases that didn't include a sample copy of the booklet or report being offered.

The main benefit of leaving out the sample booklet is cost savings: Including a sample booklet can add another 10¢ to 70¢ or more per release being mailed, depending on the cost to print the booklet and the weight of the booklet (which increases postage). For example, a tip sheet or slim pamphlet adds less cost than a bulky special report, book, or manual. If the extra 10¢ to 70¢ per piece is significant to you, omit the sample booklet and pocket the savings.

Be sure to put a line after the close of your release that says, "Editor: Review copy of [title of booklet] available upon request. Call Joe Jones at [insert phone number]." Some editors may insist on seeing a copy of the booklet before they'll promote it in their publications, so offer to send a copy free to any editor who requests it. The editor can get the information instantly via fax or e-mail.

If your free booklet is slim and inexpensive, or if cost is not a factor, include a sample copy with each release you mail. Doing so certainly can't hurt. And some editors may pay extra attention when they open the envelope and see your report or pamphlet.

Using key codes

Some practitioners use key codes in the address. For example, when someone makes a request for a copy of the free booklet, you may include "Dept. 105" in the address to which the request is made. By counting the number of requests for this tip sheet addressed to Department 105, you know exactly how many responses were generated as a result of mailing this press release to the media.

Some practitioners take this a step farther and put a different key code on each individual press release; the key code indicates the specific publication the release was sent to. Therefore, the press release going to *Computer Decisions* would have been key-coded "Dept. CD," while the next copy, being mailed to *InfoWorld,* would have been key-coded "IW."

The advantage of individual coding of releases keyed to publications is that it lets you know how many responses were generated from each publication, not just the entire mailing. With this knowledge, you can fine-tune your distribution list, hitting only those publications that generate a high level of response. The major disadvantage of key-coding each release with a different key is that it's time consuming: You have to do it one release at a time. I don't think it's worth the time and trouble, but do whatever seems best for you.

Special event, gimmick, or timely issue

The press is always looking for a story that captures the public's imagination. Therefore, if you have a special event, timely issue, or unusual human-interest story, or if you can add some sort of hook or angle to your release, you'll have a better chance of gaining coverage.

Editors are interested in stories that are substantial and of value yet have an unusual twist or gimmick to them. If you can be a bit different (albeit in a relevant way), you will get noticed.

Figure 15-2 shows a news release that's a perfect example of a story with an offbeat angle. This company rents mailboxes — a pretty mundane business. But the angle for this story was the unusual, prestigious location of its mailbox address: the Empire State Building.

Mentioning that the Empire State Building is one of the few buildings in the country with its own private zip code and post office is a nice added touch, because some editors like to include a bit of trivia or little-known information in their articles.

A successful promotion that my PR agency did for our client IKEA was the "Sharing the Caring Program." In addition to being an event-driven PR promotion, it's a good example of the PR principle of "Show, don't state."

FROM: Empire State Communications, 350 Fifth Ave.
New York, NY 10118
CONTACT: Arthur Goodman, phone 800 447-0099

For immediate release

**NOW BUSINESSES NATIONWIDE CAN ESTABLISH
A BRANCH OFFICE IN NEW YORK CITY'S
PRESTIGIOUS EMPIRE STATE BUILDING-
FOR A LITTLE AS $35 PER MONTH**

New York, NY - Want to give your company added prestige and
impress your customers? NYC-based entrepreneur Arthur
Goodman has a suggestion: a "branch office" in New York's
most distinguished and memorable location: the Empire State
Building.

Goodman's company, Empire State Communications, provides
mail receiving, fax, telex, and telephone service for businesses
nationwide that want to establish a branch address in New York
without physically having an office there. And the price is right:
Empire's service starts at $35 per month.

"Our service allows firms nationwide to immediately and
inexpensively establish a New York presence at one of
Manhattan's most memorable-and impressive-addresses," says
Goodman. "The Empire State Building is a status symbol
worldwide. And the address is easy for your prospects to
remember; no multidigit P.O. box number is necessary."

What types of companies use Goodman's Empire State service?
" It's for small out-of-town companies that want to convey an
image of a larger, more substantial firm through a prestigious
New York City address, as well as large corporations that feel
they should have a New York City location but don't want the
expense of renting costly office space," he says.

How does Goodman's service work? For a small monthly fee,
Goodman's clients obtain the right to use his Empire State
Building address as their own in letterhead, business cards, and
advertisements. "We act as their New York office," says
Goodman. "They can receive mail, phone calls, telexes, and fax
transmissions, just as if they were physically located in New
York.

"In fact, your prospects and customers will have no way of
telling that you don't actually have a big, fancy office in the
Empire State Building," he adds.

Mail received at the Empire State location is forwarded daily by
Goodman to any location his clients specify--usually their
headquarters' corporate mailroom. According to Goodman, the
Empire State Building is one of the few buildings in the United
States with its own post office branch and private zip code
(10118)....

Figure 15-2:
Editors look
for an
unusual
hook or
angle, such
as the
"unique zip
code" that
makes this
office space
special.

Like many giant retailers, IKEA sometimes gets resistance when opening a major store in a new area: The neighbors don't want a big store in their neighborhood because of the traffic and noise. A mediocre PR tactic would be sending out a release saying, "We care about the neighborhood," with some bland statements from the CEO. In the "Sharing the Caring Program," IKEA demonstrates that it cares about the neighborhood and its people by sponsoring a free family-day fair offering education and services to help residents live better lives — everything from lead testing to health checkups. Which do you think gets more coverage in the news — the free family fair or the usual corporate claptrap?

New-product press release

The most popular type of press release is the new-product release, which is a simple announcement of a new product. The product doesn't actually need to be brand new to qualify for a new product release. Enhancements, upgrades, new models, new features, new options, new accessories, new grades, new sizes and styles, and new applications can all form the basis for a release of this type.

New-product releases are typically featured in the new-product sections of publications. Editors run short, two- or three-paragraph descriptions of the products along with a photo or drawing, if provided with the release. This type of coverage, although routine in nature, provides additional exposure for your product, builds awareness, and can generate numerous inquiries at low cost.

Figure 15-3 is an example of a new-product release that's effective because it ties in the new-product announcement with current news — in this case, the controversy over genetically engineered foods, a hot topic as of this writing.

The new-product release can work for any new product, whether it ties into a newsy hook or not.

For Immediate Release

INTRODUCING THE WORLD'S FIRST-EVER BABY FOOD THAT IS 100% PURE

Earth's Best Introduces the Only Organic Baby Food that Contains No Genetically Engineered Ingredients

UNIONDALE, NEW YORK - Parents will do everything in their power to ensure the safety and well-being of their children. And, it is the responsibility of companies who make children's products to do the same. Earth's Best, a leading brand of all natural, organic baby food, is pleased to announce that as of January 1, 2000, all of their baby food will be made without genetically engineered ingredients.

In simple terms, genetic engineering is the process of taking genes from one strain of plant, animal or virus and inserting them in another with the goal of reproducing characteristics of the original species. Some of the most common foods affected include canola, corn, soybeans and potatoes -- all popular ingredients found in baby food.

"At Earth's Best, we believe that consumers have the right to be informed. That is why we are labeling our Earth's Best Baby Food GMO-Free," said Irwin Simon, Chief Executive Officer, and a fan of Earth's Best since before it became part of the Hain Food Group. "Four years ago when my daughter was born, like all new parents, I wanted the very best for her. She started solid foods with Earth's Best, and now my twin boys are Earth's Best babies."

One of the major hazards associated with genetically modified foods includes unpredictable health effects such as food allergies brought about by the introduction of new genes to any organism or plant. Other concerns include damage to the environment as new genetic information could cross into other related life forms and cause the possible extinction of the species. In addition, unknown animal genes inserted into foods may jeopardize strict vegetarian or religious dietary constraints.

It is estimated that about 60-70 percent of the food found in grocery stores has been genetically modified by scientists. Many believe if a product is certified organic, it is GMO-Free, however that may not be the case. Farmers may be subject to unintended and undesirable cross-pollination due to genetically modified seeds from nearby farms. Earth's Best products will undergo a rigorous testing and affidavit program to ensure their products purity....

Figure 15-3:
New-product release with a news angle (genetically engineered foods).

Tie-in with current fad, event, or news

Although not always easy to do, tying in your release with a fad, current event, news story, or trend can help you maximize your publicity pickups.

For instance, after the first run of the enormously popular reality TV show *Survivor,* my PR firm did a survey to find out the differences in survival instincts and strategies between CEOs of brick-and-mortar companies versus CEOs of dot-coms. The objective: to get our name known and demonstrate knowledge of the dot-com marketplace. The survey was featured in the Japanese edition of the *Wall Street Journal.*

In 1997, virtual pets became popular, and Bob Bly sent out the release shown in Figure 15-4. Within three days of mailing it, six newspapers had called Bob for an interview; one sent a photographer and reporter to his home and did a front-page story.

What's the lead story in the news this week? Who's the hot celebrity? Which trend is all the rage? With a bit of creative thinking, you can probably think of a way to tie your organization or product to that story.

Survey-results press release

It's ironic: Journalists consider themselves in the news business, yet aside from investigative and news reporters, most journalists — trade journal editors, columnists, feature editors — have a tough time finding anything that's really new. Most of what they find is recycled and has been done before. So when you present them with real news, they'll bite — and publish.

At my PR firm, our favorite strategy for creating real news — new information — is to take a survey. It's easy to do; anyone can take a survey and tabulate the results. By doing so, you create new facts, based on numerical results, and journalists love hard numbers.

Trade-in press release

Another promotional gimmick that works wonders in PR is to publicize a trade-in. The classic example is my firm's promotion for British Knights sneakers: We offered a free pair of sneakers to couch potatoes who mailed in their TV remote controls. At my agency, I use the trade-in gimmick often. The only requirement is to have a logical reason for the trade-in: For example, you want to give people sneakers and get their remote controls so they'll exercise more and watch TV less.

FROM: Microchip Gardens, 174 Holland Avenue, New Milford, NJ 07646
CONTACT: Bob Bly, phone 201-385-1220

For immediate release

MICROCHIP GARDENS, WORLD'S FIRST "GIGAPET CEMETERY," OPENS IN NORTHERN NEW JERSEY

When 7-year-old Alex Bly's gigapet died after he dropped it in the toilet, he couldn't find a place to bury it. So his father, NJ-based entrepreneur Bob Bly, created Microchip Gardens -- the world's first gigapet cemetery -- in the family's suburban backyard.

Now if your child's gigapet dies and can't be revived, instead of unceremoniously tossing it in the trash, you can give it a proper burial in a beautiful, tree-lined resting place.

For fees starting at $5, based on plot location and method of interment (burial, mausoleum, cremation), Bly will give your dearly departed gigapet an eternal resting place in Microchip Gardens, complete with funeral service and burial certificate. "Even gigapets don't last forever," said Bly. "There are pet cemeteries for dogs and cats; now gigapets have one too."

To help owners get the most pleasure from gigapet ownership, Bly -- author of 35 published books including _The "I Hate Kathie Lee Gifford" Book_ (Kensington) and _The Ultimate Unauthorized Star Trek Quiz Book_ (HarperCollins) -- has written an informative new booklet, "Raising Your Gigapet." The booklet covers such topics as purchasing your first gigapet; taking the pet home; care and feeding; and play and discipline. Gigapet burial rituals and the origins of Microchip Gardens are also covered.

To get your copy of "Raising Your Gigapet," which includes complete information on the Microchip Gardens gigapet cemetery, send $4 to: CTC, 22 E. Quackenbush Avenue, Dumont, NJ 07628.

Figure 15-4: This press release got my co-author, Bob Bly, on the front page of a local daily newspaper.

For Calyx & Corolla, a national florist, my firm did a trade-in for Mother's Day: Send in a toy gun (to promote nonviolence) and get free flowers (see Figure 15-5).

Contact: Lauren Weinberg
Jericho Communications
212/645-6900 x 110

THIS MOTHER'S DAY, GIVE YOUR MOM
THE GREATEST GIFT OF ALL...A TOY GUN
Calyx & Corolla Asks Children Nationwide
to Help Prevent Gun Violence by
Trading in Their Toy Guns for Flowers

SAN FRANCISCO, CA April 25, 2000 – Every year, over four thousand children are killed unnecessarily by guns. Calyx & Corolla, The Flower Lover's Flower Company, is lending its support to mothers around the nation who are fighting to keep guns out of the hands of children. Over the next several weeks, Calyx & Corolla is inviting children to participate by trading in their toy guns for a flower for their mother this Mother's Day.

"Flowers are a symbol of peace, harmony and the very best of nature, as are our children," said Ruth M. Owades, CEO and Founder of Calyx & Corolla. "Calyx & Corolla is pleased to offer this trade-in to encourage children to exchange their toy gun for a token of peace, a flower for their mother."

The first 1,000 children who turn in their toy guns can receive a gift for their mothers this Mother's Day, compliments of Calyx & Corolla. This gift, a spray of dendrobium orchids and a classic glass bud vase, will be sent directly from the grower, via FedEx. Participating children should send a toy gun and name, mother's first and last name, address, and phone number (for proper delivery) to:

Attn: The Greatest Gift of All
Jericho Communications
304 Hudson Street, Ste. 700
New York, NY 10013

In addition, Calyx & Corolla has created a special Mother's Day bouquet and will donate a portion of the proceeds to benefit the Million Mom March organization. For additional information, please log on to www.calyxandcorolla.com/mmm.html or call 1-800-800-7788....

Figure 15-5:
I think the cleverness of trade-ins is what attracts editors and readers to these stories.

Call-to-action press release

Create a cause or a call to action and publicize it. One example is the "Strike Back" promotion, described in Chapter 1, that got me front-page coverage in *USA Today*. All I did was urge baseball fans to boycott baseball games one day for every day the Major League Baseball players remained on strike.

Another example was the "Cursing for Chips" promotion we ran for a snack-food manufacturer. At the time, New York City Mayor Rudolph Giuliani was running a campaign to improve the quality of life for New Yorkers. We said that living in New York was stressful, so one way to improve the quality of life would be to reduce stress. We encouraged people to "blow off steam" — by swearing aloud. They came to a booth on a busy street corner in Manhattan; if they swore in front of us, they got a free bag of potato chips.

Chapter 16

Going Public in Cyberspace: Your Web Site

. . . .

In This Chapter

▶ Creating a virtual pressroom

▶ Making your pressroom easy to use.

▶ Marketing successfully on the Internet

▶ Promoting your product online

▶ Driving traffic to your site

. . . .

*T*he Internet is changing the way business is done, and public relations is no exception. Everybody knows it makes sense to be customer driven when designing a Web site, especially if you're doing business online. But that's no excuse to forget other major audiences, including the media. For a company doing PR, an important application of technology on the Web is the *virtual pressroom* — the section of a company's Web site designed specifically for use by the media.

Reporters on deadline don't want to click through three or four pages of content just to find an executive's name, a financial statistic, or a product specification.

In this chapter, I provide a plan for you to serve the media well at your site and to make it easy for them to find it.

Designing a Media-Friendly Web Site

If you're a manufacturer or a service provider, plan to provide extensive informational options that make it easier for your company and your products to get mentioned as accurately and thoroughly as possible. A chemical manufacturer, for example, might allow journalists to access chemical formulas, research studies, applications briefs, and material safety data sheets for each of its products.

The top three things journalists want to find quickly when they visit a site are deep financial information (for public companies), a file of historic press releases, and readily available contact information (e-mail, phone, address).

One survey of editors shows that only 65 to 75 percent of companies are offering these basics. When asked how often they're required to phone, fax, or e-mail a company for information that could have been offered on its Web site, all answers ranged from 30 to 55 percent of the time.

Use the sections that follow as a quality check to make sure your site has what the media is looking for.

Company background/history

Often lumped under a section titled "All About XYZ Company," this information may sometimes include so many different pieces of information that you should consider making it a separate section. Here are some types of information you can include:

- What the company does
- Mission statement
- Industries/applications
- Philosophy
- Founders and an explanation of how the company got started
- Historical markers and milestones
- Philanthropic events and charity sponsorships

Another key piece of information you can offer is a list of customers. Case histories or customer success stories are also valuable.

If part of what you offer new clients is confidentiality, posting a list of customers and the projects you performed for them violates that confidentiality. Be sure to get permission from all customers you list on your site; then note on the site that all customers listed have given their permission.

Key management

Read business articles and you notice that journalists like to give descriptions of key players of the companies they're writing about. So, make executive bios available to journalists on your Web site. Be sure to provide

✔ Where managers hail from

✔ Individual biographies/background

✔ Responsibilities

✔ Contact information

✔ Links to their e-mail addresses

It's amazing to me how many companies hide contact information. A high percentage of sites have addresses and phone numbers on their sites, but most are almost impossible to find. Journalists need this type of basic information. Always have an e-mail and phone number available for the PR director or whoever is the company's main contact for the press.

You can also list key personnel, but be warned: Web sites are a ripe source of information for headhunters who want to steal your employees. So if recruiters are actively raiding companies for people, you may opt not to list your personnel on your site.

Press release archive

Archiving all of a company's press releases for online retrieval on a Web site has become common practice. On larger corporate Web sites, some search engines give the visitor the option of excluding press releases from the documents being searched by keyword — otherwise, the results would be overwhelming. If you decide to offer a press release archive online, I suggest you include these parts:

✔ Chronological listing (most recent first) of release announcements, including the date of the release followed by the title

✔ Downloadable photos of your products

✔ E-mail link and phone number of your PR manager or main media liaison

✔ E-mail hot links to press contacts, resources, or quoted sources, when applicable, within the body copy

Financial information

More and more publicly traded companies are making their financial data available online. At a minimum, you should include

- Key current financial data for the year and by quarter (taken from annual and quarterly reports)
- Historic financial information

An added bonus, especially for financial reports and stock analysts, is charts backed up with Excel spreadsheets showing the financial history of the company.

Increasingly, larger public companies are putting both their annual reports and their proxy statements online. Be aware of how your print document translates for the Web.

Product/service catalog

Customers and prospects come to your Web site for product information, so there should already be plenty of it for journalists to reference. The product information available to the media on your site should include the following:

- Product or service descriptions and specifications
- Up-to-date pricing and availability
- Mini product photos you can click on for larger views and more information

Article/white paper library

The coverage you receive from major media helps establish credibility with other media and makes them more comfortable in running your story. Therefore, your Web site should give journalists access to press clippings and other evidence of the major media coverage you've already received. You should

- Include HTML or PDF color images of the covers of major magazines where your company has been featured in a cover story.
- Provide links to these articles if they're posted online at the publications' Web sites.
- Provide links to the e-mail addresses of the authors of those articles.

Trade show list

Journalists want to know where you'll be and the industry events where you'll be speaking or exhibiting. Your Web site is an ideal place to post

✔ Shows that the company attends, promotes, or sponsors

✔ Links to releases associated with shows

✔ Links to specific trade show sites or sponsor sites

✔ An option to schedule a booth visit

Locations/facility information

In the cyberspace age, you can easily forget that people want you to have a physical presence, not just megabytes of text and images on a server. Be sure to include

✔ Maps to headquarters and major regional facilities, including sales offices

✔ Links to an online map source (such as MapQuest [www.mapquest.com], Yahoo! Maps [http://maps.yahoo.com], or Google Local [http://maps.google.com]) for more detailed directions

✔ Site capabilities (what is manufactured there or major activities/services)

✔ Number of employees at each facility

✔ Links to e-mail addresses of facility managers or key authorities for each site

Avoiding "Speed Traps" on Your Web Site

Nothing annoys Web browsers faster than *s-l-o-w* sites. Here are two suggestions to keep your site easy and fast:

✔ **Don't use snazzy graphics that take too long to download.** Keep your users' systems in mind — not everyone has a high-speed Internet connection (although significantly more people do than did the first time I wrote this book five years ago).

> ✔ **Don't emphasize entertainment (animation, special effects, graphics) over content (information), especially on business-to-business sites.**

Keep in mind that most editors are too busy to waste time navigating poorly designed sites. With reporters, having a well-designed site is even more crucial. Come deadline time, an easily navigated Web site may mean the difference between being included in an article or excluded.

Ensuring Your Site Is User-Friendly

Do you know for a fact that the reporters and journalists you're spending so much time driving to your site can actually use it? Is your pressroom available from the home page or do reporters have to go searching to find it? And what about when you're featured in the media and customers and prospects visit your site — can they find what they're looking for? Or do your graphics take so long to load that they don't wait? Do you even know?

If you don't know the answers to these questions, you should. These are all questions of *usability*, a fancy term for making your Web site user-friendly. You see, no matter how well written your press releases are, if your site is confusing, illegible, or slow, people won't find what you want them to find. Media people won't have the patience to search for your PR contact or wait for your fancy graphics to load. And when you get press coverage that drives customers and prospects to your site, if they can't find what they're looking for, they won't bother.

According to Lori Berman, Manager of Web Technologies and Services at Boston-based Commonwealth Financial Network, outside of the design of your site, you need to focus on:

✔ **Navigation:** Navigation is how a visitor finds his way around your site. Navigation tools appear on your site in the form of tabs, buttons, or links. Navigation can be placed anywhere but is generally found along the top of the page or down the left side. Your navigation must be clear and written in the "language" of the visitor, not your own. Although you may think a common acronym is very clear, someone outside of your field (yet still in your target market) may not know what it means. For example, an insurance company with an expertise in variable life insurance should spell out those words instead of using abbreviations like *VL* or *VUL* for the navigation labels.

✔ **Readability of text:** How people read online materials is very different from how they read print materials. Content on your site needs to be "readable," which is a combination of how legible the words on the screen are and how understandable the writing style of the content is. Here's what makes a site readable:

- **Font types:** The easiest to read online are Arial, Verdana, and Tahoma — in fact, those fonts were designed for online reading.

- **Font size:** Present your content at a minimum of a 10-point font. If your audience is mostly over age 65, consider a larger font size of 12 points.

- **Color contrast:** The contrast between the text color and its background is very important for legibility. Black text on a white background presents the highest contrast and is, therefore, most desirable for reading ease.

✔ **Scanability:** When reading online, visitors will naturally scan until finding what they're looking for. PR writing is perfect for easy scanning. Write in an inverted pyramid style, with the most important information in the first sentence. Use titles and headlines, bold text to highlight main points, and bulleted lists when applicable. Also, link important points to more detailed information deeper in the site or somewhere on another site.

Another aid to scanning is to chunk your content into small pieces, keeping sentences to less than 20 words and paragraphs to no more than six sentences.

Because many languages are read from left to right (including English), the upper-left corner of the page is prime real estate and English readers' eyes will fall there first. Our eyes are also drawn to larger or bolded text, and links, which aid scanning efforts.

By applying some general usability principles to your Web site (and other online communications), you significantly increase the chance that a visitor to your site will find what she needs — easily! This helps your image *and* saves you time. Nice benefits!

✔ **Content:** The content on your site does not necessarily have to be original; it just needs to be viewed as useful by those who visit it. Keep the information fresh and up-to-date. Visitors to the site should know that there is a person who is devoting time to it, caring about what is being provided on it, and making changes and updates. However, you have to make sure that the information that you are providing, in addition to being useful, is well organized. One of the biggest hurdles with providing information online is that there is so much of it available. Don't overwhelm those using your site.

Understanding the Three Cs of E-Success

Internet specialists talk about the three Cs of e-business: commerce, content, and community. It's important to take this business model into account when creating your site. Understanding these concepts and then implementing them into your strategy will help to ensure your success.

The first C, commerce, refers to the Web site's ability to permit the consumer to buy online. Without e-commerce, an e-mail can only generate online leads or offline purchases; you cannot have true one-step mail order on the Internet.

The second C, content, refers to the information and services available on the Web site. Web sites that display only product information are not as interesting to Internet users as Web sites that offer useful information and tools. (An example of a tool is a page I saw on a health Web site. After you enter your height, it displays your ideal weight.) The better your content, the more users will favor your site.

The interactivity and graphic nature of the Internet may, on the surface, make it attractive as a marketing tool. But Web surfers are drawn by content, not graphics. Animation and Day-Glo colors may make a Web site lively and inviting, but content-rich sites are what attract browsers and keep them long enough to become buyers.

Are you tuning in to the term *content?* What people used to call *editorial* is now "content." On the Web, much of the content is created not by professional publishers or writers, but by users, buyers, and consumers — people sharing and talking with each other, rather than a publisher deciding and controlling what they read. (This is a precursor to the current blogging craze, which you can read much more about in Chapter 17.)

The third C, community, refers to the relationship that users have with the Web site and each other. It's the online equivalent of a neighborhood bookstore, café, or coffee shop. Web surfers begin to feel your site is a good place to go and spend time, especially with other visitors. People who study Web world more than I do say there are three communities out there:

 ✔ Internet communities that serve as a marketing and advertising tool

 ✔ Extranet communities designed to strengthen relationships with trade partners or customers

 ✔ Intranet communities that facilitate knowledge sharing within an organization

Chat rooms and forums can help build this sense of community. When you see people in postings talking not just to the person who originally posted the message, but also by name to each other — as they argue a point or share opinions — you know you're on a site with a strong sense of community.

Remember to measure Web surfer activity. Those who visit and buy know you better than those who visit sporadically or never buy. Factors you can measure include *hits* (visits to the Web site), *page views* (the specific pages visitors click to), *duration* (amount of time spent on site), and *conversions* (number of click-through visitors who make a purchase).

You can track traffic by time of day, day of week, and day of year. Use this data in network planning to ensure sufficient bandwidth to handle peak periods. Remember what happened to Internet toy retailers when they got more Christmas orders one year than they could handle? Customers were irate, and the share prices of those dot-com companies plummeted.

Designing a Sticky Web Site

A *sticky Web site* is one that people want to linger on, spend time with, and revisit frequently. The stickier the site, the more business it will generate (if it's an e-commerce site and not just an advertising site consisting of product literature posted on Web pages).

If you have the first C, commerce, taken care of, you'll increase your stickiness and sales by strengthening the other two Cs, content and community. If the content is relevant and interesting, people will use your site more — and buy more. If the site has a real sense of community, they'll visit often to see what's happening.

National Geographic increased e-commerce by surveying its gift shop to determine the most popular item. It turned out to be greeting cards. As a result, its next e-campaign featured a set of wild animal cards, with four cards displayed per page. An e-mail encouraged prospects to click onto the site to view the sample cards. The prospect could then choose to e-mail electronic versions of any card to a friend. People liked what they saw, and the opt-out rate to the e-mail was less than 0.04 percent. The click-through rate was 32 percent, and the campaign added 25,000 new names to the *National Geographic* e-list within three weeks.

Brainstorming More Ways to Make a Profit Online

Here are your marching orders to put the Web to work promoting your business:

- ✔ **You must have a Web site.** There's no way around this today. You need a site if only for added credibility. But it also enhances customer service and sales. In a recent study conducted by Thomas Register and Visa USA, 30 percent of businesses said their primary reasons for moving to e-commerce were speed and convenience. In addition, the survey respondents indicated by a margin of two to one that they would give preference to a supplier who could accept online purchasing transactions.

    A Web site establishes instant credibility. It provides anytime access to you and the information about your services, making life easier for you and your prospects.

- ✔ **You must give people a reason to visit your site.** Internic, the governing body that controls Internet domain names, reports that there are more than 1.5 million Internet sites. So why in the world should anyone take the time to see yours? If you have your picture, your brochure, or a cute saying, who cares? People care only about themselves. If you don't give them an appealing reason to zip over to your site, why complain if they don't visit it?

- ✔ **You must give people options to buy.** If you don't list your products and services at your site, with different ways to make purchases, you will miss sales. Remember that some people are still extremely nervous about buying anything online. Give them both online and offline options to buy, including a toll-free phone number, street address, and fax number.

- ✔ **You must constantly change your site.** You may get people to visit your site once, but how will you get them to return? Make sure to continually add new content. That's what keeps them coming back again and again. So, present special offers, news, and additional products to buy.

- ✔ **Use your sig file to promote your Web site.** Your *sig file* is that four- to eight-line paragraph at the end of every one of your e-mail messages. The Internet allows you to promote yourself in your signature (or sig for short). It's your opportunity to list your Web address and give people a reason to visit it.

Because your e-mail messages travel the Internet, get seen by potentially thousands of people, and are usually archived at giant databases like `www.dejanews.com` where they can be retrieved, you never know who will see one of your messages or when. If your sig file has your Web address in it, you just promoted your Web site.

✔ **Print your Web address on everything.** Every ad you run, commercial you air, business card you hand out, catalog you mail, and press kit and brochure you distribute should contain your Web address. Use the offline world to promote your online presence.

✔ **Participate in online discussion groups.** Join e-mail discussion groups where your target prospects gather. Do a search at `www.liszt.com` to find the groups for you. Hang out at the site to get a feel for the nature of the group, and then post relevant responses to the list. As you do, you'll be promoting yourself and your business. And if your sig has your Web address in it, every time you post a message, you'll be promoting your Web site in a perfectly acceptable manner in conformance with Internet etiquette. You'd be surprised at how many journalists sit in on or monitor discussion groups dealing with their area of coverage.

✔ **Cross-promote yourself in partnership with related Web sites.** Offline, we call it *networking* and *co-op marketing*. You can do the same thing online. Find Web sites that serve the same market you do and join forces with them. Maybe advertise on their site. Maybe exchange links. Create online allies to help you make money online.

✔ **Always give your Web address in media interviews.** Whenever you're speaking to the press, but especially in broadcast media, tell listeners they can get more information on your topic at your Web site, and give the Web address (technically called a *URL*). Some media have policies limiting "plugs" and the mention of toll-free numbers, but right now, no one stops you from mentioning your Web site. I guess because the Web is perceived as an information medium and toll-free numbers are perceived as marketing devices, the media have fewer qualms about airing Web information. Take advantage of this policy now by always mentioning your Web address.

✔ **Experiment.** The Internet as a vehicle for commerce is relatively new. Most of us are applying everything we have ever learned about marketing to this new medium. We have to think out of the box, stretch our minds, and create new ways of doing business online. We have to be willing to take risks and try new ideas. Some of this may cost money. Or time. But as Flip Wilson said, "You can't expect to hit the jackpot if you don't put a few nickels in the machine."

Just the FAQs

Add a Frequently Asked Questions (FAQ) page to your Web site. This section is a page listing, in question-and-answer format, of the most commonly asked questions and a brief answer to each. The benefit? You'll get fewer e-mails asking you the same basic questions if you have this information instantly available online. A FAQ page saves you time, keeps your customers happy, and increases your sales.

Driving Traffic to Your Web Site

Successful Web site owners report that they spend 70 percent of their marketing budget on media outside the Web to direct prospective customers to their sites. Here are a few techniques you can use to boost your site traffic:

- **Put your Web address on all promotions — direct mail, catalogs, card decks, fax marketing, space advertising, press releases, invoices, and renewals.**

- **Use search engines.** Write a short, compelling title and description tags for each page. Focus on one keyword phrase and use this phrase in page description tags, headlines, body copy, and alt tags. The keyword makes it more likely that someone doing an Internet search on the subject will be directed to your page.

- **Encourage prospects to register with you to build your e-mail database.** Offer a resource and document center, free demos, catalogs, samples, a drawing, or a free e-mail newsletter subscription. One of my firm's clients, Internet herb and vitamin marketer AllHerbs.com, sends out a regular e-mail newsletter to its database of 700,000 members. The e-mail newsletter — which generates a response rate of 30 percent — is a mishmash of useful information about herbs, useful facts, and special offers. For instance, AllHerbs.com's Valentine's Day offer was free, all-natural chocolates with any purchase of $40 or more.

- **Consider testing *banner ads*.** Try offering some of your content in exchange for a free banner ad. But test cautiously. Banner ads have been steadily declining in effectiveness, with click-through rates averaging only half a percent.

- **Send out press releases promoting your new site and the information it contains.** These press releases can focus on content (free information visitors can get on the site), community (online forums and discussion groups), or commerce (breadth of product line or special offers).

✔ **Link your site to other sites.** Set a goal of submitting a certain number of link requests per week. Search on your keywords to identify the relevant sites to which you want to link and then submit to those. Consider associations, magazines, consultants, and complementary sites.

✔ **Build strategic partnerships and alliances.** List your products on another company's site in exchange for a small royalty on any sales. For example, a site selling gourmet pancake batter can list another site's maple syrup. Consider submitting articles for an e-mail newsletter in exchange for a Web link and additional promotion.

✔ **Make it sticky (refer to the "Designing a Sticky Web Site" section, earlier in this chapter).** Offer your prospects a reason to keep coming back. Good content, free resources and tools, contests, and drawings work well.

  • If people aren't flocking to your Web site, do a little offline (paper) promotion. Example: Print postcards introducing your Web site and send them out to everyone on your mailing list.

  • Internet direct mail is a powerful tool for driving people to your Web site. You can also use e-newsletters or e-zines.

✔ **Include your Web address on letters after the signature line.**

✔ **Develop a bookmark with your Web address on it and mail it with fulfillment of your products.**

✔ **Offer a weekly update of some sort to keep people coming back.** Write an e-mail newsletter you can push to your prospects to remind them about your Web site.

Making sure search engines can find your Web site

The search engines you should focus on are Google, Yahoo!, and MSN.

Yahoo! is a human-powered search directory, and if you want your site to be found by this type of search engine, you must submit the Web address and a description of the site to them. Sometimes, there is a fee for this or a fee can be paid if you want it done sooner rather than later.

Search engines try to make searching easy for their users and to provide exactly what the searcher is looking for. In order to create a site that's easy for search engines to find, you should focus on on-page considerations and off-page considerations.

On-page considerations

On-page considerations include the text and images on your Web site and the code behind your Web site that you (and your Web designer) have control over, such as the following:

- ✔ **Use HTML.** The software used to build your site affects whether spiders can access it. Sites designed in Macromedia's Flash, for example, are inaccessible, while a site built in HTML will automatically be accessible to the spiders.

   A Flash site may be the best choice for your company because of the animation capabilities. In that case, a well-designed Flash-based site should also offer an HTML version, which will make it easier for search engines to find and index. This will also make it easier to view for any visitors whose browsers or computers don't have the latest technology.

- ✔ **Include a site map.** Good site structure is important and a site map helps the search engines see how all the pages link together.

- ✔ **Add new content regularly.** There is nothing a search engine likes more than relevant and unique content that is kept up-to-date and refreshed regularly. That will keep the search engines coming back for more. For example, a press release archive, organized chronologically and updated frequently, is exactly what the search engines are looking for.

Off-page considerations

Off-page considerations are how your site fits into the context of the Web, such as which sites link to yours. This is something that you can influence but over which you don't have control.

Anyone can put up a site, fill it with content that appears to be relevant, and position the company as an authority — even if it's not. That's why search engines look at factors outside the control of the Web site owner. *Remember:* Their goal is relevant results for their users — not good rankings for Web site owners.

Search engines prize link popularity — in other words, how many sites link to your site (those are *inbound links*) and what types of sites link to your site. If other sites related to the subject are linked to your site, you'll have a much better chance of ranking well. But if your site is an island and doesn't have many relevant inbound links, search engines won't find it, and even if they do, they won't consider it.

Obtaining inbound links

The best strategy for getting inbound links is to wait for them, even though this strategy requires patience and a long-term view. A site that is worthy of links will get them. If your site offers information and material that is useful to others, it will be found and other sites will link to it. However, these links are only effective if they're relevant to the content on your site. For instance, a link to your site from your cousin's online wedding album won't help you much.

If you publish an article in your local newspaper, you should have a link included in the article that duplicates your search words. In fact, an extremely effective tool for this purpose is an online press release service such as PRWeb.com. When they post your release (which should always include a link to your site), it automatically generates a link back to your site. The more releases you put out there, the more links back to your site.

You can also find other sites where your company's white papers and articles can be published. In return, you get a link back to yours in the byline.

You can also buy links, often in the form of an ad banner. Or you can ask for them, as part of a reciprocal linking effort whereby you agree to exchange links with the owner of another site.

Don't link for the sake of linking. Be careful of reciprocal link requests that have no relation to your industry. Make sure the sites you link to (and who link to yours) are relevant to your business. A good example of one that isn't is a dog food site linking to a Viagra site. Reciprocal linking has become a huge business and search engines are starting to smarten up about it. They will penalize sites that link to each other for the sake of linking, and it won't be long before they'll be able to detect when it's been purchased for the purpose of link popularity rather than relevance.

Again, this strategy requires patience — indeed, it can take a year or more — and it's often a question of experimentation. The best thing you can do is choose the keywords or search terms you want to rank well for, and then go to Google and do a search to see who is currently ranking well for those terms. Look at what they're doing, how the site is structured, what keywords they're using. Pretend you're a search engine — analyze what they're doing, and then do that for yours.

Keying in to keywords

Which words will a prospect or reporter type into the search query box to retrieve your Web site? These are your target keywords — the words that will bring your site up. According to Lori Berman, Manager of Web Technologies and Services at Boston-based Commonwealth Financial Network, your target keywords should always be phrases at least two or more words long. Stay away from general words or phrases that will be relevant for too many sites.

More specific phrases will give you a better shot at success. For instance, rather than *financial* or even *financial services,* a more targeted keyword phrase would be *retirement planning.*

Here are some general rules to follow about the location and the frequency of keywords on a page:

- ✔ **Include your keywords in the title of your pages.** Every page on a Web site has a title as part of its HTML code. Terms appearing in the title are considered higher in relevancy than terms lower on the page.

- ✔ **Place your keywords high up on the page.** Search engines prioritize pages based on how high up on the page words are used. They assume that the more relevant a topic is, the earlier in the text the topic will be presented.

- ✔ **Mention your keywords more than once.** A search engine will also take notice of how often keywords appear compared with other words on a Web page. Words mentioned more often are deemed more relevant and will thus be presented higher in the search results listing.

- ✔ **Make your keywords bold.** To emphasize your keywords, make them bold and the search engine will take notice.

- ✔ **Put your keywords in the code.** Your keywords must also be included in the code underneath your site. You need a good "title" to the page (these are the words that appear in the bar at the top of the browser and in the blurb that shows up on the search engine results) that includes your keywords as well.

Using paid search (or pay per click)

The disadvantage of natural search — when your site comes up "naturally" in the search engine results thanks to the success of both your on-page and off-page efforts (as described above) — is that it can take up to a year to deliver. Paid search, on the other hand, literally takes minutes — if you're willing to pay. Paid search (or pay per click [PPC]) makes sense as part of your branding and advertising budget but unless you're selling a product and can make money from each visit, it's tough to measure the value of each visitor or "click" — which is what you're paying for.

The *paid-search* process (which is when you buy or bid on specific keywords so that when those keywords are typed into a search engine, your ad is presented to the user) is simple to start and test out. You can tell the paid ads from the "organic" search results because the ads are usually under a different banner or display the phrase *sponsored link.* Sometimes the ad is placed along the right margin of the page and has a different background color, to distinguish it from the rest of the page.

Dozens of services offer a paid-search model, but it's best to start with one of the big guys (such as Google Adwords, Yahoo! Search, or MSN adCenter, one of the newest entries into the market). The smaller, less-popular ones offer cheaper keywords, but that's because they're less frequented by searchers. Quality varies greatly, so until you know what you're doing, start with major players because they do monitor quality.

Google Adwords is the easiest, most user-friendly service, as well as the quickest. They'll walk you through the process of setting up your first campaign and choosing your keywords. They even have people you can speak to live if you need help on your first campaign. And according to Scott Jangro, cofounder of MechMedia, Inc., a consultancy focusing on organic search and pay-per-click search engine optimization, you'll start seeing traffic within 10 to 20 minutes. Yahoo!, by contrast, reviews every ad before it goes up so it can take a day or so to start seeing traffic.

Each service is slightly different, but here's the general idea of how paid search works: You first determine a specific amount that you're willing to pay each time a person clicks on your link after using a specific term during a search. For example, you may bid 25¢ on the term *financial planning*. Every time a user enters those keywords during a search, your site comes up in the results, and the user clicks on the link, you're charged 25¢. If another company bidding on the same term is willing to spend more per click, their site shows up higher in the search results than your site does. You can adjust your bid on that term to come up higher (and then they may do the same) so it's essential to watch your ads closely to see where they're showing up.

But because paid-search ads are so easy to do, unless you plan carefully, you can easily waste a lot of money. So here are a few things to keep in mind:

- ✔ **Design (or write) a compelling ad.** You only have 70 characters to get your message out. (That's about as long as the first two sentences of this paragraph.) So your ad copy must be compelling and catch your prospect's eye. It must be relevant and contain enough information that your prospects know what they're clicking through to. If it's not, you'll get lots of clicks (that you'll pay for) from people who are just curious or confused. The clearer your ad, the better the quality of your clicks. More clicks is not necessarily better.

- ✔ **Manage your keywords.** You can select 1, 10, 20, or 1,000 keywords for your campaign (or anything in between). You can choose between a broad match (any of the words in your phrase) or an exact match. Be careful with broad matches because those people can be looking for something completely different from what you're offering. For example, a "mustang" searcher might be looking for horses, not cars. You can put in negative keywords (such as *free,* a common word used by people who have no intention of buying) so your ads won't show up. You can exclude words too, called negative keywords.

✔ **Manage your spending.** Set budgets for how much you want to spend per day. It can be a big money waster if you're too busy to manage it. For each keyword, you choose how much you're willing to spend. You can bid whatever you want (a penny, 50¢) for each click through to your site, depending on what your competition has bid. Some people spend $50 per click. You can tell the service the max you're willing to spend on any given click. It's all up to you. That's why you have to experiment and figure out which keywords are the most valuable to you, and then focus your attention and your budget on those.

✔ **Give it a couple days.** Although driving traffic takes no time at all, it does take time for a campaign to settle down. You have to spend enough money to get some traffic to your site and then see if those clicks convert to actual sales or qualified leads. If not, revise your keywords, tweak your text, or up your bid. Then watch carefully. Most important: Watch your costs and, if possible, track your return on those costs.

Chapter 17

Getting a Grip on New Technology — Blogs, Webcasting, and Podcasting

*T*hings continue to move at lightning speed in cyberspace. When we published the first edition of this book in 2000, blogs didn't exist, iPods didn't exist, podcasts didn't exist, and RSS, if it existed, was too technical for anyone to pay attention to. But things have changed. And they will continue to.

PR practitioners have just begun to experiment with the latest new media. Like at the beginning of the Internet, it's the Wild, Wild West out there in the blogosphere. There are no rules and very few conventions to follow, not to mention a boatload of hype, which makes assessing the real value of any of these tools difficult.

Even so, assessing the tools is our goal in this chapter. When it comes to blogs, podcasts, RSS, and webcasts, we put these tools in context and tell you only what you need to know, for now at least.

Using Blogs for PR

Though people have been voicing their opinions on the Internet for years, *blogs* (short for *web logs*) add a new dimension to the conversation. A blog is basically a Web site where everyone and anyone can get published (because they are, in essence, publishing themselves). Every blog has a blogger behind it, running the show, voicing his or her opinions, and inviting others to join the conversation.

Most blogs are nothing more than personal journals or diaries, a place for a blogger to rant. But some bloggers, who are experts in a field, make it their business to evaluate and recommend resources and expound on trends in their blogs — and those blogs have a following. Some companies may even provide corporate blogs, a place in cyberspace for consumers to share their experiences, give advice, and articulate their likes and dislikes. That means companies, large and small, need to listen to and act on that feedback.

Overlooking this medium and assuming it's just a fad is a mistake, especially if you're working anywhere near the technology industry, where real-time information disseminated to the public needs to be monitored on a consistent basis. Plus, on average, news and issues discussed in the blogosphere are at least one to two days ahead of the major media. In public relations, that one or two days can make a big difference. To understand the importance of blogs even further, just check out the following facts:

- ✔ At the end of September 2005 there were more than 20 million blogs and that number is said to be doubling every five months. Most important, credible research points out that more than twice as many people read blogs as write them.

- ✔ A survey conducted in late 2005 by Backbone Media discovered that corporate blogs are giving established corporations and obscure brands the ability to connect with their audiences on a personal level, build trust, collect valuable feedback, and foster strong relationships, while at the same time benefiting in ways that are tangible to the sales and marketing side of the business.

- ✔ Another 2005 survey, this one by *Cool News,* was designed to find out how marketers actually view blogs. It found that 64 percent of respondents believe blogging has some level of importance as a marketing tool, while 18.5 percent noted that it is very important.

For PR purposes, blogs represent another very important online marketing tool to watch and integrate into your bigger PR campaign in three ways:

- ✔ Monitoring blogs in your industry
- ✔ Pitching to bloggers in your industry
- ✔ Creating your own blog

Monitoring the blogs in your industry

For the first time, blogs allow companies to listen to the conversations that are occurring, particularly those related to issues that are important to their business. Blog-watching can be cheaper, faster, and less biased than staples of consumer research like focus groups and surveys. And certainly there are valuable insights to be uncovered.

At the very least, you should be aware of the major blogs in your industry, and someone in your company should be charged with monitoring them. A quick check of your RSS reader (see the "Using RSS to monitor the media" section, later in this chapter) a few times a day will keep you on top of the issues and allow you to seize opportunities.

If you're managing a big brand, it's worth hiring a service to monitor the chatter and what's being said about you in the blogosphere, such as Intelliseek (`www.intelliseek.com`). Even PR Newswire has added blog watching to its service offerings.

Every PR practitioner should monitor and observe the blogging landscape on behalf of your company or your client. There are two ways to do this: You can search for the items you're interested in or you can monitor certain media outlets and be notified whenever your item is mentioned. For example, if I am being talked about on the Internet, I need to know it. I need to know who is saying what, on which blog, and who is responding to it. Then I can decide whether or not to respond.

Using RSS to monitor the media

RSS, stands for either *Real Simple Syndication* or *Rich Site Summary*, depending on whom you ask. The beauty of RSS is that it allows you to quickly review new content from a variety of Web sites and blogs. The majority of blogs, and more and more newspaper sites, are providing an RSS feed of their content. Each time a Web site or blog adds content, the RSS feed is updated and if you subscribe to that feed, you're notified. That way, you don't have to go searching for the information.

Here's how you handle RSS:

- ✔ **Viewing an RSS feed:** An RSS feed does not display correctly in a standard web browser, so in order to view one, you'll need an RSS reader. There are several free Web-based services, such as Bloglines (`www.bloglines.com`) or My Yahoo! (`www.myyahoo.com`), as well as a number of stand-alone applications that you can install on your computer. The most popular is NewsGator (`www.newsgator.com`) but there are many more, for Mac and PC. They're free to try but usually cost $15 to $30 to own.

- ✔ **Subscribing to an RSS feed:** After you have your reader installed (or you've created an account for a Web-based tool), you can begin to subscribe to RSS feeds. All the RSS readers offer an easy way to subscribe to feeds. Many blogs also provide a quick link to add the feed to one of the popular online tools such as Bloglines, NewsGator, or My Yahoo!.

  To find an RSS feed on a blog, just look for the small *RSS* or *XML* graphic on a page, or the term *syndicate*. Usually clicking on the link will provide you the URL for the RSS feed.

Each time you open the RSS reader, all your feeds are checked for new content. Any feed that contains new content is highlighted. Some feeds provide the entire body of the article, others provide a short synopsis. In either case you can easily click on a link and be transferred to the appropriate Web page to read the news or posting.

Searching the blogosphere

RSS feeds are perfect for terms you need to monitor closely, like your company name, the names of your principals or clients, or the competition. But if you want to do a one-time search for a term or keyword in the blogosphere, try Technorati (www.technorati.com) and Feedster (www.feedster.com), two search engines that specialize in blogs. You simply enter your search term and review the results, which are generally displayed chronologically, with the most recent one first, sometimes just a few minutes old. The results of these searches can turn you on to other blogs. You may discover a blog that always has the latest information within your industry, and you should add that blog's RSS feed to your reader.

PubSub is another free service that allows you to create an RSS feed to monitor a set of search terms. For example, let's say you want to monitor the blogosphere for any time Lance Armstrong is mentioned. Create a free account on PubSub, enter your search terms ("Lance Armstrong"), and PubSub creates a custom RSS feed. Then subscribe to this feed in your RSS reader. Each time a blogger writes about Lance, it will be shown in your RSS reader. In fact, as soon as it's published, you get it. And it highlights the phrase for you. One drawback to PubSub, however, is that it only monitors RSS feeds and major press release services. News outlets that do not provide RSS feeds are not indexed.

No matter which service you're using, make sure that your search terms are not too broad, otherwise you can quickly become overloaded with results. Tweak your search terms as you go to narrow or broaden your results.

Responding to negative posts

As you monitor the online media, you're likely to come across both positive and negative comments on your brand, ad campaign, or products. But what do you do when you come across a negative blog posting about you, your company, or your client?

First of all, there's no need to panic. The whole point of a blog is to encourage discourse. You should, however, respond immediately because rumors can spread instantly. You could have 25 bloggers spinning it within 5 minutes.

When you come across "constructive criticism" or a blatantly negative comment about your company, product, or ad campaign, respond head-on with facts, statistics, and information about the thought process behind the decision or product being criticized. Offer information and give the blogger an opportunity to get involved in the issue that concerns him or her.

Things happen quickly online and time is of the essence. But you must balance timeliness and thoughtfulness. Before publishing your posts, look objectively at what you've written and ask yourself as objectively as possible whether it could be taken the wrong way. If you're not sure, ask someone else for his or her perspective. Poor or hasty communication can hurt you or your company easily and quickly.

Stay away from vitriol and emotion. Don't be emotional or impulsive. Remember, the Web is public — anyone and everyone can find and read what you've written. Do your best not to offend anyone out there in cyberspace. Comments and posts can easily be taken the wrong way or misinterpreted. If that happens with something you write, apologize right away and be genuine about it. Don't try to explain.

And if you absolutely must say something negative or controversial, do it directly to the blogger or writer via e-mail, not in a public comment.

Pitching to blogs

Over 20 million blogs and counting. Needless to say, it can be overwhelming. If you plan to use blogs as a media outlet, don't try to reach all blogs or all bloggers. It's not like buying a list of media outlets and blasting a release to them.

Blogging is redefining the way we get our news and information. Assuming that trend continues, that means reading the newspaper or watching the nightly news is no longer the only way to get information. In the near future, we may go to blogs before we go to the newspaper, as they are rapidly becoming more and more influential, so you can't ignore them. You must pitch to blogs, but in a slightly different way (which I discuss in the "Approaching bloggers" section, later in this chapter).

Knowing what to look for in a blogger

The most effective strategy for working with and influencing the top bloggers is to identify the top bloggers in your industry (that is, those that have the biggest following and whose opinion is most respected), and focus on them. You should look at:

- **Links:** Look for a blogger who links out a lot and has a wide variety of interests. That's an indication of openness. If a blog is more of a personal diary of rants and ruminations with few links and outside material, don't waste your time.

- **Comments:** Blogs with lots of comments are a good indication of an engaged readership.

- **Commercial interests:** If you see advertising on a blog, you'll know that the blogger may be open to all sorts of arrangements.

Approaching bloggers

When approaching blogs for media coverage, many of the same rules apply as when you approach a more traditional form of media: Do your research, understand the readership, and pitch only appropriate stories.

But there's one huge caveat: Don't "pitch" bloggers in the traditional sense. They aren't traditional journalists or reporters. Don't send them your generic press release, because they won't know what to do with it. Bloggers instantly detect and are not receptive to anything automated or generic. If you want them to respond, you have to tailor your approach for each blogger. You must understand the blogger's perspective and speak to him in his language.

Bloggers are independent spirits. Most are not used to working with PR people and the writing and "reporting" they do is a by-product of their main interest, whether it's political or an industry expertise. Also, they're very sensitive to being manipulated by PR companies and corporations.

So instead of "pitching" bloggers, you must identify each blogger relevant to your business and then contact him or her directly. Instead of your standard press release, use the e-mail address usually provided on the blog to send a personal message introducing yourself and the company you represent. Ask permission to send the blogger company news and announcements. If you've targeted properly, most bloggers will say yes. The simple fact that you ask first means a lot to them.

Here are some guidelines for approaching bloggers:

- ✔ **Do your research.** Read relevant blogs every day, or hourly, if things are changing that fast. Read not only the blogs you've identified but also the blogs linked from those blogs. And don't worry about exclusivity. Bloggers thrive on community. They're there to share information.

- ✔ **Start by posting to the blog.** Don't use the comments section to blatantly promote your or your client's products. Instead, post a response that is part of the conversation. That way, they know you're reading their blog, which in itself is essential. Engage in a dialogue, which is what blogging is all about anyway.

- ✔ **Don't deceive.** Be upfront about who you are, who you represent, and what you want.

- ✔ **Don't try to influence the blogger's point of view.** Instead, inform him of yours and involve him in the dialogue.

- ✔ **Don't get too personal too soon.** Even though blogs are a more informal medium and bloggers usually post lots of personal information, keep the tone of your initial outreach businesslike. Then according to the tone of the response you get, you can match the blogger's informality.

✔ **Only send relevant announcements to your blogger reporters.** Stay engaged, and continue to read their blogs so that you're sure to always send relevant announcements. Treat them with the respect they deserve.

✔ **Make RSS feeds available for your news releases and other announcements.** If a blogger covers your industry, she'll subscribe to the feed and get the important information that way. Most blogging software includes the ability to make a blog available via RSS. If you don't have a blog, there is simple software available to create RSS feeds for your content.

Keep in mind that in the blogosphere, anything goes. Anything you send to a blogger, whether intended for publication or not, can be posted almost immediately. And the blogger is under no obligation to abide by journalistic guidelines.

Creating your own blog

One main reason to have a blog of your own is that it will make it easier for bloggers to include you in their blogs. It will allow them to see what you've done, what you've said, and what others are saying about you.

You can start your own blog right now and be up and running within an hour. The potential benefits of having a blog are many. Here are just a few:

✔ **Blogs build buzz.** The blogosphere is an alternate universe where bloggers link to and post on each other's blogs. If you make the time to become part of the blogosphere — to find the blogs important to your community, your industry, the media who cover your industry — then you won't be able to stop the buzz.

✔ **Blogging builds your brand.** A blog contributes to your brand by expressing your unique voice and ideas and allowing consumers to build a community around your brand.

✔ **Blogging provides a channel to monitor consumer chatter.** It especially allows you to get early warning signals on problems and other issues.

✔ **Blogging presents a human face and voice for your company.**

✔ **Blogs build link popularity and visibility from all sorts of search engines.**

Using a blog for business

Launching a blog is relatively easy. Plenty of free or very inexpensive software or Web-based applications, like Blogger.com, provide design templates ready to go.

But to do it right, you need a blogging strategy, which will allow you to look ahead and plan what to write and how you'll use it to accomplish your PR and marketing objectives. Otherwise, you'll get the blog out there, post a few times, and then let it languish in the blogosphere, which looks really unprofessional. This happens more often than you might imagine because blogging takes time and thought (someone has to do all that writing) and often, the high-profile executive or CEO whose face and voice is supposedly behind it gets too busy to actually do it.

So before you launch a blog, you should

- ✔ **Have a clear purpose.** Consider how your blog will deliver value to your target audience. Your blog's key strategic objectives can include

  - Informing your target audience of new products and services

  - Providing customer service and support

  - Communicating the "human" side of your business

  - Encouraging readers to post comments or take action

  - Creating an ongoing dialogue with prospects, customers, and clients

- ✔ **Research other blogs that affect your industry.** Your blog will fit into a context of lots of other blogs so be sure you know which ones your media contacts and customers are looking at also. Just search the keywords that relate to your business and you'll find the blogs that reach your target market. Look for their distinctive voice, style, and content. Most important, to see how they're received, read the comments posted.

- ✔ **Choose a blogging service.** Hosted blog services like Google's Blogger (www.blogger.com) and Typepad (www.typepad.com) offer affordable, nontechnical tools to get your blog up and running with minimal hassles. Most blog services allow you to customize your blog.

- ✔ **Create a content strategy.** Successful blogs focus on a particular theme or niche. Choose an appropriate name for your blog that reflects your business brand identity and overall objectives. Your blog should provide relevant, meaningful, exclusive information of value to your target market — information not easily found anywhere else.

Taking in some blogging tips

Follow this advice for maintaining a successful blog:

- **Develop a strong blogging voice.** The overall style of your blog should be in line with your brand and designed to meet your marketing objectives. It should be written in the first person and the tone should be open and credible, conversational and jargon-free, like someone writing off the top of his head (even if it isn't).

- **Write short blog entries.** The most successful blogs are very narrowly focused on one small issue, don't try to cover everything. Blogs with the greatest readership get to the point and make effective use of posting titles. Blogs are meant to be read quickly, so write in a way that's easy to skim. Keep it short and sweet so visitors can pop in, read up, and click on.

- **Post a few times a week.** Your blog needs new content on a regular basis to be successful. Choose a regular time for writing and posting blog entries. At a minimum, post a new entry at least once a week, preferably two or three times a week.

- **Link as much as you can.** Cite other blog posts, Web sites, and articles related to your post. Use your links to thank bloggers who write about you. Other bloggers will see this and want to write about you, too. Figure 17-1 is an example of a highly linked blog post from Steve Rubel's Micropersuasion.com.

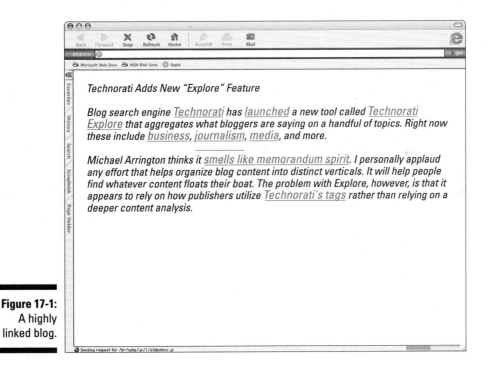

Figure 17-1:
A highly
linked blog.

✔ **Check spelling and grammar, and proofread for typos.** Doing so is essential if you want to be taken seriously.

✔ **Make sure your name and company name are prominent and clear.** Include a photo of the blogger and details about the company's services and products.

✔ **Encourage readers to leave comments.** One of my co-authors, Bob Bly, is a master at getting people to contribute to his blog. His biggest secret is this: Ask a provocative question. Figure 17-2 is an example that generated lots of response.

Promoting your blog

Here are some great ways to promote your blog:

✔ **Submit to blog search engines.** Beyond the traditional search engines, such as Google and Yahoo!, there are search engines and directories that track blogs exclusively and which thousands of people search every day. Submit your blog's URL to these sites for free:

- Blogdex: www.blogdex.net

- Blog Search Engine: www.blogsearchengine.com

- Daypop: www.daypop.com

- Moreover: www.moreover.com

- Popdex: www.popdex.com

- Technorati: www.technorati.com

- Yahoo!: www.yahoo.com

✔ **Ping each time a new post is published.** The blog search engines offer a system whereby you notify (or *ping*) them, either manually or automatically, each time a new post appears on your blog.

✔ **Use trackbacks and tags.** Look for the "trackback" link at the bottom of a post, next to the permalink and comments link. Trackbacking notifies a blogger that one of his posts has been featured on another blog. It's a nonintrusive way of letting a blogger know you're interested in what he has to say. *Tags* are categories and keywords for blog posts. You'll often see keywords on the navigation bar of a blog. If you click on one of the keywords, it will show you all the blogs that are categorized under one of those tags. If someone finds your blog and wants to read all the articles on a particular topic or keyword, tags make this very easy.

✔ **Include a growing blogroll.** You'll see a blogroll on the navigation bar of many blogs. It's essentially a list of favorite blogs or related Web sites. This is one of the ways people hop from one blog to the next and help promote each other's blogs.

✔ **Participate on other people's blogs.** Devote a certain amount of your time to actively commenting on and linking to blogs that are related to your industry and topic. Focus especially on blogs that get high traffic. And be sure to include your blog address in your e-mail signature so that your blog will reach many new readers who see your post.

✔ **Make it easy for readers to subscribe to your blog via RSS.** Give lots of options so people can choose the one they prefer.

✔ **And one last thought: Don't be discouraged if your company blog only has a few subscribers.** More is not better in this case. If someone sub-scribes to your RSS feed, it means they want your information and they are keenly interested in what you're doing. Make it easy for her and she'll post about you.

Figure 17-2:
An example
of how to
generate a
response to
your blog.

Subject line: Jumping on Bandwagons:

It always surprises me how many marketing people jump on trends and become "instant evangelists" for the new thing – whether it's blogging, podcasting, or SEO copywriting – mainly, it seems, because it IS new.

They so badly want to believe that their beloved gimmick is the "holy grail" or marketing ... the silver bullet ... despite the fact that such has never been found – and, I am convinced, never will be.

I'm of a different school – the "show me" school. And in marketing, that means showing me that a new tool or trendy technique has a proven track record of generating a positive ROI.

Until that happens for a new marketing technique ... whether it's blogging or whatever ... I can't see getting excited about it. Why would you?

It does seem to me that the people who are quick to embrace the "next big thing" – even though it's far from certain to be so – are mainly the consultants who want to peddle advice on that marketing method to unwary clients.

So the consultants make money whether it works or not. But the clients lose big time when it produces zilch in results.

Right?

Podcasting

First of all, what is a podcast? The term *podcast,* which is a combination of the terms *iPod* (a brand of audio player) and *broadcast,* is basically a radio talk show. But instead of listening to it on the radio, you listen on an MP3 player. And you don't need to have an iPod to listen to a podcast. Any MP3 player will play podcasts — even your computer's media software, such as Windows Media Player, QuickTime, or iTunes.

When you add RSS code (see the section "Using RSS to monitor the media," for more on RSS) to the audio file, the file becomes searchable, so people looking for information on your topic will find your podcast and listen to it, which wouldn't be possible with a normal audio file. So you can reach a wider audience using podcasts.

Subscribing to a podcast is the equivalent of signing up to receive an e-mail newsletter with one very big exception: Unlike e-mail, subscribing to a podcast puts you in control of when you get the content. Nothing is pushed to your e-mail inbox.

Keeping in touch with the media via podcasts

For PR purposes, podcasting presents a new and very powerful method of communicating directly with the media, many of whom already receive information by subscribing to newsfeeds.

In fact, more journalists subscribe to RSS feeds than ever before, and the number is growing — particularly in the trade media. The best part for journalists is that your news isn't competing with all the press releases crammed into their e-mail in-boxes. So why not make it easy for them to cover news about your company and its products with podcasts?

Cisco Systems, for example, offers a selection of podcasts for the media in the "newsroom" on its Web site. Topics include everything from a recording of its CEO unveiling a new education-focused initiative, to Cisco executives and health leaders from major metropolitan hospitals showcasing a new product, to a discussion of the role of Cisco technology at the racetrack.

You can offer your latest press conference or analyst call via podcast. You could *stream,* or offer a regular monthly or weekly podcast to which journalists can subscribe and receive up-to-the-minute company news.

You could even make your next in-person press conference more exciting by giving each editor an MP3-compatible USB flash drive with the contents of the press conference.

Getting started with podcasting

Podcasting is not as easy as blogging, even though they get lumped together as new media tools. As a marketing tool, podcasting is far safer than blogging because you control the message, which is what PR is all about anyway.

The reality is that producing a podcast is a lot of work. Production values are very important. Also, podcasts need to be entertaining and relevant.

The actual creation of a podcast is surprisingly simple. In terms of hardware, all you need is a computer, a microphone, and a broadband connection.

Free software such as Audacity (`http://audacity.sourceforge.net`) allows you to record it. Then it's a matter of saving the file as an `.mp3` and uploading it to your server.

After it's uploaded, your podcast is ready to be distributed. Here's a list of current systems through which you can do that:

- ✔ BlastPodcast (`www.blastpodcast.com`)
- ✔ FeedDemon (`www.feeddemon.com`)
- ✔ iPodder (`www.ipodder.org`)
- ✔ Podcast Alley (`www.podcastalley.com`)

You can also "pitch" to podcasters (some of whom are also bloggers). Find one who is podcasting on your topic and who has a following or large audience and reach out to him as you would a radio show producer. In the same way that you search the blogs, you search for podcasts on your topic. Then you approach the podcasters in the same way that you approach bloggers (see the "Approaching bloggers" section, earlier in this chapter).

Pitching is more appropriate here because podcasters are looking for content in the form of guests for their podcasts, But be careful about what you say and who you say it to: Bloggers and podcasters are not journalists. They aren't required to be fair, balanced, or accurate. They bring their personal bias to what they write every day and could have some very negative things to say, which spreads like wildfire. Before you agree to do a podcast, do your homework. Listen to podcasts the podcaster has done and decide if that environment would be appropriate for you.

Webcasting

A webcast is a live, interactive online conference or event that uses the Internet to broadcast a live (or delayed) audio and/or video transmission to a targeted group of users who log in for the event. They generally happen in real time, so there is an opportunity for two-way communication between a participant and the conference leader or across the team or group, via instant messaging applications or other software.

On paper, this is an ideal way to host a press conference without anyone leaving his desk. In addition to their broad reach, webcasts are cost-effective, easy to use, and visually dynamic — featuring slides, graphics, and even live video. They allow you to provide a fuller presentation for the audience because they combine audio and visual elements.

However, in reality, most journalists probably won't have the time to sit at their desks and watch your webcast. And even if they do, will you get their full attention? Many people in online meetings are multitasking — checking and responding to e-mail, filling out expense reports, and accomplishing other tasks that divide their attention.

Also, not everyone can participate in webcasts. The media is owned by major corporations that have rules about what you can do with your computer, so you can't be sure journalists will be able to access it.

Our firm had planned a global webcast for a big, multinational client, but their own internal technology wouldn't support it without it costing a lot more. So we stayed with the traditional tools.

There's an age factor here also: In general, the more experienced journalists are troubled by technology and often the older ones need to be approached in the way that is familiar to them. As of 2005, they still want things delivered traditionally.

Part V
Creating Buzz

The 5th Wave   By Rich Tennant

In this part . . .

*N*ow is the time to turn up your PR efforts to full heat. Buzz is king when it comes to PR, and in Chapter 18, I show you how to get it through viral marketing and more. Staging special PR events is a big part of the buzz machine; in Chapter 19, I outline how to do it. In PR, timing is everything, and Chapter 20 helps you take advantage of timing to maximize your PR results. Sometimes the heat you face is negative, so I include Chapter 21 to guide you in coping with any PR crisis. Finally, Chapter 22 shows you how to measure your PR results and return on PR investment.

Chapter 18

Getting Hits from Buzz Marketing and Viral Marketing

*M*ost marketing efforts are carefully calculated pitches choreographed by professionals to convey a specific message to a target audience, and it's obvious. Buzz marketing, on the other hand, is just as carefully calculated but it doesn't appear to be so. It's a combination of creative grassroots tactics and creative PR stunts that capture the attention of consumers and the media who then begin to talk or spread the word about your company in a way that is entertaining, fascinating, and newsworthy.

In this chapter, you find out what makes buzz marketing so effective, the four elements of buzz marketing, how to determine the right moment for buzz, plus eight things you can do right now to get the buzz going.

Understanding the Difference between Buzz Marketing and Viral Marketing

Buzz marketing is the overall volume of noise about a product or service and it includes all sorts of tools, such as viral marketing, word of mouth, press coverage and more.

Viral marketing, an element of buzz, is restricted mainly to the online space, because that's where things are easily passed around, whether they be viral e-mail messages with jokes or links to Web sites, photos, or JPEG files of static images or video clips.

For a brand, one of the most successful viral marketing campaigns has been Burger King's Subservient Chicken. To promote a new chicken product from a company known for beef, their ad agency, Crispin Porter, created an irreverent Web site where people could go and give commands to the chicken. The link to the Web site was sent to 1,000 people as a test and it immediately mushroomed into millions of hits to that site.

Humor is one of the staples of viral marketing, but if you decide to do it for your company, be aware that you're asking someone to send something to someone he knows. Therefore, whatever that person sends is a reflection of himself. The question to ask is, "Would *you* pass this on to somebody?"

If you create a video clip for viewers to watch, pass it as a link rather than an actual clip via e-mail, and keep it short. Two to three minutes is the maximum; shorter than that is even better.

Examining the Effectiveness of Buzz Marketing

What makes buzz marketing so effective? It's trust — or lack of trust, actually.

You see, trust is eroding in both traditional and emerging forms of marketing. Have you noticed that *self-promotion* is often preceded by the word *shameless?* It's because people just don't believe what companies say about themselves anymore.

Meanwhile, people do believe what others say about those same companies. Those others include the people in the media, beloved experts and celebrities, as well as friends and family — in other words, other consumers. The beauty and the essence of buzz marketing, when done correctly, is that it puts people you know (or at least people you feel you know) at the center of the equation.

For example, according to the Travel Industry Association, friends and relatives are the number-one source for information about places to visit, flights, hotels, or rental cars. A survey in *Self* magazine found that 63 percent of women cited "friend, family, or co-worker referral" as one of the factors influencing their over-the-counter drug purchases. The high-value impact of buzz is verified over and over in survey after survey, whether it's the 53 percent of moviegoers who rely to some extent on a recommendation from someone they know or the 70 percent of Americans who rely on the advice of others when selecting a new doctor, or your own experience of polling family and friends when considering something new.

Boning Up on Basic Buzz Techniques

Buzz marketing is a new and different animal in the PR arena. It will evolve because PR practitioners are beginning to recognize the value of buzz. In this section, I give you some background on buzz before I tell you how to start your own buzz, when to do it, and what the advantages are.

Educating people about your products and services

In order for the media and other people to get a buzz going about your company, you must give them the information they need to spread the word, and you have to provide it in a format that is easy to digest and easy to understand. If they don't know enough about your company, they can't spread the word about it. That's why you need to put the information into the hands of the media. Educate by using the tried-and-true PR materials available (especially press releases), but because buzz is less formal, don't hesitate to provide samples, put on seminars, or even take reporters to lunch.

Identifying people most likely to share their opinions

To get the buzz going, you must focus your attention on the "opinion leaders" or "hubs" in the world of your market. There are four kinds of hubs and the common denominator among them is that people listen to them.

Regular hubs

Regular hubs are folks who serve as sources of information and influence in a certain world or market. The people they connect with trust them and listen to what they say. For example, Prostate Net, a prostate cancer advocacy group, enlisted barbers to spread the word about free cancer screenings to the most-at-risk group: African American men. Identify the person(s) or group(s) that your market trusts.

Unlike big-time experts and celebrities, regular hubs are easiest to reach and to develop relationships with, so here are a few traits to look for when trying to identify regular hubs in your area:

- ✔ **People who are connected:** Their job or position requires that they come into contact with a lot of people. They're good networkers and they create links between their local network and the outside world.

- ✔ **People who are ahead in adoption:** Though not necessarily the first to adopt a new technology or idea, they're open to them.

- ✔ **People who are information-hungry:** They read everything, especially material that will help them do their jobs better.

- ✔ **People who are vocal:** They write, they speak, they're out there. They need content. They have a blog or a newsletter (or both) in which your product or service could be featured.

Expert hubs

Expert hubs are folks who go beyond making recommendations. They're experts and specialists on a particular topic, and people listen to them because of their expertise and credentials. For example, Michael McLaughlin is an author and expert on the consulting industry. Thousands read his regular e-mail newsletter, Management Consulting News, which makes him an expert hub on management consulting. Identify the person in your industry who functions as a respected expert. (You don't need to know these people personally.)

Social hubs

Social hubs are people who are charismatic, socially active, and trusted by their peers. One example is Lois Weisberg, one-time commissioner of Chicago's Department of Cultural Affairs, who's been described as "the type of person who seems to know everybody." In a small town or neighborhood, a social hub–type person is often symbolically referred to as "the mayor" of his or her social group, community, or area of interest. Identify people you're aware of who fit this description.

Mega hubs

The media, celebrities, politicians, and other really big names make up the mega hubs. These people stand out because they're connected to millions of people. Obvious examples are Oprah Winfrey or Dr. Phil. Of course, the attention of mega hubs is the hardest to get, but if you succeed, the buzz will keep on coming. But keep in mind that "mega" is relative. Think about people you know of who would be considered "mega" in the market of your customers. For example, Michael Masterson is the publisher of *Early To Rise,* a daily e-mail newsletter that goes to more than 400,000 people. His readers respond almost religiously to his recommendations. Identify whose blessing would translate into gold for you.

Providing tools that make it easier to share information

After you've identified the hubs or media outlets in the best position to reach your customers (see the "Identifying people most likely to share their opinions" section, earlier in this chapter) and then educated them about your product or service (see the "Educating people about your products and services" section, earlier in this chapter), you must make sure that they have what they need to spread the word. Create entertaining or informative messages designed for passing along in an exponential fashion, often by e-mail or other electronic forms (instant messaging or via their cell phone). But it doesn't have to be electronic. For example, a family-owned florist based in Chicago, recently put on a stunt that was picked up by local media. On a busy street, they gave out bouquets containing five roses to curious onlookers. Each bouquet came with a printed coupon that read: "Share the love!" and asked that each rose be shared with five other people to "make new friends and share goodwill to neighbors."

Studying how, where, and when opinions are being shared

Tracking the buzz after it's going is important, and you can do this easily on the Internet. One way to track what people are saying about your company is to set a Google Alert or Yahoo! Alert for news on your company. The alerts make monitoring a developing news story or keeping current on a competitor or on your industry very easy. Just go to www.google.com/alerts or http://alerts.yahoo.com and type into the field the word or phrase you'd like to track. They'll send you an e-mail every time that word or phrase hits the news.

Yahoo! also offers a free service called the Buzz Index, which proposes to measure public engagement with brands, products, people, technologies, and broad concepts. They tabulate buzz by counting the number of people searching for a topic on a given day, dividing by the number of users visiting Yahoo! that day, and multiplying by a constant factor. This can give you a good idea of interest in your brand (and your competitor's brands), the effectiveness of your buzz marketing campaign, as well as broad cultural trends. You can find out more at `http://buzz.yahoo.com`.

Listening and responding to supporters and detractors

If you do it right, most of the buzz you receive will be positive. But because it's a medium that you can't control (the way you can with advertising), some of the buzz may be negative. What you can control, however, is how you respond. So, as you keep track of the buzz, listen closely to what is being said and respond quickly and personally to all those who require a response.

Listen and respond to both positive and negative conversations. The best methods to use when responding to feedback are the most personal. For example, send a personalized letter from the president of your company addressing the issues. Sometimes even a phone call is in order, when the issue is delicate and you want to make sure the person knows that it is being taken seriously. This small effort can go a long way in this culture of pseudo-personalized responses and autoresponders. You should also have a toll-free number available as an option for feedback with a real person on the line.

Determining the Right Moment for Buzz

Timing is everything, especially when it comes to buzz. It has to be spread at the right time in order for someone to act on it. So think about when the market or the specific hubs you want to approach are most likely to talk. Are they most likely to talk:

- ✔ When something related has happened in the world?
- ✔ When they first hear about your company?
- ✔ During a particular season?
- ✔ When they receive a surprise from you?

If, at these moments, you can capture their attention and provide tools that make it easy for them to spread the word, they are more likely to do so.

For example, election seasons are perfect opportunities to capitalize on what's happening in the world. During a recent 2004 election season, Domino's Pizza piggybacked on what they knew would be a big story: voter registration. They got a lot of press by simply delivering voter registration forms with every pizza.

Certain techniques are considered unethical by the PR industry. Be aware of them and take care not to engage in any of these techniques:

✔ Impersonating people or hiding your identity

✔ Deceiving people or hiding your involvement in a PR effort

✔ Vandalizing or damaging property as part of your product promotion

✔ Manipulating or corrupting honest opinions

✔ *Spamming* (sending bulk or unsolicited e-mail or other messages without clear, voluntary permission)

Generating More Exposure with Buzz Marketing

This section will give you tips and techniques to get more people talking about you, your product, or your company. It will also let you know who to go to, how to identify them and the best way to create favorable conversation.

Certain qualities that a product or service has make it more conducive to buzz. You don't have to have any or all the following qualities, but if you can highlight them or add them, you'll find it easier to get buzz:

✔ **Excitement:** People talk when they're excited, especially in the early stages of using a product or service. For example, the iPod has garnered tremendous buzz since it was introduced because it's changing the way we listen to music (and other things), so that makes it exciting.

Excitement is subjective, of course, and if you're developing a new product, you're probably excited about it for your own reasons. But I'm talking about excitement of your customers here, not your own excitement. What often makes a product exciting is that it's new and never seen before, or that it provides a new spin on something old.

That's not to say that everything new is necessarily exciting. During the Internet heyday, everything was new and everyone was convinced they were creating a revolution. But if your product or service truly has the potential to change the way we do something — listen to music, read, take in information, and so on — it could be considered exciting. Your new, improved cheese grater may be better than any other on the market, but it's unlikely to revolutionize the way we cook.

✔ **Complexity:** Complexity is a double-edged sword. Make it too complex and no one talks about it because they can't figure it out. But if you give them a forum to talk, especially a place where both prospects and current customers can exchange information, buzz flows naturally. For example, some speech-recognition software is complex and challenging, but if the manufacturer provides a forum for users to chat and help each other, it's more likely to create buzz.

✔ **Personal experience:** People talk about things they've personally experienced (such as hotels, airlines, or books).

✔ **Expensiveness:** People talk to reinforce that they made the right decision in purchasing an expensive product or service because it was more than worth the cost in satisfaction and social acceptance.

✔ **Observable:** People talk about what they can see and show. The latest cell phone or the iPod are the perfect examples here, too, because they're products that are small enough to carry around and they're very visible so people can observe them, as opposed to a software application you love that lives on your computer but you can't show to anyone. The application will naturally create less buzz than the gadget.

Looking at the unique qualities of your product or service is where you can get creative and think about what would surprise people, what would delight them, and what would make your customers and prospects stop a second and say, "Wow, that's cool. I need to tell everyone about that." It could be as simple as sending chocolate and a gift card in the mail as a follow-up. Bob Bly, direct-mail copywriter (and co-author of this book), regularly sends a copy of one of his many books to prospects when they're considering hiring him. The gift makes a huge impression, mostly because it's a surprise but also because the timing is perfect.

Having a good story helps, too. LaserMonks (`www.lasermonks.com`) is an office-supply company run by, you guessed it, monks (in Sparta, Wisconsin). There's nothing unique about the product — printer cartridges, for now — but they have capitalized on their unique and charming story to create strong word of mouth and get a lot of PR, too. (You can read their story on their Web site.) In addition, the experience they provide to the customer is worth talking about: The monks pray for all their customers, handwritten thank-you notes are sometimes slipped into shipments, and when callers are put on hold, they hear a Gregorian chant. So far the strategy has paid off — satisfied customers have been telling friends and colleagues, and the media has picked up the story and spread it even farther.

Identifying Brand Evangelists and Terrorists

You ought to know who's putting effort into liking your company and not liking your company. Both groups need to be courted with accurate information.

Taking advantage of evangelists

Brand evangelists are people who love your brand and your company. They believe most strongly in the strength and superiority of your product or service. They provide those third-party endorsements that everyone believes, and they're as good as (and sometimes better than) a press clipping.

But who are they? You may not have to look too far to find them; simply notice who's excited about your business. They may be your customers or even your employees. You'll know them because they communicate the most with you and about you. They call you on your cell phone. They call your offices. They send you e-mail messages. They refer their friends and family to you or your company. They may even sometimes annoy you but don't be annoyed. These are your best advocates.

After you've identified the evangelists, make sure they have access to any information they want or need so they can spread the word. Here's how:

✔ Provide recognition — awards, certificates, gift cards — to say thank you. Offer visibility or "15 minutes of fame" by featuring these evangelists in your marketing.

✔ Provide tools — your business cards, brochures, and other information — to make it easier for them to spread the word.

✔ Recruit new advocates, educate them about the benefits of your products, and encourage them to talk.

For example, Paul Holmes is an evangelist for the PR industry. He writes a weekly newsletter, writes a column in the trade publication *PR Week,* and hosts an awards program that matters to the industry. If he used my agency as an example, it would create buzz for us and, therefore, bring business our way. So we make sure he has accurate, factual information about us and we keep him in the loop on what we're doing and what we've accomplished.

A brand evangelist is somebody who is enthusiastic about a brand and has the means and the wherewithal to spread the word. One good example is Spike Lee, whose love and passion for the New York Knicks is highly visible, influential, and a wonderful association for the Knicks. His enthusiasm is contagious. People look for what he says about the Knicks and that gets the fans buzzing. Plus, his towel-waving antics at playoff games in the late '80s almost became part of the game. He got the whole stadium waving towels and maybe even brought the Knicks as close to a championship as they've been since the early '70s. That's a successful brand evangelist. You can't pay for that kind of coverage.

Gathering and using testimonials

Testimonials are quotations from clients who are raving, in their own words, about how great you and your company are and how much you've helped them. That's what makes testimonials so credible. But getting testimonials takes some effort. You must make it easy for your clients to provide them. Here's how:

- ✔ **Listen.** Keep your ear tuned for comments from happy customers, and then capture those comments on paper and ask, "Do you mind if I use this as a testimonial?" You should always get permission to use testimonials, and a formal signed permission form, if possible. But written permission via e-mail is often easier to get and is sufficient. Always, always thank them for it. Go even farther and give them something special — a gift or exclusive access to information — for taking the time to share their opinion.

- ✔ **Give a model.** The ideal testimonial provides concrete results or return on investment that anyone reading it can also expect to achieve. It often also describes the situation the person or company found themselves in so that others can relate to it. Give customers a model for a testimonial so they don't have to start from a blank page, and a list of questions to stimulate their thoughts.

  Here's an example:

  When I began the Marketing Mentor Program, I had no previous experience in marketing. Today, as a result of our work together, I have been able to get more than 30 meetings with prospective clients for our company. I have also been responsible for bringing in 11 new projects.

  Here are some questions you can ask your clients to stimulate this type of testimonial:

  • What do you like best about [fill in the blank]?

- How has [fill in the blank] helped you or your business achieve its goals?

- What concrete results can you point to after working with [fill in the blank]?

✔ **Create one for approval.** If your customer wants to give a testimonial to you, but she simply can't find the time to focus on it, you can also write a testimonial and have her simply approve it.

Some people believe that more is better when it comes to testimonials, that quantity is the key to their effectiveness. So there's no reason to retire of any of them, even if they've been around a while, as long as they're still relevant.

Whatever strategy you choose, make asking for testimonials a standard part of your evaluation process at the end of a sale, project, or process.

Compliments can sometimes prevent you from getting a much more useful testimonial because you may be so flattered that you forget to probe further to find out what exactly affected your clients and customers. When someone offers a compliment, don't stop at "thank you." Ask what they mean, what they liked, what specifically had the strongest impact on them. Then piggy-back on the positive by asking for suggestions, improvements, and anything you can do to improve your current offerings.

Giving them a taste

You can get a tremendous amount of marketing and PR mileage from a gener-ous sampling program, because allowing people to experience your product or service makes it easier for them to spread the buzz. This is even true for those who sample but don't buy. You never know who they'll talk to.

If you're marketing intangible services or talents, your "sample" can be any of the following:

✔ A free consultation

✔ A presentation

✔ Tips and tricks or white papers

✔ A free critique

✔ A promotional item with an image of your artwork

✔ A demo reel

✔ A few ideas provided on spec

Creating and supporting communities

Communities create a sense of belonging, which makes it easier for your advocates to connect with others like them. There are simple and inexpensive ways to do this with technology. Here are a few ways to create a community around your product or services:

- ✔ **Create user groups and fan clubs.** Then bring in your best customers or fans to brainstorm ideas. If you have the budget for it, the best strategy is to organize a meeting where you fly them to your headquarters and host a daylong session, treating them like royalty and showing your gratitude for their efforts. (This alone can create its own buzz.) You can find out a lot from them, and they'll no doubt be excited to help out. If that approach isn't financially feasible, you can coordinate a virtual conference and give them special access via phone and Web. Also, be sure to let them know when one of their ideas is used — yet another good buzz stimulator.

- ✔ **Support independent groups that form around your product.** Enable grassroots organization such as local meetings and other face-to-face participation (more about this in Chapter 17).

- ✔ **Host discussions and message boards about your products.**

Dealing with brand terrorists

On the other side of the equation are the brand terrorists. These are people who spread rumors and urban myths like wildfire. Anyone can be a brand terrorist. They could be your competition or a disgruntled customer. Or sometimes they're simply unhappy customers whose complaints get swept under the rug and go unaddressed. They spread the word — but not the word you want them to spread.

One of the weapons in their arsenal is anti-corporation Web sites. These are sites that are created by people who have something to say about your company and, without your permission, post a Web site outlining their ideas, charges, accusations, and so on.

If brand terrorism were done in simple press releases, it wouldn't be such a big deal. But now, thanks to the Internet, it can be created and posted and available for everyone to see. Put that together with viral marketing, and you have a dangerous situation. You can't let this happen, which is why monitoring the Internet for such campaigns is essential — that way, you can find out about it as soon as possible. When someone is making false statements or accusations, they must be corrected.

What you have to do is respond to their pointed criticisms with your accurate information. If they claim that your product has 82 percent fat, you respond with the accurate information, plus complete background on your statistics. Engage them in an open conversation. They shouldn't feel rejected just because they have a negative point of view. The approach to brand terrorists should be: "We appreciate your constructive criticism. We'd like to hear it and we will address it."

Leveraging the Web and E-Mail for Maximum Buzz

One sure way to get the buzz going is to recruit celebrities to use or wear your product or somehow associate themselves with your company. Millions and millions of people look at celebrities every day. They're big influencers.

Samantha Slaven Public Relations specializes in generating this type of buzz for her clients, many of whom are companies that make and sell women's fashion and accessories. One of the main PR strategies she uses to generate buzz is to get celebrities to wear and/or carry the clients' items and then get the clients exposure in the press based on these celebrity "fans." And she does this mostly via e-mail.

After Slaven and her clients have selected the items they want to focus on for the season, they send out an e-mail blast to the top celebrity publicists with a JPEG photo of the item, a fun description, and an invitation for them to receive complimentary samples for their clients in the size and color of their choice. Sometimes they offer these items to the publicists as well.

Then they capture a photo of the celebrity wearing the item and e-mail it to all relevant fashion/accessory editors at the weeklies, celebrity-oriented media, and top fashion and women's magazines, naming the piece the "'it' item of the season!" This strategy usually results in several press hits, or at least ups the buzz factor of the client in the editors' minds.

Stunts are another way to generate buzz because they can generate continual press coverage. In the late '90s, I worked with Ken Hakuta (of Wacky Wall Walker fame), who started an Internet site called AllHerb.com, which was basically another me-too vitamin site.

AllHerb.com sought to differentiate itself by positioning itself as "the most authentic resource for herbal medicine available today." So we hired an unusual and captivating spokesman — a shaman, tribal healer and herbalist from the Amazon rain forest of Peru — to share his ancient wisdom and inter-act with visitors at the site. We gave him a computer and he answered e-mail from people all over. As you can imagine, this created an enormous amount of buzz about the e-commerce site, not to mention the traffic it drove to the site.

For a store opening, for example, you have to get the whole town talking and this won't be done with a simple press release. Ideally, you want your com-pany or product or service to become part of pop American culture — at least until the next trend takes over. In 2003, a guy who went by the name of "Bill" started a phenomenon called "flash mobs," which were essentially perfor-mance art projects involving large groups of people who had been mobilized by e-mail. Bill would spread his message to thousands of people through viral marketing about where to meet and what to do. At the appointed time and place, a mob would suddenly materialize in a public place, follow the instruc-tions, and then disappear. On one evening in Manhattan, for example, 500 people fell to their knees in the Times Square Toys R Us before the store's to-scale Tyranosaurus rex for 10 minutes. This not only got the whole town talk-ing, but also got a lot of media coverage.

Measuring and Tracking Buzz

The truth is, buzz is very hard — if not impossible — to measure. Agencies like Lime PR and Promo Agency, which specializes in generating buzz and online press, create ads just for viral marketing. They start the process and track it wherever it goes. There are all sorts of "buzz-meters" that claim to measure buzz by, for example, searching for the popularity of certain words and brands in selected blogs over time.

But even companies that consciously do buzz marketing don't necessarily know how buzz works. Word of mouth is hard to track or measure. After all, most conversations are private and ephemeral. Nobody keeps a record.

You can measure buzz in a few ways:

- **Sales:** The most obvious measure is an increase in sales. It probably has something to do with the buzz you've generated.

- **Impressions:** If you're using viral marketing techniques, you can mea-sure the number of hits to a Web site or click-throughs on a link in an e-mail message. Plus, things that are hot get picked up by blogs, maga-zines, and Web sites, so your press coverage will increase if you get the buzz going.

✔ **Word of mouth:** This is more difficult to measure than sales or impressions, but you can do research after an event or stunt to find out how attendees heard about it. If there is an online component to your campaign, you can ask that question before granting access to a Web site.

Meeting the Legends of Buzz

Examining how the legends of buzz used it to their advantage may further inspire your own efforts. Check out their stories:

✔ **P. T. Barnum:** Of the legendary Barnum & Bailey Circus, P. T. Barnum was one of the originators of public relations. In every city the circus played, Barnum would march his elephants through the town in what came to be known as the Pachyderm Parade. This created a ruckus in the town, generating lots of press and getting the buzz going about the event — before people even knew it as buzz.

✔ **Hotmail:** A more recent but already classic viral marketing legend is Hotmail, one of the original free, Web-based email services. Without spending a cent on advertising, Hotmail went from zero subscribers at their launch on Independence Day 1996 (they tied into that holiday on the idea that the e-mail service was independent of a user's computer) to 12 million subscribers in only 18 months.

Here's how: At the bottom of every free message any user of the service sent, was added this simple tag: "Get your private, free e-mail at `http://www.hotmail.com`."

As users used the service to correspond with their network of friends and associates, everyone who received a message also had a chance to sign themselves up for the free — and that's an important element of this successful campaign — service. It quickly rippled across the Internet.

Why did it work so well? Besides the fact that the timing of their service was impeccable, their viral marketing tool was built in. It required no additional effort or vehicle to spread the word. Plus, it was a very simple message, making it supremely simple to spread.

✔ **Shel Horowitz:** Buzz marketing works especially well in local communities, where momentum can be gathered quickly over the short distance. Shel Horowitz, copywriter and consultant, used buzz to save a mountain in his local community.

In November 1999, a local developer announced a plan to build 40 trophy homes abutting Skinner State Park in Massachusetts. Local conservationists expressed variations on "Oh, this is terrible, but there's nothing we can do." Horowitz said, "Oh, yes, there is something we can do!"

The article about the developer appeared on a Friday night. By Tuesday, Horowitz had drawn up a petition, posted a Web page, called a meeting for two weeks later, and sent out press releases and flyers about the formation of "Save the Mountain."

He expected 20 or so people at the first meeting; he had over 70! Over the course of a year, 35 local activists fought the project on every conceivable level, harnessing the outrage felt throughout the valley and using PR and buzz marketing to turn that outrage into a powerful — and highly visible — public force.

And they did make a difference. Within two months of starting the campaign, they had established themselves firmly in the public eye as a can-do organization. The discourse shifted from "There's nothing we can do" to "Which of the dozens of ways to pursue this will be most effective in stopping this development?" Collectively, they used their powers of persuasion and skills at reaching the public with a strong message to block the project.

In the end, a wealthy benefactor stepped forward, publicly stated that she was inspired by the group's efforts, and wrote the state a check to buy and preserve the land. The state took title in December 2000.

Chapter 19

Staging Publicity Events

· ·

In This Chapter

▶ Attracting people and press coverage

▶ Setting your budget and objectives

▶ Coming up with event ideas

▶ Planning your event

▶ Gauging the success of your event

· ·

*W*ho says publicity stunts are passé? Outrageous staged events designed solely to show up on the evening news still get the job done when they're clever and fun.

Calvin Klein's Living Billboard in Times Square was a giant bottle of "perfume" with many models swimming in it.

Store openings for IKEA, one of the leading home furnishings retailer, have become famous for the Fun Factor Challenge in which four area residents are offered the chance to compete in a series of fun, friendly challenges. It's a three-day, three-night stay that benefits a worthy cause — and gets a lot of publicity for IKEA.

If you compare the cost of events (even pricey ones) and the exposure they generate (if they do), it's often a significant savings over the cost of advertising to advertise in the very broadcast and print media that cover your event.

In this chapter, I walk you through the steps of putting on an event that can achieve multiple objectives. I also cover how to control your costs while getting great press (of course) and the criteria for evaluating the success of your event.

Drawing Crowds and Gaining Publicity

Special events — such as grand openings, pony rides for children, barbecues and square dances, picnics, and Halloween parties — are effective publicity vehicles in two ways:

- ✔ **They help market your company, product, or service to the public.** People attend the event, come to your store for the free hot dogs or ice cream, and then browse and buy while they're there.

- ✔ **They're promotable and can get you a lot of press coverage.** Many editors like special events and cover them.

If the event involves free food, gifts, rides, or other giveaways, many editors at least announce it in their papers, typically in a schedule of events or things-to-do-this-week column.

If the event is based on a clever gimmick or angle, many editors not only put it in the calendar but also may give it broader feature coverage, both as a preview and as a post-event story. This leverages the time and effort spent putting on the event, because you not only promote yourself to those who attend but also, through the publicity, reach thousands of additional prospects who did not come.

Spiderman snares kids but loses sales

Maximizing the selling opportunity at special events is important. For example, a local department store advertised that Spiderman would be at the store's grand opening to pose for photos with the kiddies and give away autographed comic books. When we got there, the line of parents with children to see Spiderman went around the store, with a 50-minute wait.

Spiderman stood in front of the toy department, where he shook hands and posed with young fans. To my amazement, no Spiderman or other superhero toys or comic books were displayed near him! In fact, no such display was set up anywhere in the toy department! The store blew an opportunity to sell thousands of dollars' worth of Spiderman and superhero action figures, dolls, costumes, and other comic-book paraphernalia. Don't you make this same mistake!

Also, the only announcement of Spiderman's appearance came in free-standing newspaper inserts and ads. The store didn't drum up any free publicity. You might say, "What do you expect? It's just a guy dressed up in a Spiderman costume. No news there."

Here's where being creative and clever could have made the difference. What about writing and distributing a press release in the form of a tongue-in-cheek, question-and-answer interview with Spiderman? If such a release had been sent with some action photos of Spidey striking a dramatic pose or shooting a web, I guarantee that at least one local editor would have enjoyed and run this release as a feature article, thus generating publicity for the store.

Here are some quick suggestions for creating special events that not only draw big crowds but also gain publicity:

- ✔ **Tie the special event to current events or news.** For instance, a store selling 1950s and other nostalgia items could have had an Elvis Presley memorabilia sale tied to the U.S. Postal Service's widely publicized introduction of the Elvis stamp.

- ✔ **Tie the special event to a holiday, anniversary, or other observance.** Virtually every day is the anniversary of some famous person's birth or death; the anniversary of some important event; or a holiday, commemorative day, or day of recognition. For example, you might give 25 percent off any item in your store to left-handed people on National Left-Handers Day.

- ✔ **Involve local celebrities.** For example, invite the DJ from a popular local radio station to serve as the master of ceremonies and to sign autographs. Celebrities draw crowds and generate press coverage. Stores often call on celebrities to help promote grand openings.

- ✔ **Make your own news.** When a union of social workers was not getting a lot of press for its strike against a state agency unwilling to grant them a small wage increase, I suggested that they make a video greeting card and send it to the agency's director. On the video, families served by the agency pleaded with the director to end the strike, because the scab workers who were replacing the striking workers did not know the families and their special needs. The PR angle? We sent the video greeting card not only to the agency director but also to all local TV news programs.

- ✔ **Feature an unusual, interesting, or creative event as part of the day.** For example, to promote your pizza parlor, you can truck in ingredients and attempt to get everyone present into the *Guinness Book of World Records* by having them help you make the world's largest pizza.

Setting a Budget and Figuring the Cost

The biggest drawback of events is their cost, and the second biggest drawback is the sheer amount of work they take to put on. When planning an event, the best place to start is your budget because it will dictate the scope, the size, and even the creative approach to your event.

Once a client asked me to submit ideas for a promotional event. Figuring he was thrifty, I presented several concepts that would work on a modest budget. He became enraged and told me he wanted *big* ideas. He wanted something really spectacular. When I came back with the spectacular ideas, he paused a second and told me they were great, but that he couldn't afford them. The point is: Establish a budget first and then frame an event you can do within your budget.

I've worked with event budgets ranging from $30,000 to several million dollars. With a $500,000 budget, you can afford to do a travel promotion with an appearance by a pitcher from the baseball team that won the last World Series. When your budget is smaller, you may have to stick to something simpler — hot-air balloon rides or just hot dogs in the parking lot.

The biggest plus of events is their unique ability to dramatically demonstrate a message and make it come alive. PR is the art of demonstration. You just can't *say* you're environmentally friendly or technically savvy; to get the public to believe you and the press to quote you, you have to demonstrate that these claims are so. Consider this example: When the Park Central Hotel in New York City wanted to communicate the message that the improvements being made at the hotel would improve the quality of service for guests, it offered a day of free "personal renovations" in the lobby, where visitors could get hairstyling, massages, and manicures (more on that event later in this chapter).

Controlling Event Costs

A general guideline is that a special event always costs at least ten times more than a print promotion (for example, mailing a press release). There's no getting around it — events cost time, money, and effort.

However, you can take several steps to control costs and keep the event budget at a reasonable level:

- ✔ **Keep the event local.** Hold it in your own town or the nearest city, not the city where the annual industry meeting is held, 2,000 miles away.

- ✔ **Allow only essential personnel to attend.** Having executives travel to the show or conference wastes your budget and their time.

- ✔ **Be a scrooge about expenditures.** For example, at events where wine is served, I tell the waiters to ask attendees whether they want more wine instead of automatically pouring more in the glass. The savings are considerable.

- ✔ **Shop around for everything.** You would be shocked to discover how prices for seemingly comparable services and items vary. For instance, many so-called B-list celebrities who are very well known and are crowd pleasers will work for a fraction of the cost of a superstar with a slightly bigger reputation who doesn't buy you much extra as a draw.

ZINGER

Fine smokes feed old folks

Cigar smoking, once a hot trend, has faded in recent years, and our client, Club Macanudo — a New York City cigar club — wanted to demonstrate that cigar aficionados are people with taste who appreciate the finer things in life. Our agency created the "Ultimate Cars, Premium Cigars Road Rally" in which participants in 25 luxury and collectible cars drove through New York's Westchester County.

At each rest stop, drivers were given a fine cigar to smoke. Onlookers could see happy people driving beautiful cars, smoking, and enjoying their cigars. The event proceeds — which included the entry fees plus sales of humidors to the crowd attending the event and its awards banquet that evening — benefited City Meals-on-Wheels, a nonprofit organization providing food to elderly New Yorkers. The event was covered in the *New York Post* and the *New York Daily News* and on WB Channel 11 among other media.

Determining Your Event's Theme and Concept

Demonstrating a key message should always be the reason for and key objective of any promotional event. Look at your product or service. Identify the key messages you want to communicate. Now get creative and, using the methods outlined in Chapter 5, brainstorm ways to use events to demonstrate these messages.

Here are some examples:

- Carvel Ice Cream wanted to modernize its image as a place that really cared about kids. To animate the message, it brought free ice cream to 55 schools in the New York tri-state area with the best attendance records.

- To support the launch of IKEA's line of a.i.r inflatable furniture, I helped conduct the IKEA a.i.r Open Golf Tournament benefiting the Asthma and Allergy Foundation of America (AAFA). We covered a golf course with room settings by using the inflatable furniture and other IKEA furniture. Soap opera stars Jackie Zeman and Julian Stone were on hand to raise money to send 100 children with asthma and allergies to the AAFA's summer camp. Media coverage included the *Los Angeles Times*, Reuters, CNN, and local affiliates of all major networks.

✔ Another client of mine, the Park Central Hotel in New York City, wanted to publicize a $50-million renovation. That may sound like a big deal, but it's actually far from a record in the world of high-priced hotel renovations. To draw attention and press coverage, the hotel sponsored a "Renovate Yourself Day" in its lobby. People could come in for a free facial, manicure, hairstyling, massage, shoeshine, and even a consultation with a plastic surgeon who used a video imaging system to show people what they'd look like before and after a face-lift or tummy tuck. The event — and the hotel's renovation — got coverage on all four network affiliates, national TV, and a feature story in the *Daily News*.

Events like these can help elevate you above your competition, because you're playing on a different field. The creative theme and the fact that you're doing an event are what set you apart from your competitors who may publicize a company only by doing the usual press release (for example, "Hotel Undergoes $50-Million Renovation"). Yawn.

With a little creativity, you can apply this kind of thinking to come up with an event to publicize your own business. Just follow these steps:

1. **Decide the key message that you want to communicate and whom you want to reach.**

   A local dry cleaner, for example, may want to compete with other dry cleaners — for example, a national chain — by showing that the local store is a cornerstone of the community.

2. **Think of a way to demonstrate the message.**

   In the example in Step 1, how can you prove — not just *say* — that you are a part of the community? Perhaps you can make some kind of donation or offer a service.

3. **Decide how you tie that donation or service to your product or service.**

   A dry cleaner cleans, so perhaps the dry cleaner can sponsor a "Clean Up Happytown Day." Residents come to the messy downtown park for a cleanup effort; the dry cleaner provides the garbage bags, entertainment, and refreshment for the volunteers. And what does a dry cleaner clean? Clothes. So maybe the dry cleaner invites local residents to bring in old clothes, which the dry cleaner then cleans and donates to a local shelter.

Planning the Event and Logistics

Although a clever theme and a creative approach can make your event, poor planning can break it. Event planning is a detail-oriented task, so assign someone on your team who's good at details to handle it.

Here are a few tips to help you plan your event:

- ✔ **Determine the number of attendees, the location, and the exact time and day of the event early in the planning process.** Many of your needs depend on the season, weather, time of day, and day of the week on which you hold your event.

- ✔ **Visit the event site as early as possible in the planning stage, both before and during the creative process.** Take your team to the site for part of the brainstorming process.

- ✔ **Do a mental walk-through of the event from start to finish.** Write down each of the major steps and the tasks involved with each. Prepare a schedule with deadlines, and assign people to each task. Specify when every detail will be completed and by whom. Double-check timing on everything that must be ordered. Allow time for delays; they happen more often than not.

- ✔ **Communicate regularly with all vendors, participants, and volunteers to make sure that they're on schedule.** Ongoing communication helps them maintain a comfort level and makes them less likely to pull out. If they do pull out, you'll know about it in time to find a replacement.

- ✔ **During the mental walk-through, visualize the event.** Do you need sound, lighting, décor, signage, tents, a stage, a band shell, heat, air-conditioning, entertainment, music, toilets, dressing rooms, water, security, food, drinks, storage for supplies, a coat room?

- ✔ **Make a rough floor plan of the event.** Make sure that you have enough space. Keep updating the floor plan as the event proceeds.

- ✔ **Leave out no details, no matter how small.** The success or failure of an event is in the organization and the precision of details. If everything is perfectly organized and all the details are correctly done, your event is more likely to be a success.

- ✔ **Write down everything.** Make detailed checklists. Go over them again and again. The more often you review them, the more details you can add.

✔ **Make an agenda or time line for the event itself.** Everything must be perfectly timed, in many cases to the second. Have rehearsals until you get the timing right.

✔ **At a pre-event meeting, give all staff and participants an information package.** The package should contain any press releases (refer to Chapter 8) regarding the event, an overview, the event agenda or time line, the responsibilities of each person, staff schedules, a layout or map of the event, a schedule of breaks for the staff, location of rest areas, and location of food and beverages. Give out uniforms at that time if you want your people to wear them.

WARNING!

A word about timing. You may ask, "How can we make sure our event isn't ruined by a hurricane or overshadowed by a scandal or crime that steals the headlines that day?" The answer is: You can't. Unforeseen events happen all the time, and there's nothing you can do about them. That's what makes events so risky.

For example, in 2005 a lot of planning went into an event my firm scheduled for a major retailer in downtown Chicago at the same exact time the city scheduled the White Sox World Series Victory Parade, one of the great sports stories of modern day. (The Sox hadn't won the Series since 1917.) Needless to say, that dampened the effect on our event. I'm fond of telling clients who want to do an event that, if they name any major news event — a war, an airline crash, a political scandal — I can tell them about one of our special events that the headlines preempted that day. It's just a risk you take.

Publicizing Your Event

The tools for reaching the press discussed throughout this book — phone, e-mail (Chapter 16), press releases (Chapter 8), pitch letters (Chapter 11), and meetings — apply equally to promoting events. Because events are more time critical than many other promotions, I suggest that you e-mail or fax your materials for faster delivery and a slightly greater sense of urgency.

Should you create some sort of clever invitation to lure the press to your event? If the concept doesn't intrigue them, they won't go, no matter what you send. But if the event is appealing, they'll come. A press release announcing the event does fine as an invitation.

As for TV coverage, watch the evening news. On most local affiliates, the last story is always a light feature piece. If your event catches the producer's interest, this is the spot in which it will probably run.

Measuring Event Results

My measure of a promotional event's success is simple: If it doesn't get major press coverage, it's a failure.

The event itself is important, but it's the PR effort to promote the event that makes or breaks it. As I discuss in Chapters 8 and 11, the key is strong press releases widely distributed to the appropriate media outlets and diligent telephone follow-up to all of them, with an eye toward convincing as many as possible to cover the event.

I don't care how many people came or the impression you made on them. Given the time, expense, and sheer work involved in sponsoring an event, it's only worth the cost and trouble — in my mind — if you get media coverage.

Thousands of people turned up to watch the IKEA a.i.r Open Golf Tournament. Throughout the golf course, in the open air, pieces of IKEA's new, inflatable a.i.r furniture were blown up and displayed.

Those thousands of people in attendance saw the new furniture, but the real benefit was the press coverage, which gave us more than 40 million media impressions. (A *media impression* means that a person saw, read, or heard about the product in the media. If a TV news story covers an event and the viewership is 100,000, that counts as another 100,000 media impressions for that campaign.)

When bad news happens to good events

Events are risky because coverage of your event can be preempted by the news of the day, and that's a factor you cannot control. As I mention earlier in this chapter, this has happened so frequently that if you name a world crisis, I can probably tell you the PR event I was having that day.

Baseball player Cal Ripken, Jr., appeared one morning for my client Itsy Bitsy Entertainment at a major licensing trade show in Manhattan. I found out the night before his appearance that

Vice President Al Gore was coming to the city! Fortunately, Gore arrived in the afternoon. Had he come in the morning, I guarantee the press would have covered the Gore visit and ignored our Cal Ripken promotion. Fortunately, that was not the case, and the event helped Itsy Bitsy make the front page of the *New York Times* business section. But it could have easily gone sour; we were extremely lucky.

A large, well-attended event can attract as many as 5,000 people, but a well-publicized event can reach hundreds of thousands more through media coverage. Attaining that press coverage is the real objective of promotional events.

The shorter the event, the smaller the window of opportunity for the media to cover it. Whenever possible, I make an event two days to maximize the opportunity for media coverage.

Chapter 20

Spotting and Seizing Opportunities

*T*he reason that so many companies get so little PR is that they don't show up. Opportunities present themselves every day, yours for the taking. But most people never see them. In this chapter, I show you how to condition yourself to spot PR opportunities as well as act to take advantage of them.

Remembering the Importance of Timing

I already said that part of getting a feel for PR is to consume media from the point of view of the PR professional, not as the general public. Doing so is especially important in the quest to identify and exploit PR opportunities. When you read the papers and watch the evening news with an eye toward spotting PR opportunities, you notice patterns emerging that you never really paid attention to before. For example:

✔ On April 15, the evening news always does a feature story about the last-minute taxpayers — every year.

✔ On the last day of public school, the media run stories on preparing for the summer and finding activities to keep kids busy and entertained.

✔ Stories on how to give flowers, buy flowers, or arrange flowers always run around Mother's Day.

The fact is, the media are always going to do "built-in" stories. And because they're always looking for a fresh angle to an old story, that's where you come in. If you can provide that fresh angle in a way that promotes your product, company, or cause, you can ride the coattails of the story they were already planning.

An example is "Petting Day at the Post Office," a campaign we did for a pet manufacturers association. The objective was to promote pet ownership as healthy by demonstrating that pets help relieve people's stress.

We know that TV always sends cameras to the post office the evening of April 15 to do a short feature piece on last-minute taxpayers standing in line to file returns. We put a petting zoo in the post office and invited frazzled taxpayers to pet a cuddly puppy or kitten after finally getting their returns in the mail.

Naturally, the cameras turned to the petting zoo, showing the once-nervous taxpayers now relaxed and smiling as they petted the animals. The reason the campaign succeeded: timing.

The quintessential light campaign? To be sure, it's a little fluffy (pun intentional). But actually, it demonstrates an important message — the need to reduce stress — in a visual (and highly memorable) way. Sure, the campaign is cute. But it's also on target with the client's strategy.

Few things are as stressful as preparing your tax returns, and April 15 is the only day of the year when the broadcast media universally focus on taxes. If we had put up a petting zoo anywhere else at any other time of the year, I am convinced that Petting Day would not have received nearly as much coverage as it did.

Reacting to Current News and Events

Opportunities can be keyed to one-time events as well as recurring events. For a decade, *Seinfeld* was the leading comedy on TV, so the ending of the show was big news. Now, the people behind *Seinfeld* said many times that it was a show about nothing. So for one client we devised a campaign we called "Thanks for Nothing, *Seinfeld*."

The objectives were to reach a particular target audience — the demographics of which just happened to match the same audience *Seinfeld* reached — and get 100,000 consumers in this audience to sample a bag of potato chips.

Because *Seinfeld* was about nothing, nothing was what you had to do to get a free bag of these chips. Any consumer who sent in a bag or envelope containing nothing would get a free bag of chips. This campaign received enormous media coverage and won several PR awards. In fact, the *Seinfeld* people asked to use the story in their own promotions for the last *Seinfeld* episode.

Looking for an Opening

Do you have a marketing problem that PR can solve, but you can't think of an angle that would appeal to the media? If you think creatively, chances are you can find some way to tie it in to current events or news.

Astor Chocolate is a fine chocolate maker with a brand awareness problem: Nobody knows who they are. Yet when you stay at a fine hotel, the chances are 70 percent that the chocolate left on your pillow at bedtime is an Astor.

How to tie this in with anything? After some brain-stretching, we came up with "The 'Square One' Academy Awards Wake-Up Call." Every year, the Academy Awards show runs longer and longer, forcing people who want to watch until the end to stay up later and later. In this campaign, we promised that if you contacted us, you could stay up as late as you wanted and not oversleep, because we would give you a wake-up call along with free chocolates for your pillow.

To maximize your PR coverage, strive to go where the cameras already are. Now, where are the cameras on the Fourth of July? At the fireworks. How about on Labor Day? At the lake and shore, filming the bathers and boaters.

Another of our clients, Progressive Boat Insurance, wanted to show that it cared about the safety of the boat owners it insured. We came up with "Keys, Please," which was a variation of the liquor campaigns encouraging people who become inebriated at bars to give their keys to friends who can drive them home: We offered, during the Labor Day weekend, a free towing service for boat owners who got too drunk to drive their boats safely (see Figure 20-1).

Note that promoting safe boating is not only good for Progressive Boat Insurance's image, but it also literally goes right to the bottom line: The fewer boating accidents its policyholders have, the lower the dollar amounts of policy payouts.

Figure 20-1:
Progressive
Boat
Insurance
"Keys
Please"
press
release.

For Immediate Release

Contact: Tim Schramm
Jericho Communications
212/645-6900

PROGRESSIVE LAUNCHES *FIRST-OF-ITS-KIND* PILOT PROGRAM FOR BOATERS THIS LABOR DAY

*"Keys... Please" Program Urges Boaters
To Have Fun, Safely*

Cleveland, OH, August 30, 1999--- It's Labor Day... a time for everyone to get outside and enjoy the last rays of summer. With the waterways jammed with summer-end revelers taking their boats out for one last spin, it's important to realize that safety on the waterways is equally as important as safety on the roadways.

That's why Progressive Watercraft Insurance is launching *"Keys... Please,"* a new pilot program to help provide boaters with a safe and fun holiday weekend. The program is providing a free towing service for those boaters who have had too much to drink and are concerned about operating their boat safely. As an added safety feature, for people who find out at the last minute that they have more guests than life jackets, Progressive is also loaning out adult and child-size life jackets throughout the entire weekend.

This unique program will be offered throughout the weekend for all boaters on Lake Erie (the "Flats"). Throughout the day beginning Friday, September 3 through Monday, September 6, Progressive will be patrolling the area in a specially marked boat....

"Our number one concern is that people have fun but also act responsibly this Labor Day weekend," comments Jeanette Hisek, Product Manager, Progressive Watercraft Insurance. "We developed this program because it exemplifies everything Progressive stands for – serving people the best that we can, reducing risks, and responding fully to their needs and concerns. We want everyone to have fun this Labor Day and to do so in the safest way possible"....

Getting Messages Noticed Quickly

Lots of mid-size and large PR firms tell their clients that public relations is a strategic process and that they should be patient for results. And doing the strategic planning, as outlined in Chapter 2, takes time.

But almost no client is patient for results. If I don't get lots of press for my clients — and fast! — they'll be unhappy and restless. So how do you get the campaign off to a quick start after the strategy is approved?

The surest and quickest way to get PR is to go where the press already is and grab your share of the existing media spotlight. Doing so is a lot easier and more effective than trying to get them to haul out that spotlight and bring it just for you.

Seasonal or holiday tie-ins are perennial favorites. Linking your message to current events requires faster thinking and action, but it can work wonders when you pull it off. When there is a hot news story and you come up with an idea to piggyback on it, your window of opportunity is extremely short — typically a week and rarely more than two weeks (O.J. Simpson and Monica Lewinsky had unusual longevity). After that, it's old news and the campaign won't work.

Chapter 21

Knowing What to Do in a PR Crisis

....

....

*T*he more prepared you are, the better the chances that you can survive a crisis — however long the odds of its occurrence are — if it comes. If you're skeptical of the need for crisis planning, keep this fact in mind: Many companies never have more than one crisis, because the first crisis they have puts them out of business. I wrote this chapter so this doesn't happen to you.

Defining a PR Crisis

I define a *crisis* as an event, rumor, or story that has the potential to affect your reputation, image, or credibility in a negative way. Examples include everything from product tampering (remember Tylenol?) and contamination to alleged discrimination or lawsuits (Wal-Mart is a recent example of the latter). The stock market once dipped on a false rumor that former Federal Reserve Chairman, Alan Greenspan, had been killed in a car accident.

Most small businesses think that "crisis PR" is the concern of only Fortune 500 companies. But a crisis can strike any organization at any time. For your business, potential crisis situations may include the following:

✔ Public health issues (for example, a toxic spill or a cancer-causing product)

✔ Safety and security issues

✔ Financial and business issues

✔ Environmental issues

- ✔ Disasters (product tampering, service outages)
- ✔ Business practices and ethics
- ✔ Worker misconduct
- ✔ Legal issues
- ✔ Accidents and disasters (driver accidents, crashes, fires, building collapses)
- ✔ False advertising
- ✔ Customer complaints
- ✔ Out-of-stock products

If you think that your tiny business, out of the public eye, is invulnerable to a crisis, you're wrong. Smaller businesses, which often rely on one or two key customers, can lose that business at the drop of a hat. For this reason, I advocate planning for any possible crisis that could occur.

Developing a Crisis Management Plan

Having a crisis plan is like buying insurance. Nobody wants to spend the money or invest the time until a crisis happens, and then everyone panics because they don't know what to do. This can kill a company or destroy a brand.

Making sure a plan (that outlines exactly what you're going to do) is in place before something happens is a very worthwhile use of your time and money. The moment the crisis happens is the wrong time to come up with a plan. You need to know simple things like answers to the following questions:

- ✔ Who makes the decisions?
- ✔ How do you get in touch with the CEO at home?
- ✔ Who's available? What if the crisis occurs at 3 a.m. in the Far East? Three key people — the head of PR, the head of legal, and the CEO — might need to talk in the middle of the night. If you have no plan in place, try to find them all at that hour and then try crafting a response. It's not easy.

In this section, I provide you with an outline of crisis response procedures and responsibilities for employees most likely to be involved in handling a crisis situation. A crisis alert may come from different levels such as customer service, sales, e-commerce, international, and so on.

Identifying a crisis

If a crisis is identified, the senior employee is responsible for:

- Collecting information and preparing the crisis fact sheet.

- Requesting assistance from the crisis communications team via the crisis administrator. When a crisis occurs, you won't have time to find the lawyer's phone number or locate the CEO on the weekend. That's why the Crisis Communication Team is established in advance. This team includes any and all resources you may have to call in the event of a crisis: the top decision-maker, your legal expert (in house counsel), your top communications person (that could be you), and all division heads. Basically, it includes anyone with expertise on a potentially relevant subject and in a position to make a decision and/or the people with the most expertise on issues that could be raised.

- Contacting the deputy crisis administrator (in the absence of the crisis administrator).

- Sequentially calling all crisis communications team members if neither the crisis administrator or his deputy can be found.

Assessing and reviewing the crisis

After the crisis administrator has been contacted, he is responsible for:

- Gathering and recording all pertinent facts on the crisis fact sheet

- Assessing the scope and nature of the crisis, including damage or potential damage

- Alerting the appropriate members of the crisis communications team

- Determining the timing and format of the crisis communications team meeting (either in person or by conference call)

- Contacting additional parties (appropriate employees or external individuals) to secure their involvement

- Disseminating crisis fact sheets and other relevant information to crisis communications team members

The crisis communications team meeting

The crisis communications team meeting will involve

- ✔ The election of a crisis manager, based on the nature and scope of the crisis
- ✔ A crisis debriefing, including new developments/updates, by the crisis administrator

Planning a crisis response

After the crisis communications team is assembled, under the leadership of the crisis manager, the team is responsible for immediately:

- ✔ Planning a crisis response and ensuring its execution
- ✔ Establishing communications strategies to address the crisis situation (for example, selecting an appropriate spokesperson)
- ✔ Allocating responsibilities to the crisis communications team members
- ✔ Identifying crisis situation response tactics to be implemented by others (employees or external individuals)
- ✔ Monitoring the media via the public relations team (see Chapter 12)

The crisis manager must ensure, at all times, that the crisis response is being executed by the crisis communications team as well as additional employees and external individuals.

Communicating with key publics

Throughout the crisis, it is imperative that the crisis communications team communicates with the company's key *publics* or stakeholders (that is, any group that may have a heightened interest in what the crisis is). For instance, if you're a publicly held company, the shareholders fall into that category. If it's about a product distributed via retail, stakeholders include your retail customers. And it always includes the press.

- ✔ **Employees:** When possible, employees should be informed about a crisis situation before the media are informed. The crisis communications team must determine the most efficient way to communicate with employees (for example, in staff meetings). Be sure to keep the "front-line" employees — such as the switchboard/receptionist and customer service call center reps — updated on where to direct customer questions and incoming calls regarding the crisis.

✔ **Affiliated parties:** Be sure to keep affiliated parties (such as vendors) in the loop on crisis situations they're affected by or play a role in. The crisis communications team must determine the method and scope of communication.

✔ **Consumers:** In crisis situations, it may be necessary for the company to communicate directly with consumers without the assistance of the media. The crisis communications team must determine the best method of communication (for example, e-mail, direct mail).

✔ **Media:** An extremely influential public. One thing all of your key publics will have in common is that they read the morning newspaper. So the press is the most important group to focus on. (See more about this in Chapter 11.)

Remembering the Rules in a Crisis

The first rule in a crisis is this: Facilitate information in a quick, accurate, and timely manner. How quickly you communicate the facts to the victims, press, investors, shareholders, and other audiences determines, in large part, how you emerge from the situation. The faster you move, the better the message is received. The longer the public guesses, the worse off the company.

Here are some other critical rules for acting in a PR crisis:

✔ **Always tell the truth.** Do not be misleading or dishonest.

✔ **Be prepared.** Have a communications plan in place before disaster strikes. Don't wait until it happens to start thinking, "What do we do?"

✔ **Act as though you care.** Demonstrate compassion.

✔ **Move quickly.** Don't stand there stunned.

✔ **Make fast decisions and swift adjustments.** If you're faced with having to spend money to clean up the situation, do it now (while it seems as though it's your choice) instead of later (when it seems as though you're acting only because of pressure).

✔ **Never say, "No comment."** If you don't have an answer, say so and then get it.

✔ **Return all calls from the press promptly.** Every day you do not respond to an accusation, the bad press the situation generates gets exponentially worse.

✔ **Don't avoid the press.** Actively seek opportunities to get in front of the cameras and tell your story.

✔ **Admit when you messed up, apologize, explain how you're going to fix it, and then do what you promised.**

✔ **Always carry a checklist of important contacts' phone numbers (home phone of CEO, cell phone of legal counsel, and so on).**

Demonstrating Care and Compassion

I say throughout this book that PR is an art of demonstration — showing rather than stating your message — and crisis management is no exception. When you just *say* that you care and are sorry, people are cynical. When you *demonstrate* compassion and caring in a dramatic and distinctive way, people not only believe your message but also pay attention to and remember it.

For example, years ago I was handling PR for an off-Broadway play. Well, the play got a terrible review in the *New York Times,* which usually spells death for such a production. We felt that the *Times* critic had made a mistake and wanted to get this message across without sounding like sour grapes. We sent out a press release saying, "Even *The New York Times* Makes Mistakes!" The gimmick: If people found a typo in the *New York Times,* they could send it in to us and we would mail them a free ticket to the show. The campaign generated a lot of press and demonstrated the point — that reviews do not have the final word on a piece of art or entertainment, but are just one person's opinion — in a fresh, credible, and nondefensive manner.

Another client, a retailer of home furnishings and accessories, published the wrong phone number in its catalog, and suddenly some poor guy was getting hundreds of phone calls every day. Our solution? Not only did we pay for a new phone number for him, but we also refurnished his home with our client's furniture absolutely free. He was delighted, and the press loved the story.

Customer service surveys show that, if a customer has a problem but you resolve it quickly and correctly, the customer actually becomes more loyal to you than he was before the problem occurred. It's the same with a PR crisis: If you resolve the crisis quickly and get your story out to the media, the event can actually *strengthen* your brand image — which is why I see most crisis management as an opportunity rather than a threat. Properly handled, response to crisis is a showcase for great leadership. It can increase corporate visibility in a positive way, highlighting character and competence.

For example, when a food-delivery client of mine was being widely viewed as promoting unsafe driver safety on "rushed" deliveries, we had to demonstrate a different example. My client was getting blamed because its advertising stressed fast delivery. The truth, however, was that the company could deliver faster because it had a more efficient cooking operation than its competitors.

To demonstrate this message — that our fast delivery was due to faster cooking, not reckless driving — we held a contest among company employees nationwide. The winning cook was the subject of a full-page profile in *People* magazine and appeared as a guest on both the *Late Show with David Letterman* and *Good Morning America.*

Another client, a clothing company, called to tell me it would be several weeks late in delivering initial shipments of a much-promoted new clothing line. We immediately sent out a release on the theme "Caught with Our Pants Down," saying that we had screwed up and would be two weeks late. To dramatize the message, we said that for the first 1,000 people to send their pants to us (actually, a pair of underwear), we would make a donation to the homeless in their names and send each of those 1,000 people a free pair of our product.

Thinking of Every Crisis as a Red Alert

When the threat got really serious in the old *Star Trek* series — like when the Romulans were about to attack — Captain Kirk invariably upgraded the ship's status from yellow alert to red alert. I advise my clients to treat any PR crisis as a red alert. The keys to doing so are to

- ✔ Make the situation a management priority.
- ✔ Have plans in place before crises happen. If you wait until they happen before creating a plan, you're too late.
- ✔ Respond with same-day speed. "Tomorrow" isn't good enough.

In crisis plans for large corporate clients, we say that every one of the top management people is always "on call." If a crisis occurs, every key decision-maker must be available within two hours — by phone, if that's the best they can do, but preferably gathered in the same room. After they're in the room (or connected with the people in the room via speaker phone), no one leaves until consensus is reached on what's to be done. The person managing crisis communications should have the home phone numbers of all executives in the group and shouldn't hesitate to call them at any time of the day or night.

Not having the team together slows decision-making, which can be devastating for PR purposes — the media's job is to investigate and get at the truth, and their deadline for doing so is tomorrow (for print), tonight (for broadcast), or even now (for the Web). For example, one American shoe manufacturer was faced with a rumor that a street gang wore its sneakers. They responded like a snail rather than in a flash, and the brand was destroyed.

Managing a Crisis with Success

Remember Dorothy's famous line to her dog in the film *The Wizard of Oz* — "Toto, I've a feeling we're not in Kansas anymore"? The next time you get that queasy, "We have a problem" feeling in your business, and your concern has to do with media exposure that threatens to damage corporate reputation, take a deep breath, get calm, and put the following tactics into practice:

✔ Make every effort to gather the pertinent facts, quickly assess the situation, and respond to key audiences in an open and honest manner.

✔ Enact the necessary measures to swiftly resolve the situation without jeopardizing the integrity and safety of your company, your co-workers, and your customers.

✔ Appoint executives to a standing crisis communications team who will be called on in times of crisis to make decisions and determine policy. Members should include the CEO, COO, CFO, PR manager, marketing manager, and customer service manager at the very least. Appoint one member of the team — typically the PR manager — as the primary liaison between the team and the public. Also appoint a deputy crisis administrator to serve as the backup for the primary administrator.

✔ Educate employees, especially top and middle managers, about your crisis procedures.

✔ Establish communication strategies to address crisis situations. Select the appropriate spokesperson. Create press materials. Communicate your crisis response to all key audiences: employees, government agencies, vendors, consumers, and the media.

✔ Continually monitor the media for signs of escalation. If signs are apparent, adjustments may be required. Remain objective and be willing to make the necessary adjustments. Remember that changing your strategy is okay if your original plan isn't working as well as you thought it would.

✔ At all times, take pains not to create the perception that your organization doesn't care or lacks integrity.

✔ Be as objective as possible when evaluating data, analyzing consumer and media reactions, and making judgments about the effectiveness of your crisis communication program. Is the media coverage positive or negative? What key message points are being made in media stories about the crisis? If they don't reflect your key message points, perhaps you could communicate them more clearly, credibly, or dramatically.

✔ After the crisis has passed, put together a post-crisis summary report. It should include the cause of the crisis, extent and tone of media coverage, suggested improvements in the crisis response process, ways to implement those changes, and possible alterations to company policy and procedures.

✔ After you have overcome the short-term threat, work to rebuild the goodwill from each of your key audiences over the long term.

Chapter 22

Evaluating PR Results

*T*he public relations industry has tried to take on the measurement issue for years and develop a system to give empirical value to PR results. So far, the industry's efforts have left us with a good-news/bad-news situation.

The good news is that the PR industry has developed a number of different formulas to calculate results, most notably *advertising equivalency* (AE) and *media impressions* (MI). The bad news is that both of these formulas are flawed, are limited in their use, and leave you with comparative value, not empirical value.

Generally speaking (and understandably so), advertising budgets are significantly larger and part of their budgets includes a mechanism to research and evaluate results. Sometimes the cost of that research and evaluation is equivalent to an entire PR budget. Therein lies the dilemma for the PR industry.

What you will find in this chapter, then, is a variety of ways to both analyze your public relations results and, equally as important, ideas about how to communicate them to the people within your organization who control the purse strings.

Measuring by Advertising Equivalency

The way advertising equivalency (AE) works is to simply look at the media outlet in which a PR placement runs, how long it is, and its position within the medium (for example, front page versus back of the magazine). You then compute what placing an advertisement of the same size and in the same location would cost. For instance, if you secured an article in the *New York Times* on the third page of the Metro section, and the article ran a quarter-page, how much would it cost to run an ad in that spot? Or for TV, if you place a spokesperson on *Good Morning America* at 7:55 a.m., how much would it cost to run a commercial there? You then take all your placements, compute their values, and add them together, and you have your AE for that PR campaign.

I've said that PR achieves marketing objectives at a small fraction of the cost of advertising, and the AE clearly shows why this is true. If you're a do-it-yourselfer, your out-of-pocket costs for mailing a press release to a few hundred media outlets is only a few hundred dollars. When you add up the equivalent ad-space cost for the pickups of that release, you often find that paying for the space would have cost thousands or even tens of thousands of dollars or more.

A major flaw of the AE formula: It is, in a sense, unfair to your PR program, because a press pickup is often more effective as an influencer of the consumer's mind than a paid ad of equivalent size. Consumers view advertising skeptically, precisely because they know that it's a sales effort from a paid sponsor. But consumers view PR as objective because the source is a neutral reporter or journalist, not a paid promoter. In fact, many consumers are unaware that much of what they read, see, and hear in the media originates from PR agencies rather than from the investigative work of journalists. So the key assumption of the AE formula — that an ad of a certain size, space, and location, has equal value to a PR placement of like size, space, and location — is wrong.

For example, best-selling author, Matthew Lesko has a very successful business in which he self-publishes books on how to get government grants and loans for everything from buying a house to learning how to play the piano. I did not only Lesko's PR but also his direct-response TV commercials at the same time. I would book Matthew on press interviews, he would talk and then give the toll-free number (this was pre-Internet), and people would order the book like mad. When he went on *Larry King Live,* we sold about 30,000 books in the first half-hour after the show via phone orders.

One day, we booked Matthew on the *Oprah Winfrey Show* as part of a panel. Although this was before Oprah's Book Club came into existence, the show was still considered the best spot on television for promoting a book. (To give you some idea how effective TV PR is on the top talk shows, I once booked a chef on *Donahue,* which had a smaller audience than *Oprah,* a week before Thanksgiving. That one appearance drove the chef's book to the number-one spot on the *New York Times* bestseller list.) The *Oprah* booking for Matthew did not have quite the same results, but orders still skyrocketed. So I figured: If an interview on the show worked, why not run our direct-response ad during the show? If there is ad equivalency, then by definition we should have similar results.

Well, we didn't. Not even close. In fact, the commercial generated almost no orders at all.

Making Media Impressions

Media impressions (MI) measure how many people see your message. For instance, say that your press release is picked up in a women's magazine with a circulation of 200,000 readers. You've made 200,000 media impressions. To calculate the media impressions for print media, you take the circulation figure and multiply it by 2.5. Therefore, the 200,000 circulation times 2.5 gives you 500,000 total media impressions.

The reason you multiply the print circulation by 2.5 is that it's assumed that a newspaper or magazine, although one person purchases it, is passed on to and read by others. In the publishing industry, this phenomenon is known as *pass-along circulation.*

For television and radio, media impressions are simply the audience that watches or listens to the show as computed by a national rating agency such as Neilsen or Arbitron. If you're a guest on a radio talk show reaching an audience of one million, you've made one million media impressions.

Now, the problem with media impressions is that they base specific distinctions on general assumptions. Take the 2.5 factor by which you multiply readership. To start with, that number is not consistently used throughout the industry. I use 2.5 as my multiplier to be conservative. But whatever factor you choose, how do you know that a newspaper or magazine has actually been passed on to other people?

The 2.5 multiplier has been used for years. If it was accurate back then, then logically it should be reduced today. Why? Because people don't have the same relationship to print that they once had. During the Depression, it was considered good manners to leave your newspaper on the train so that someone else could read it. Today, we don't share nearly as much. And numbers show that younger people don't read as much as they used to, so the theory that the daily paper is passed around the family needs revising. Recycling also must be affecting that pass-along habit: Many of us now feel guilty if we don't get that paper in the blue bin as soon as we're done. After it's recycled, it can't be passed around.

Increased *vertical publishing* (creating narrow-interest magazines catering to specific market niches) may also affect pass-along circulation. When there was one *People* magazine, everyone who liked *People* wanted to read it. Now there is *Teen People* and *People en Español* and *People.com.* The parent getting regular *People* isn't going to want to read a pass-along copy of *Teen People* from her teenager. Publications are increasingly being targeted just for you, indicating that the multiplier should be lower.

And other problems exist with MI. Using viewership numbers as calculations can be misleading. Just because the evening news has a 350,000 viewership on an average night doesn't mean that anywhere near that number of people are watching your story. Just because a newspaper has 200,000 readers doesn't mean that many people are reading the section, column, or article that you're in.

And then there's the same issue as with ad equivalency. MI assumes an equal relationship of attention between an ad and editorial content — a mistaken assumption that often penalizes PR.

Although neither AE nor MI has real empirical value, each has some value. Both measures are useful in comparing one PR campaign or initiative to another. They can show whether your PR efforts are working better or worse than they were previously, or whether one tactic has outperformed another. But that's about as far as they go.

Using Key Message Points

A somewhat more valuable — albeit more-difficult-to-compile — measure of PR performance is *key message points.* You begin by identifying, in the planning stage of your PR campaign, the key message points you want to convey. A potato-chip company, for example, may have as a key message point: "Our potato chips taste lighter." Another may be that the chips are less oily.

You deliberately work key message points into all your PR campaigns and materials. When you get media coverage, you analyze the stories and count the key message points. You then add up all the times key message points are mentioned to get a total count. If your key message point is "fewer calories" and three articles mention your lower calorie count two times each, you get six key message points.

A common mistake that amateurs make is to seek, get, and be thrilled about publicity that is devoid of their key message points. People love to see their names in the paper or tell their relatives and friends, "Watch the news — I'm on TV tonight." But if you don't communicate a key message point during the exposure, what good is it? How has it helped your business? Publicity that doesn't contain your key message points is a waste of your time and money.

Market Research Isn't Always the Answer

Ad people use focus groups to test their ads. They have used focus groups for decades, but focus groups don't always give accurate results. If focus groups worked all the time, you would never see a bad ad. Well, here's a shocker: There are lots of bad ads.

The cry from everyone hiring a PR or advertising firm is *accountability*. "We want to see direct sales from every dollar we spend!" clients shout. Business owners and managers are hoping for the day when every ad or PR campaign drives an immediate sale. Certainly, the rise of *e-commerce* — the ability to buy products over the Web — provides a new electronic link between marketing communication and purchasing. It would be a great accomplishment for the practice of PR if we could always directly tie a sale of the product to an article in the newspaper, but for many categories of products and services, it's not a reality. People don't make most of their purchases or become loyal customers in a split second. It takes time.

Companies like loyal customers because convincing the loyal ones to buy more costs far less money than converting someone to your brand for the first time. By striving to make every aspect of your marketing mix generate an immediate sale, you risk taking the focus off building a personality for your brand — an image that a customer can relate to and be loyal to.

A good example is IKEA. When IKEA opens a new store in a city, just by reputation they get enormous sales volume in the first two days they're open. How much more money would they have to spend to reach out and convince that many people to come to the store if no one felt a relationship with the IKEA image?

Of course, some ads or PR campaigns turn a company around in such a way that there is an immediate lift in sales. I think the Pepsi Challenge of a couple of decades ago had that effect. It happens in PR, too. When Dan Rather mentioned one of my clients, Ken Hakuta — who was selling the Wacky Wall Walker toy — it started a nationwide fad.

Watching the Word Spread: Hiring Clipping Services

Print coverage spreads everywhere fast. It gets syndicated and picked up over the Internet. It could even be read on the 6 o'clock news in Des Moines, Iowa, and you wouldn't know about it. That's why you have to track it.

I need my client CEO to hold the Dallas Morning News in his hand so he can see how effective the PR campaign we're running is. Clipping services make this possible.

For print and the Internet, the first thing to do is sign up for free news alerts at both Google (www.google.com/alerts) and Yahoo! (http://alerts.yahoo.com/). Both search engines offer a simple way to be notified every time an article with the company name, keyword, or keyword phrase you choose is posted in a news article.

But even with news alerts in place, you won't see everything, because some pieces that run in the newspaper won't run on the Web, and vice versa.

So if you're serious about tracking your press coverage, you also need a *clipping service* — a company that collects articles from newspapers and periodicals as well as tapes from broadcast coverage.

In the "old days" (actually not so long ago), it used to take six weeks for the clips to come in. Now, you can be notified the day of (or within the hour, depending on your budget), and you can get your hands on the clips the same day or the day after.

For print clips, don't just order the text of the article. You also need the actual page from the newspaper so you can see how and where the clip is placed. Are you buried in the left corner of page 11 or on the cover of the Business section? Does it have a photo? If you only get the text, you'll be missing important information and will, therefore, be shortchanging your evaluation of the program.

For TV, getting clips is even more important. You might think it would be easy enough to get the clips directly from the TV stations but that's not their job. They aren't in the business of providing tapes for you, and asking for tapes could easily strain your relationships. You can tape the program yourself, of course, but you won't have a professionally edited version for your library and for future PR usage.

The best option is to hire a clipping service. It will provide you with a professionally edited clip that shows the beginning of the show, the teasers about your segment, and your actual segment.

TV clips are also important because they allow you to evaluate and critique every television appearance you make, with the goal of making each one a bit better. When you're on the air, you don't know how you look, and you can't tell how your body language comes across.

As for how to find a clipping service, start your search at the Web site of the Public Relations Society of America (`www.prsa.org`).

Measuring Inquiries and Sales

If your goal is to generate inquiries or orders rather than to build brand awareness or positioning, you may find it easier to show a direct relationship between PR and sales. This type of public relations is sometimes called *direct-response PR,* because, like an infomercial, direct-mail package, or mail-order ad, its goal is direct response (an inquiry or order) rather than image building.

Marketers traditionally think of public relations as an image-building, rather than a direct-selling, activity, yet PR is one of the most cost-effective and successful methods for generating large volumes of direct inquiries and sales. One of my former clients, Trillium Health Products, used a toll-free number in infomercials selling juice machines. We got the company's juicing expert to do a 20-minute segment on a radio talk show on WBZ in Boston. The callers were invited to phone for a free information booklet on juicing, which contained juicing information but also was a promotional piece for the machine.

Approximately 50,000 listeners called for the free juicing information. Of those, 10 percent bought a $350 juicing machine. That comes out to gross sales of $1.75 million for a single radio placement.

The marketing objectives in direct-response PR are as follows:

✔ Get not only the client's name in the media but also the address, phone number, and Web site so that the client can be reached easily by potential customers interested in finding out more about the product or service.

✔ Generate inquiries directly from PR items as they're published or broadcast.

✔ Increase both the quantity and the quality of sales leads generated by PR — that is, get the greatest number of qualified prospects to inquire about the client's product or service as a direct result of the PR coverage.

✔ If it's feasible, generate direct sales or walk-in trade or traffic from PR items.

In your press releases, include the toll-free number you use in commercials, ads, and direct mail for taking orders. If you sell on the Internet, include your Web address as well.

If you do direct-response PR, make sure that the producer or editor will allow you to feature your phone number or Web address. Without this contact information, you won't get direct orders.

One author who self-published a how-to book went on *Oprah* without checking whether the show would give her toll-free number for orders. It wouldn't and didn't, and her book was not in bookstores. She sold only a handful of books.

Marketing professionals serving clients who seek to generate leads and sales via direct response traditionally recommend such vehicles as direct mail and advertising. Although I believe in direct mail and advertising and frequently use both, they are expensive. Consider direct mail: The cost per thousand for a direct-mail package might be $600, including printing, mailing, postage, and lists. If the response rate is 2 percent, you're getting 20 leads for every 1,000 pieces mailed, at a cost of $30 per lead.

The advantage of direct-response PR over direct mail (and direct-response advertising) is that it generates the same type of direct inquiry or order at a fraction of the cost per response. On the other hand, although you can roll out a direct-mail package that generates a certain percentage of responses to a large number of mailing lists and mail it again and again, you can use a given press release usually only once. (Of course, there are exceptions.)

Therefore, direct-response PR does not necessarily replace traditional direct-mail and print advertising as a response-generating tool, but its cost-effectiveness does suggest that you should almost always use a direct-response PR campaign to supplement or augment direct-mail and space advertising. Experience shows that an offer that works well in direct-mail and direct-response space ads usually works in public relations campaigns, too.

Taking the Long View of PR Success

The bottom line is this: If your PR is successful, it will increase your overall revenues and profits over a period of time. If you're getting a lot of media placements, your audiences are excited, your sales are growing, and the phone is ringing, chances are you have a good PR program; if not, you probably don't.

In most cases, PR can be evaluated in comparison to what came before it, what came after it, and by anecdotal observation. How is your business doing now versus before you started the PR program? Here's a case study to illustrate this point.

A successful New York matrimonial attorney was interested in enhancing his image and developing a strong profile as one of the nation's top authorities. The strategy was to position the attorney as an expert in all areas of family law. Because principals in major cases are inundated by requests for interviews from the media, an outside expert who can provide thoughtful and insightful commentary on legal issues of the day is a valuable commodity to a journalist or reporter.

The PR strategy? When the press covered a high-profile trial (the Trump divorce), the PR counsel and legal counsel prepared pitch letters featuring the attorney's observations on that particular issue, suggesting that journalists use him as a source of "expert legal opinion" in stories they were preparing about the case.

This strategy resulted in a steady flow of publicity as the press became aware of his credentials and began to rely on his expert commentary. The placements ranged from ABC-TV's *Primetime Live* to *Larry King Live* to articles in *Harper's Bazaar*. In addition, the attorney was booked by his PR agency as a regular lecturer for an adult seminar entitled "The Legality of Love." With this newfound publicity and notoriety, even a British journalist took note of all the media attention this attorney was receiving and featured him in a major story in London's *Daily Mail*.

This exposure became an invaluable addition to the attorney's business and following. Calls for consultations poured into his office and, over the course of a year, led to a substantial increase in his total client base. After a year of PR efforts, the attorney and his PR firm are now contacted daily by television producers, magazine editors, and radio commentators for ideas regarding upcoming feature stories and scheduled programs.

Demonstrating Viability of the PR Department (Even in a Crunch)

Here's the thing about PR: It's a great investment if you have a successful program. But the definition of success depends on your company's goals. If you spend $10,000 to do a PR program and revenue increases by a multiple of that investment, it's worth it.

But many people (read: bigwigs) don't really understand how PR works. If you want its viability to be perceived and understood, it's your job to educate the decision-makers. You must always be demonstrating the benefits of your PR program to the people who are allocating the PR dollars.

How should you promote your PR program to them? That depends who your internal audience is. Choose the measurement that will resonate the most with that person or committee. One idea, depending on your budget, is to set up a mechanism to tie sales increases to your PR efforts. You could also use actual customer feedback or show the correlation between peak sales periods and peak PR periods.

The onus is on the practitioner to educate the audience in how PR works and how much value it brings — not once, but on a regular basis, even if it's an audience of one.

Part VI
The Part of Tens

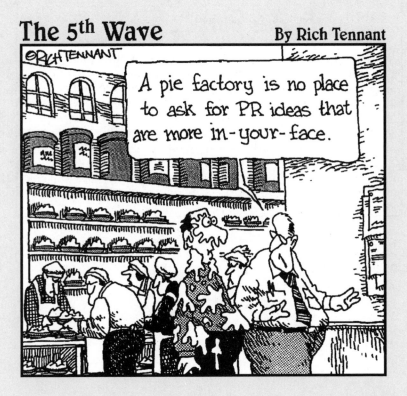

The 5th Wave   By Rich Tennant

A pie factory is no place to ask for PR ideas that are more in-your-face.

In this part . . .

*E*very media maven worth his salt knows David Letterman's Top Ten lists. Well, here are some of our own top ten lists for PR. Chapter 23 presents ten of the most successful and creative public relations campaigns of all time. In Chapter 24, I debunk ten PR myths. Chapter 25 outlines ten reasons to do PR. Chapter 26 shows you how to avoid no-noes with ten things you should never, ever do in PR. And Chapter 27 gives you guidelines for making your PR writing as focused as a laser and as clear as crystal.

Chapter 23

The Ten Greatest PR Coups of All Time

In This Chapter

▶ Overcoming bad publicity

▶ Changing an image to generate appeal

▶ Targeting your audience

▶ Creating PR campaigns that get the job done

What makes a PR campaign great? Two things. First, it has to achieve and surpass its objectives, achieving results beyond what anyone had a right to expect. Second, it has to be memorable — the kind of campaign people will remember 10 years or even 100 years later. If the campaign also pioneers or improves on an innovative idea, practice, or technique, that's icing on the cake.

In this chapter are, in my opinion, the top ten PR coups of all time — stellar examples of using public relations to achieve difficult marketing objectives, all of which stand the test of time. I hope that this list inspires your thinking (and mine) to similar heights.

Lucky Strike

Edward Bernays is widely known as the "father of public relations" for his groundbreaking work in the field. One of his most famous campaigns from the early 1900s was to position Lucky Strike, one of many brands, as the premier cigarette for women. (Keep in mind that this was well before tobacco use was linked to cancer.)

R. A. Patterson founded Lucky Strike in Richmond, Virginia, in 1871. The name refers to what miners made when they found gold during the gold rush — a "lucky strike." Bernays realized that most cigarette marketing at the time was either generic or male oriented. By positioning Lucky Strike as a woman's cigarette, he hoped to capture a dominant share of half of the total market.

In those days, it was acceptable for women to smoke only at home, if at all — and certainly not in public places. A research study commissioned by Bernays on behalf of Lucky Strike showed that women perceived smoking in public as a sign of freedom. In his PR campaign, Bernays positioned Lucky Strike as the "Torches of Freedom" for American women.

Results of this campaign include the fact that Lucky Strike became the number-one cigarette for women. Plus it changed the way both smoking and women were perceived by society.

John D. Rockefeller

John D. Rockefeller, Sr., America's first billionaire, had a reputation for being a ruthless businessman. The public saw him as cold, calculating, controlling, and greedy. And there was some truth to this image: Rockefeller once gave his groundskeeper $5 as a Christmas bonus, only to dock him the same amount of pay for taking Christmas off as a holiday.

What the public did not know was that Rockefeller was an active philanthropist. He had tithed 10 percent of his income since he was a child, and by the time he reached his 66th birthday, that amount approached $100 million.

Bothered by the bad press he received, Rockefeller hired consultant Ivy Lee to change his image. Lee had once been paid $25,000 — a huge sum in those days — for a single day's work with Charles Schwab, CEO of Bethlehem Steel. Lee had shown Schwab how to be more efficient and get more done by making a simple to-do list each day.

Lee immediately began publicizing Rockefeller's generosity and charitable activities, which were not common at the time. One of Lee's ideas was to have Rockefeller carry a roll of shiny dimes and give them away to children in public, with a photographer always present to capture the photo opportunity. Rockefeller gave away more than 30,000 dimes during his lifetime.

This changed and enhanced his reputation and is the beginning of a lifelong strategy for how the Rockefellers promoted philanthropy and the importance of being involved with worthy causes.

Tylenol

Tylenol is a classic case of good crisis planning and execution. In 1982, seven deaths resulted from poisoned Tylenol pills. When reports that someone had tampered with Tylenol and that people had died as a result hit the evening news and front pages, Johnson & Johnson responded by immediately pulling $100 million worth of the product off the shelves in a single day.

The PR was simple but powerful: Johnson & Johnson did the right thing. It didn't harm anyone deliberately or even through a mistake or accident; someone tampered with its product. It could have happened to any manufacturer that sells its products in pharmacies and grocery stores. But instead of pointing out this fact in its defense, J&J focused on solving the problem rather than laying blame somewhere else.

The company was available to the media throughout the crisis to answer questions and provide information. It used daily opinion polls to accurately gauge public reaction and adjust its communications strategy accordingly.

J&J did not ship Tylenol again until a tamper-proof bottle had been designed. When the improved container was ready, J&J reintroduced Tylenol with a major media campaign that included a 30-city teleconference. Within a year, Tylenol had regained its 70 percent market share.

Bill Clinton's 1992 Presidential Campaign

Although history will determine Bill Clinton's place in the rankings of presidents and of men, few dispute that he ran a masterful campaign to beat incumbent George Bush in the 1992 presidential race. Clinton's campaign manager deliberately steered him away from the traditional hard-news venues and toward TV programming targeting a younger audience.

A turning point was Clinton's appearance on the *Arsenio Hall Show,* during which he played his saxophone on national television. Stunts like this humanized him as a candidate and highlighted his relative youth compared to his opponent.

A series of TV roundtables, including one on MTV, showed Clinton as able to answer tough questions. Actually, most of the attendees for these roundtables were idealistic college students who asked big-issue questions (for example, whether Clinton is pro-choice) that made for good television. At the same time, the audience's lack of in-depth political and foreign affairs knowledge — compared with professional journalists — allowed Clinton to avoid complex issues and tough-to-answer questions.

Even back then, rumors of Clinton's marital infidelity were circulating. He immediately went on *60 Minutes* and vigorously denied these accusations, cutting them off before they mushroomed.

The New VW Beetle

When the original VW Beetle was introduced in the 1960s, its low price and odd, bug-shaped appearance made it a popular economy car. But when the New Beetle was introduced in 1998, the price was no longer rock bottom.

What made the New Beetle so popular? In part, a promotional campaign that exploited the nostalgic appeal of the Beetle — people bought it because they remembered it fondly from their youth. According to a Volkswagen press release, the New Beetle "instantly rekindled the magic of its legendary namesake."

A number of creative public relations initiatives helped make the introduction of the New Beetle a success. In March 2000, Volkswagen sponsored a "New Beetle Cup Race" in conjunction with the Atlanta Auto Show, with half a million deutsche marks as prize money. Volkswagen also did an innovative Internet promotion, selling special color editions of the New Beetle only over its Web site. To appeal to die-hard Beetle enthusiasts, VW also introduced New Beetle collectible trading cards. The cards were issued only to people who purchased the car or visited the VW Web site.

Traditionally, car manufacturers publicize their new models by offering test drives to editors of specialized car and consumer magazines, like *Road and Track* and *Consumer Reports*. Breaking with that tradition, VW offered test drives of the New Beetle to editors and producers of more general media outlets such as *USA Today* and *Family Circle*.

Driving the New Beetle brought back fond memories of their teen years to these editors, generating massive media exposure for the car. By turning to consumer media instead of the usual automobile publications, VW immediately moved the campaign to a new playing field on which no other car was competing for attention. Tremendous media coverage followed.

Cabbage Patch Kids

PR can start trends or work to accelerate them. Such is the case with the Cabbage Patch Kids, a line of odd-looking dolls launched by Mattel in the early 1980s.

From the beginning, Cabbage Patch Kids were not positioned as ordinary toys; children were urged to "adopt" Cabbage Patch Kids as if they were their babies. Each doll came with an "adoption form" — blue for boys, pink for girls — imprinted with the doll's name.

Children were encouraged to write their names on the adoption certificates as the parents and take good care of their kids. By mailing in the forms, they enrolled in the Cabbage Patch Kids Parents' Association and received congratulatory notes in the mail. A year later, the adopted dolls received birthday cards from their maker. This campaign transformed Cabbage Patch from just another plaything to a companion. Many children began collecting multiple Cabbage Patch Kids and forming families.

At holiday time, stories appeared in the press saying that stores had a shortage of the dolls. Parents stampeded to get Cabbage Patch Kid dolls for their kids. I don't know whether there was really a shortage or if it was just a rumor started by the toy company to stimulate sales.

More recently, Mattel created a Web site at www.cabbagepatchkids.com serving as an online community for these doll owners and their parents.

Domino's Pizza Meter

I discuss in detail in this book the various campaigns my PR agency did for Domino's Pizza when it was my client, and my favorite of those is the Pizza Meter. My agency measured the number of pizza deliveries to the White House, Pentagon, and CIA, and found that whenever there was a national crisis, the number of deliveries went up to feed government officials at late-night office meetings. We sent a press release about this occurrence, generating huge media exposure for Domino's.

The reason I include the campaign here is that it had an unusually long life. When we did the campaign, we realized that the Pizza Meter didn't have to be a one-time PR initiative — the pizza delivery could be monitored continuously throughout the year.

My agency did this monitoring, and at the end of every year, we did the Pizza Meter campaign again, showing the big events of the year and how accurately the meter predicted them based on pizza deliveries. There was no end to how many times we could get a whole new wave of media exposure by recycling this idea annually. We didn't even need a new twist; the major events spurred the increase in pizza deliveries. We eventually did 41 different Pizza Meter campaigns over a 12-year period.

IBM Big Blue versus Gary Kasparov

In 1997, IBM conducted one of the most brilliant PR campaigns ever: It challenged world chess champion Gary Kasparov to play an IBM computer specifically programmed to be good at chess. The computer, Big Blue, contained a special-purpose chip capable of evaluating 2.5 million chess positions per second.

In our technological age, one of the most dramatic and emotional issues is man versus machine: Elevator operators are unemployed because elevators are automatic. There are fewer bank tellers now because of ATM machines, fewer telephone operators because of voice-activated phone systems. Pitting IBM against the world chess champion was the ultimate man-machine challenge.

The campaign was a no-lose proposition for IBM. If Big Blue won, it would dramatically demonstrate the superiority of IBM computing technology. If Big Blue lost, people would still be impressed that a computer could play competitive chess with a grandmaster at all.

Big Blue won, and Kasparov lost, shocking many in the chess world. But the event was actually good for the world of chess — not since Bobby Fisher has chess received such media attention.

Gillette Sensor Razor

The PR campaign for the introduction of the Gillette Sensor was a first and maybe a last: The new razor made *Fortune* magazine's list of the top ten new product introductions of 1989 — but the product wasn't available until 1990.

The name Sensor implied high technology, and the SensorExcel for Women looked more like a Star Trek phaser than a razor. Advertising touted a unique rubber grip on the handle that gave the shaver more control for a closer and safer shave. Because of the rubber grip, your hand won't slip even if the handle is wet, so you won't get cut.

The incredible PR campaign for Sensor achieved more than 800 media placements worldwide in 19 countries. Media running stories included *Good Morning America, CBS Evening News, Newsweek, Forbes,* the *Wall Street Journal,* the *New York Times,* and the Associated Press.

Howard Stern and Sirius Satellite Radio

In 2006, Sirius Satellite Radio signed a five-year, $500-million contract with Howard Stern, one of the most successful radio personalities ever. Many people said the amount of money was ridiculous and far beyond what Stern is worth. But look at the PR it generated.

With two main players (XM and Sirius) in the fledgling satellite radio industry, Sirius was third in a two-horse race. The marketing cost to build its customer base, convince people to pay for its service, and then buy from the second fiddle would be, I estimate, approximately a gazillion bazillion dollars.

Stern's pre-switch publicity might just be one of the most successful media plans that a brand has undertaken. *Newsweek, New York* magazine, daily newspapers across the country, *60 Minutes,* the *Late Show with David Letterman,* and the *O'Reilly Factor* — these are just a few highly read and watched media outlets that picked up the story. But it's not just the quantity of coverage that's worth noting; it's the sheer variety. Stern's media blitz has crossed almost every demographic and ideological subset of the media. He has become not only an entertainment story, but also a business story and a human-interest story, appealing to both liberal Democrats and conservative Republicans. And what has he taken with him to all these reaches of the media? The Sirius brand.

But the reason this is perhaps one of the greatest PR coups in modern history is because, for his final six months on traditional radio, the feud between Stern and his employer was played out on the air in front of 7 million people, fueling the PR fire. For example, he was forbidden from saying "Sirius Radio," so instead he said "uh-uh-uh," and everyone knew what he meant. He had four hours of airtime every day and he used it to promote where he was going next — on somebody else's dime! Everything they did to try to stop him had the opposite effect, just as Stern planned.

For its $500 million, Sirius gets all this plus it reaches every type of audience, sends a key message to the entire country, and picks itself up off the competitive mat. And this doesn't even include the listeners who will surely sign on with Sirius just to listen to Howard. The final coup will be if Sirius does become the number-one satellite radio station. Stay tuned. . . .

Chapter 24

Ten Myths about PR — Debunked

*I*t's ironic: One purpose of PR is to get good press and avoid bad press, but PR itself has had pretty bad press over the years. The public image of PR has been produced in part by corporate flacks who made their living covering up toxic spills and oil leaks; by hucksters hovering around Paris Hilton or P. Diddy; and by Hollywood operatives keeping drug-addicted movie stars' rehab schedules out of the papers.

Your first step toward becoming a successful PR practitioner is to separate myth from reality. What really goes on behind the scenes in journalism and PR? How do stories make their way from the mind of the publicist to the front page of the newspaper? What is the relationship between PR and media professionals? I'm going to set up and knock down some of the common misconceptions about public relations.

Press Releases Don't Work Anymore

Reality: Press releases do work, and they are often the most cost-effective and least time-consuming form of PR. No PR tool is simpler to use or as effective as a basic, well-written, short press release based on a strong hook or angle. Press releases still work. They work well. They're easy to produce and inexpensive to distribute.

I agree that, done *wrong* (as many people do them), press releases can be a waste of time and money — yours and the media's. But done *right* (as explained in Chapter 8), press releases are one of the most hardworking, result-getting marketing tools going: Nothing beats them.

"Legitimate" Media Snub PR

Reality: Much of the "news" you read in the newspaper, hear on the radio, and see on TV has its origins in PR materials sent to the media by organizations and corporations looking to promote their causes, products, or services.

My reply is that prestigious and well-respected publications such as the *Wall Street Journal, Forbes, Fortune,* and the *New York Times* are interested in and will use good stories, regardless of whether they uncovered the story through intensive investigative reporting or a press release sent to them by a company or group like yours.

Virtually any media outlet you're seeking publicity from can be swayed to give you some coverage, provided that your materials are on target and you can offer or create a story of genuine interest to an audience. And doing so is relatively easy because there are only half a dozen or so basic themes or hooks (see Chapter 15) for news and feature stories that will interest editors and program directors.

Printed PR Doesn't Work without Follow-Up

Reality: Follow-up can help increase results, but well-written material will "sell itself" and generate lots of publicity without a single follow-up call or letter.

Follow-up is valuable and is a big part of what PR agencies do for clients. What's not true, however, is the notion that, without follow-up, printed PR materials are not effective and have little or no chance of getting published. In reality, a well-written press release containing interesting information can get wide coverage from a significant number of media outlets without a follow-up phone call to even a single editor.

So although follow-up can't hurt and usually helps, it isn't necessary, and a lack of time to follow up on press release mailings shouldn't stop you from distributing press releases or from handling your own PR.

The situation is much the same with query letters used to interest editors in running articles by or about you. Many of the successful query letters shown in Chapter 9, for example, generated acceptance and publication of the article without a follow-up letter or call to the editor. If the query letter is written according to the guidelines spelled out in Chapter 9, the letter alone will get editors to respond to you without your having to contact them.

The bottom line: PR works even if your time and resources for editorial contact are limited. Yes, it works even better if you can follow up. Follow-up is helpful but far from essential. Well-written materials state their own case with editors and get printed without your help.

You Need "Contacts" to Get Publicity

Reality: Contacts do help, but you can succeed beautifully without them. PR professionals like to talk about their media contacts — all the editors, program directors, and other media people they know and what an advantage that is in getting publicity placement. I do it myself!

Does schmoozing — network building — help? Sure. In my early years, I attended every networking function that I could, and every editor and producer knew my name. And when I called, they either took the call or called me back.

Does that mean you have to do the same intensive media networking to succeed with your PR program? Not at all. You can probably do nicely on your own without it, thank you very much.

Although networking got my calls returned, it never once got the media to publish any story of mine that they wouldn't have otherwise used. When we did our Pizza Meter campaign for Domino's Pizza, I don't think we made a single call: The story was a natural and too good for the media to resist. Same thing with the Strike Back idea I talk about in Chapter 1 — the PR campaign that produced my first front-cover story in *USA Today*.

Editors Want to Be Wined and Dined

Reality: Editors don't have time to be wined and dined. This is an extension of the myth that close personal contact with media people is necessary to getting media coverage. The intent is to get preferential treatment from editors and reporters by getting to know them personally and establishing a close relationship with them, and also by giving them perks, such as taking them out to lunch in a posh restaurant or giving them tickets to a basketball game.

Although editors are only human and some may respond favorably to such treatment, my experience is that most don't want it and would rather you not try to monopolize their time with small talk and three-martini lunches. The reason is that, like all of us, editors are busy people. But in addition to being busy, they constantly face tight deadlines. (Few editors in my acquaintance do *not* feel pressed by looming deadlines almost all the time.)

As a result, most editors prefer to keep PR sources, even good ones, at arm's length. They prefer to receive story ideas and proposals in a letter or press release rather than have the details transmitted in a lengthy conversation. Most editors and producers are print oriented and so prefer written communication; if they have questions, they'll ask. If a conversation is necessary, they'd rather it be five minutes over the telephone than a two-hour lunch.

So the truth is that it's not necessary to wine and dine editors as you might entertain an important prospect or customer. If you want to socialize, go ahead. Just be aware that doing so is unnecessary.

Snail Mail Is Awful; Overnight Delivery Services and Fax Work Great

Reality: A simple one- or two-page press release, sent to editors via first-class mail, is just as effective as fax or overnight delivery services, such as Federal Express, UPS, or DHL — and much, much cheaper. A number of distribution services and individual PR practitioners contend that using a fax is a better way to distribute news than through the U.S. Postal Service, but that's only partially true. A fax does get your material out much faster than if you print and mail it. However, I see no evidence that editors give faxed materials more consideration than mailed materials.

Similarly, a PR writer I know handled a project for a client who said, "Send all the releases Federal Express — that'll really get the media's attention." (This occurred before faxes and the Internet were common.) The cost was tremendous when compared with regular first-class mail for a 1-ounce letter, and we saw no evidence that any editor was duly impressed or took any extra notice of the material because FedEx sent it. Keep in mind that, every day, editors get many packages from overnight delivery services as well as fax messages. So sending your press release in such a manner has minimal added impact.

As for electronic submission, some magazines do welcome longer feature material sent on a CD or via the Internet, but the standard format is still a printed manuscript, and this is accepted by 99.99 percent of the magazines in the United States. If you can provide a computer file, go ahead. But it isn't necessary, and it usually won't increase your chances of acceptance.

You Can't Buy PR with Advertising

Reality: In some publications, you can.

Media and PR people have always been taught that "advertising" and "editorial" are separate. That is, the editorial department of a media organization operates separately, independently, and without the influence of the advertising department. Thus, the fact that you are an advertiser does not increase your chances of getting your press release run in the publication, any more than the fact that you are not an advertiser means the publication *won't* run your release.

But is this really true? Or can you "buy" publicity by promising to run a lot of ads? With some publications, you can. But my experience is that at the higher level, among well-known, nationally respected publications (such as the *Wall Street Journal* and the *New York Times*), you can't buy editorial space by promising to spend money on advertising, nor do the PR materials of advertisers receive even the slightest extra attention from the editorial staff. The exception may be when the advertising department wants the editorial department not to run a negative story about an advertiser, but unless you're in toxic dumping or public scandal, don't worry about this.

However, in smaller-circulation publications; in those that are more specialized or regional; and in industry-specific *(vertical)* publications versus general business *(horizontal)* magazines, the plain truth is that advertisers do sometimes get preferential treatment. I have seen it many, many times and know it to be a fact beyond dispute.

Every Fact Reported in the Media Is Checked and Verified

Reality: Most PR materials are picked up and run with almost no verification of any kind. I have found that editors rarely do much interviewing of sources to add to the material in a press release. Part of the reason is downsizing resulting from budgetary cutbacks at media outlets. Newspapers and broadcast stations simply don't have enough people to check every fact. Editors and producers tend to run PR materials pretty much as is; if they edit, it's usually for style, grammar, and space limitations, not to add or verify factual content.

I do PR for many dot-com companies and have mailed dozens of releases. I have found that 90 percent of the phone calls my clients get from editors are to verify the spelling of the Web address or the name of the company; rarely do they question the features listed or the accuracy of claims made.

Although editors may be too busy to check the statements in your releases for accuracy, they don't want to appear to be endorsing you, nor do they want to take responsibility for claims you make about your product in your own materials. So if there is doubt as to the accuracy of information, or if your copy states an opinion or makes a claim that is likely to be challenged, the editor may get out of this dilemma the easy way — by simply not printing your material.

Getting Publicity Is a Matter of Luck and Timing

Reality: Chance favors the prepared mind, and timing can be controlled. People who are unsuccessful at public relations (or anything else, for that matter) often view those who are successful with suspicion and cynicism. "Oh, they're lucky," claims the executive at one company who sees a favorable story about his competitor in an important industry journal. "They must have contacted this staff writer with the right story at the right time. When we mailed our release, the magazine wasn't interested in this topic, so they didn't run it. Now, of course, it's a hot topic, and our competitor must have suggested the story to them just when they were planning to cover it."

Do I disagree that timing is important? No. In public relations, marketing, promotion, new product introductions, and selling, timing is critical: You succeed largely because you reach your media contact, target market, or prospect at just the right time.

A strategy that works well for me is to time PR efforts with major events already going on. To launch the new children's department at IKEA Home Furnishings, we gave a free crib to any mother who went into labor on Labor Day. This tied into the holiday in a creative way, while also promoting our children's section.

It Doesn't Take A Lot of Time

Public relations that get results requires an investment of time, no matter how much money is involved. You don't write a press release and see it in the paper the next morning. Lots of time is spent writing (even if you're a great writer), developing appropriate media lists, and most important, doing follow-up phone calls before anything actually hits the press. If you're sending out a thousand press releases, you should be making a thousand calls. Spending that time is how you get the best results. The more time you put in, the more you get out of it.

Chapter 25

Ten Reasons to Do PR

I don't believe that any press is good press. And I don't think that the desire to get your name in the paper should have anything to do with the decision to invest your time in a PR program. I do, however, believe that this chapter provides ten excellent reasons why you should consider doing a PR program.

You're a Little Fish in a Big Pond

Your competitors may be bigger, may be better established, and may have more money. They probably spent more on that giant booth at the industry trade show last week, or on that full-page magazine ad last month, than you can afford in a year.

Beating someone else's ad campaign with your own paid advertising can be difficult if your competitor can afford to outspend you ten to one. But PR levels the playing field. In advertising, money buys you more media space and airtime. In PR, creative thinking wins you media space and airtime. The big companies don't have an advantage here. If anything, their bureaucratic structures sometimes hamstring them from moving quickly on creative public relations ideas, while smaller firms can move right away.

Some of the public relations techniques described in this book, such as events, can be expensive. But most can be done on a shoestring budget. Running your TV spot during the Super Bowl costs a million dollars, not to mention the $100,000 or more for producing the commercial. But sending a press release that gets you booked as a guest on the *Oprah Winfrey Show* costs only the first-class postage.

Your Product or Service Is the Best — and Nobody Knows about It

Advertising can, surprisingly, sometimes be very ineffective at getting consumers to buy your product because of a real advantage inherent in your product over another. You can write an ad that clearly communicates the advantage, but consumers are skeptical about advertising. It's precisely because you, the advertiser, are stating the advantage of your product that the reader is inclined not to believe you.

Consumers know that an ad is an ad. So when you start talking to them in an ad, their defense subconsciously goes up, and only a really great ad can penetrate that defense. PR, with its elevated credibility, never raises those defensive shields in the first place: When people read an article about you, they tend to believe that it's true, for better or worse

In public relations, you can't merely state a product or service claim, because the media is not interested in advertising your product for free for you. To get media exposure, you have to demonstrate your claim in an interesting and entertaining way. For instance, when my agency represented Domino's Pizza, we worked on a "World's Fastest Pizza Maker" contest among Domino's employees. This event dramatized that Domino's could deliver faster because it made pizza faster, not because its drivers drove too fast.

PR has two advantages over paid advertising. First, you're forced to tell your product story in a more engaging manner. Second, the consumer, reading your message in an article or seeing it on a TV show, is more inclined to believe it, because it is, in a way, "endorsed" by the media.

Your Product or Service Isn't Better than Anyone Else's

Winston March, an Australian business consultant, says that to succeed today, "It's more important to be a good marketer of what you do than a good doer of what you do." You may have cringed when you read that sentence, but the fact is that the most successful people and organizations are often the best self-promoters, not the best at making widgets or whatever it is they do.

The more PR you do, the more you, rather than your competitors, become established as the leader in your field. Read the brief case history of the matrimonial attorney in Chapter 22, if you haven't done so already. Is he necessarily a better lawyer than his competitors? It doesn't matter. As long as he keeps sending editors useful material that they'll publish, people will read his articles and consider him a knowledgeable authority.

In Chapter 11, we discuss the strategy of becoming the "go-to guy" — establishing yourself as the source the media people call on when they need an interview for a story on your particular subject of expertise. You may have said to yourself in disgust concerning a competitor, "Why is he always quoted in the media? He doesn't know anything about widget technology? That reporter should be interviewing me!"

The reason he's quoted so much is because he deliberately pursued the media for the exposure, and they came to rely on him as a good source for stories. Even if he's not as knowledgeable as you are, journalists find him clear and credible. And just as important, he's always available when they're on a deadline, any time of the day or night.

Believe me, these go-to people never have to go out and cold-call to get new business. Prospects come to them in droves, cash in hand, ready to pay their rather hefty fees for advice, service, expertise, and product — simply because they used the media to make themselves stand out from the pack.

Management Cuts Your Marketing Communications Budget

Marketing costs go up every year. Ad space costs more, printing costs rise, hourly rates of graphic design studios increase, and photographers up their day rates. Yet marketing budgets often stay flat, even though management is adding products, divisions, services, and new markets.

Public relations is arguably the most cost-effective marketing on the planet. It can achieve equal or better results than paid advertising at as little as $\frac{1}{100}$th of the cost. When your ad budget is slashed and you can't run as many ad insertions as you used to, step up your public relations efforts. PR can continue to help your presence in those media outlets that are important to you but in which you can no longer afford to advertise as frequently as in the past.

Management Demands Tangible Results from Marketing Expenditures

Twenty years ago, if managers liked the way your ads looked, or if they got compliments on the advertising from their friends and neighbors, they were happy.

But for the past couple of decades, pretty pictures haven't been enough. "What results are we getting from our marketing dollars?" management demands. "Show me the numbers."

In Chapter 22, I discuss the pros and cons of different systems used to measure PR effectiveness. If your management is numbers oriented, use these systems freely. Also do more direct-response PR designed to generate inquiries. Submit reports showing how many leads PR generated and the low cost per lead.

Traditional Marketing Isn't Working as Well as It Used To

Many marketers find that current tactics decline in effectiveness over time. Sometimes the specific promotion isn't working: Response to an ad drops off after several insertions. Other times, the nature of the media itself may be the problem: Direct-mail response rates have declined in recent years, while postage and printing costs have been rising, making it more difficult for direct mail to generate a profit.

When current tactics are underperforming, try new promotions. And make PR one of them. PR can generate significant return on your marketing dollars alone or in tandem with other marketing communications.

Desperately seeking synergy

Make sure that the objectives and messages for all your marketing communications — PR, print advertising, direct mail, trade shows, the Internet — are in synch. You don't want to negate the impact of a successful PR campaign by promoting a completely different message in your print advertising. Very few do this well but if you do, this is the Holy Grail. When PR is working with advertising, at the same time and with the same message, it is the most valuable investment of your dollar. But you must be part of the initial conversations to discuss strategy in order for this to work.

Your Competitors Get All the Good Press

One of the most dreaded phone calls for any PR professional to receive from a client or boss is, "*Big Magazine* just did an industry roundup, and we weren't listed. Why not?" The boss, understandably, is upset that journalists are so unaware of his company or product that they didn't even mention it in an industry overview.

The way to minimize such an unpleasant incident is through diligent, vigilant PR. Motivational speaker Rob Gilbert says, "The way to be there when people are looking for you is to be there all the time." You can't afford to be there with a paid ad all the time. But by conducting an ongoing PR program, you dramatically increase the likelihood that editors will think of you — and not just your competitors — when they're writing about your industry or product category.

I often hear people say, "We got lucky today," when a big story about them is published in the newspaper or the TV crews cover their event. But if they've been doing PR, it's really not luck — it's effort meeting with opportunity. Or as Pasteur observed, chance favors the prepared mind.

You Need Venture Capital

Public relations can go a long way toward helping you raise money. A few pages of press clippings in prominent publications, appended to your business plan, make an impression on venture capitalists that your carefully conceived projections do not: If you're already in *a high-profile* magazine, you must be a serious player.

You Are Media-Genic

Almost any product or service can be promoted via PR, but some are naturally more promotable than others. If you have a product or service with an inherent element of fun in it, for example — such as a trend like the Wacky Wall Walker of the 1980s — you're well positioned to gain tons of media exposure. You may as well take advantage of it.

Similarly, some people are just more "media-genic" than others. Colorful and eccentric characters have the edge, so if you're colorful or flamboyant, don't be shy. Use your natural charisma to your advantage in charming the public and the press.

You Really Enjoy Working with the Media

I never engage in PR for PR's sake: getting my name in the paper just to see my name in the paper. I value my time too much. When I contact the media to place a story, it's because the story will help me achieve a specific business goal.

That said, if you enjoy media attention, put your natural enthusiasm to work — in a PR campaign that generates results for your company and your product. After all, we tend to do more of the things we enjoy most, and better. So if being in the spotlight is your thing, go for it. Just don't lose sight of your business objectives — the end result of all this PR should be more money in your pocket. Getting your picture in the paper is only a side benefit, not the main event.

Conversely, if being in the spotlight makes you sweat, cringe, and blink, let it shine on your company or product, but not you personally. Or hire a spokesperson to stand under the spotlight for you.

Chapter 26

Ten Things You Should Never Do in the Name of PR

*T*hroughout this book, I give you a lot of the do's of public relations. In this chapter, you get the don'ts — ten things you should never do as you pursue PR for yourself, your business, or your clients.

Lie or Mislead

Rule number one: Never lie to or mislead a reporter. If a reporter catches you in a lie, she will never trust you again. The reporter will also tell colleagues, and your reputation as an untrustworthy source will spread. This will severely compromise your ongoing ability to work with the media, even when you're telling the truth.

Stonewall

Rule number two: Never say "No comment" to a reporter. "No comment" is very similar to "I plead the Fifth Amendment." In both cases, the other party automatically assumes that you're guilty.

When a reporter asks you a question to which you don't know the answer or don't want to respond to on the spot, the correct answer goes something like this: "Joan, you know we are always responsive to the media, but I'm not the right person to give you that information. I'll contact the right person and get back to you before your deadline today."

Procrastinate

As far as deadlines and commitments go, treat journalists as you treat customers. Always do what you say you're going to do, when you say you're going to do it. Journalists have deadlines that are not flexible. If you promise information and fail to deliver it on time, you'll tick them off considerably at best. At worst, the story will run without your having a chance to defend yourself, possibly resulting in a negative portrayal of you in tomorrow's paper.

Be Inaccessible

I advise executives at my clients' companies, including the CEOs, to treat any call from a journalist as the most important thing they have to do that moment. Once, I was at a press conference where NBA rookie of the year Derek Coleman was supposed to appear. Top sportswriters eagerly awaited the young superstar's arrival. When he didn't show, they waited about 40 minutes and then left.

If sportswriters give the NBA rookie of the year only 40 minutes, you'll be lucky if the media gives you 10 minutes. When the press calls, you're of interest to them only at the moment. Tomorrow, the story will have already been filed, and they won't even take your return call.

Striking while the iron is hot is the only way to get a steady stream of regular media exposure. I make it a point to be available to the media 24 hours a day, 7 days a week — whether it's on Thanksgiving Day during turkey or in the middle of the night. Most successful PR professionals I know have a similar policy of being totally accessible to the media.

Offer a Bribe

Never tell an editor or reporter, "Run my press release, and I'll advertise in your publication." Conversely, don't call an editor at a publication in which you already advertise and attempt to bully him with, "Run my press release, or I'll pull my advertising." Most print publications have three departments: editorial, advertising, and circulation. These are separate departments, and the PR professional who pits one against the other is making an error.

As a general rule, the top media outlets never let advertising influence editorial situations. As I'm fond of telling my PR clients, no one gets favors from the *New York Times*.

At trade journals covering specialized industries or smaller regional or local publications, publishers sometimes do favor advertisers with editorial coverage. But you should never be the one to bring up this idea with the editor.

If a *space rep* (a person selling ad space in the publication) approaches you with an offer of special editorial treatment in exchange for placing an ad, that's perfectly acceptable. But leave that between the space rep, the publisher, and the editor. Don't approach an editor about such a favor directly on your own.

Turn Up Your Nose

Advertising, PR, and promotion are increasingly becoming acceptable and even desirable in many industries that, a decade or so ago, thumbed their noses at it. The obvious example is the increase in advertising by professionals such as lawyers and doctors.

If you think advertising is beneath you and unprofessional, PR offers a marketing alternative that enables you to promote yourself, your practice, or your business in a more dignified and professional manner. Maybe you don't want to run commercials on late-night television or have full-page ads in the Sunday paper.

But how about a weekly column by you on your specialty in the local paper? Or a speech by you on that same topic at the library, YMCA, or Rotary club? Even for people who don't like marketing, PR offers plenty of low-key, soft-sell marketing opportunities you can like and feel comfortable with.

Bore People

David Ogilvy said, "You cannot bore someone into buying your product." Around our agency, the greatest sin is to be boring. Not because we love creativity for creativity's sake. But because in PR, boring simply doesn't work.

The most boring thing is to do the same PR, the same marketing, that everybody else does. If everyone's press releases and brochures look and read the same, how will one stand out from the other and get noticed? In PR, "same old same old" is the kiss of death.

People are bombarded by information and media messages today, and most of it, frankly, is incredibly dull. Successful PR finds or creates an element of fun in a product, service, organization, or event — one that can gain media attention while communicating a key message in an interesting, memorable fashion.

Joseph Kelley, speechwriter for President Dwight Eisenhower, once said, "Everything God created has a kernel of excitement in it, as has everything civilization invented or discovered." Saying that your product is boring because it is technical or a commodity is no excuse. What makes it exciting to the potential customer? Something, obviously, or people wouldn't buy. Your job is to find that excitement and build a PR campaign around it. There's no excuse for being a bore — at least not in PR.

Be a "No Man"

People love to kill ideas. They seem oddly eager to say no or explain why something won't work or can't be done. Saying no whenever someone proposes an idea is a copout. Such a response is too easy. Critics are a dime a dozen. But in PR, creators and doers earn annual salaries of $100,000 or more.

A lot of great PR campaigns are killed out of fear. Someone suggests a breakthrough idea that's different — *not* the same old same old — and top management says, "Why take the risk?" Because the greater the risk, the greater the potential payoff. That's true in many fields, whether it's business, PR, or investing.

I have no patience for critics. At our PR firm, I tell my employees that it's okay to have a brilliant idea or opinion I disagree with; what's not okay is *not* to have an idea or opinion. Don't just say, "I don't like it." Say what you would do instead.

In her book *The 7th Sense,* Doris Wild Helmering presents criteria to distinguish *constructive* (that is, helpful and useful) criticism from *nonconstructive* (that is, petty, denigrating, and useless) criticism. Her criteria are meant for general criticism of creative work, but they certainly apply to creation and evaluation of PR campaigns.

According to Helmering, constructive criticism has three components. To be constructive, your criticism must have all three components present:

✔ There is a contract between the people involved. The person who is making the critical comment is involved with the project, has some authority, and has been invited to do so.

✔ The negative feedback addresses a specific issue (for example, "This article ignores the current slump in tech stocks" versus "This stinks").

✔ There is direction for change (for example, "Why not talk about why now is a time to pick up good stocks at bargain prices before the market picks up again?").

Inappropriate criticism, on the other hand, has one or more of the following characteristics:

✔ It is uninvited. There is no contract. It is unsolicited.

✔ The feedback is nonspecific or broad based.

✔ The commentary is without direction for change.

When giving negative criticism, say what you *like* about the work before you say what you don't like. This approach preserves the recipient's ego, softens the blow, and ensures a positive working environment.

In a presentation skills course at Westinghouse, the instructor taught the following method for criticizing creative work. First say, "Here's what I liked," and recap at least three positive points. (If you look hard enough, it's impossible not to find at least three good things to say about almost anything.)

Then say, "Now, if it were mine to do . . ." and proceed with your list of specific criticisms. This phrase implies that what you're telling the recipient is your opinion, and not an accusation of incompetence or shoddy work on his part.

If someone gives you inappropriate criticism, especially comments that attack you as a person or demean you as a professional, say to that person, "Is there a purpose for your saying this to me?" This response alerts the person that you're aware of the demeaning tone and you want it to cease.

Sacrifice Long-Term Relationships for Short-Term Results

Many times clients have pressured me, "You've got to get this press release on the front page of the *Wall Street Journal*. Call your contacts there and put on the pressure."

I advise against strong-arm tactics in dealing with the press. The idea that any one story is important enough to jeopardize your relationship with an editor or producer is a mistake. You plan on being in business for many years. Well, guess what? That editor or producer plans on being in the industry for just as many years, too. And so will the *Wall Street Journal* and CNBC and your local TV news.

In the last several decades, businesses have discovered the concept of lifetime customer value and customer relationship management — that keeping a customer satisfied for the long term is more important than the immediate sale or the profits from it.

Treat the press as you would a customer. Don't place today's story above the long-term relationship. If the editor or producer says no and you've tried every conceivable angle to convince them otherwise, let it go. You'll want to place other stories tomorrow. Preserve the relationship so that the editor or producer will continue to be friendly and receptive when you call with your next idea.

Behave Unethically

You'll live a happier and better life when you don't violate your personal code of ethics for PR or any other business pursuit. In PR, you'll also be more successful, because editors and reporters seem to be better able than other people to spot unethical behavior. If you try to pull a fast one on the media and they spot it, it'll backfire terribly.

Other than media sensitivity, why behave ethically in business overall? For several reasons:

- ✔ **You get what you give.** If you've ever been treated unethically, you know it was an unpleasant experience. People give as good as they get. Therefore, if you want people to behave ethically when dealing with you, you should behave ethically when dealing with them.

- ✔ **Your organization's reputation is one of its most important assets.** Good business ethics maintain your reputation and enhance this asset. People who trust you are more likely to do business with you.

Consultant Paul C. Ritchie notes that, according to a survey by the Walker Group, when quality, service, and price were equal among competitors, 90 percent of consumers were more likely to buy from the company with the best reputation for social responsibility.

Unethical behavior, on the other hand, can result in ill will and negative publicity that mar your organization's reputation. This behavior can cost you customers, sales, and revenues and make acquiring the products and services you need from good vendors at favorable prices and terms more difficult. Ritchie cites a *Business Week*/Harris poll in which 71 percent of those surveyed said business has too much power and is morally responsible for the country's woes.

"One transgression by one employee can have an enormous impact — whether it is the liability incurred by not coping properly with an environmental problem or the financial penalty resulting from an engineering failure," writes Norm Augustine, chairman, Lockheed Martin Corporation. "Even more daunting is trying to restore one's collective reputation once it is tarnished."

✔ **Adhering to ethical business practices is simply the *right* thing to do.** For many of us, doing the right thing is important to our fundamental makeup as human beings, and so we strive to do right — although on many occasions we may be tempted to stray. Scientist Charles Darwin said, "The moral sense of conscience is the most noble of all the attributes of man."

If you don't feel a compulsion or obligation to do right, the other two factors — encouraging decent treatment from others and protecting your organization's reputation and good name — will have to provide sufficient motivation for you to adhere to ethical business practices.

And often, it isn't. Research shows that many workers these days feel tempted to do things that border on the illegal or the unethical:

✔ In one poll, 57 percent of workers surveyed felt more pressured now than five years ago to consider acting unethically or illegally on the job, and 40 percent said that pressure has increased over the last 12 months.

✔ According to a study sponsored by the Ethics Officer Association, 48 percent of employees admitted to illegal or unethical actions. Half of U.S. workers surveyed by the Ethics Officer Association said they used technology unethically on the job during the year, including copying company software for home use and wrongly blaming a personal error on a technology glitch.

✔ In a Gallup poll, half of those interviewed said business values were declining.

✔ In a survey of top executives, honesty and integrity were found to be the most important qualities interviewers look for in prospective employees.

In response, more and more organizations are training employees in ethics and establishing ethical guidelines for employees to follow. According to Harvard Business School Professor Joseph L. Badaracco, Jr., one out of every three American firms has ethics training programs, and more than 500 have ethics officers. Six of ten firms have ethical codes that employees are supposed to follow. Lockheed Martin even has a toll-free "ethics hotline" that its employees and suppliers can call to get advice on business ethics issues. More than 500 ethics courses are offered at American business schools.

Chapter 27

Ten Steps to Better PR Writing

You can hire a PR firm, a publicist, or a freelance writer to craft your press releases for you (refer to Chapter 8) — but, of course, you can do it yourself.

If you're a natural writer, writing press releases should be easy for you. If not, practice and you can improve. This section is a reminder to practice ten rules of good writing. Apply these rules to your drafts to achieve greater clarity and power in your prose.

Organizing!

Poor organization is a major cause of foggy writing. If the reader believes the content has some importance to him, he can plow through a document even if it is dull or has lengthy sentences and big words. But if it's poorly organized, forget it. There's no way to make sense of what is written.

Poor organization stems from poor planning. Before you write, plan. Create a rough outline that spells out the contents and organization of your release or tip sheet. The outline need not be formal. A simple list, doodles, or rough notes will do. Use whatever form suits you.

By the time you finish writing, some content in the final draft might be different from the outline. That's okay. The outline is a tool to aid in organization, not a commandment cast in concrete. If you want to change it as you go along, no problem!

The outline helps you divide the writing project into many smaller, easy-to-handle pieces and parts. The organization of these parts depends on the type of document you're writing. If the format isn't strictly defined by the type of document you are writing, select the organizational scheme that best fits the material.

Some common writing formats include

- ✔ **Order of location:** An article on the planets of the solar system might begin with Mercury (the planet nearest the Sun) and end with Pluto (the planet farthest out).

- ✔ **Order of increasing difficulty:** Computer manuals often start with the easiest material and, as the user masters basic principles, move on to more complex operations.

- ✔ **Alphabetical order:** This is a logical way to arrange a booklet on vitamins (A, B3, B12, C, D, E, and so on) or a directory of company employees.

- ✔ **Chronological order:** In this format, you present the facts in the order in which they happened. History books are written this way. So are many case histories, feature stories, and corporate biographies.

- ✔ **Problem/solution:** Another format appropriate to case histories and many types of reports, the problem/solution organizational scheme begins with "Here's what the problem was" and ends with "Here's how we solved it."

- ✔ **Inverted pyramid:** This is the newspaper style of news reporting where the lead paragraph summarizes the story and the following paragraphs present the facts in order of decreasing importance. You can use this format in journal articles, letters, memos, and reports.

- ✔ **Deductive order:** You can start with a generalization, and then support it with particulars. Scientists use this format in research papers that begin with the findings and then state the supporting evidence.

- ✔ **Inductive order:** Another approach is to begin with specific instances, and then lead the reader to the idea or general principles the instances suggest. This is an excellent way to approach trade journal feature stories.

- ✔ **List:** The article you're now reading is a list article because it describes, in list form, the most common problems in technical writing. A technical list article might be titled "Six Tips for Designing Wet Scrubbers" or "Seven Ways to Reduce Your Plant's Electric Bill."

Knowing Your Reader

With most marketing documents — articles, press releases, brochures — you are writing for many readers, not an individual. Even though you don't know the names of your readers, you need to develop a picture of who they are — their job title, education, industry, and interests. You can get a clear picture of your reader by studying some of the publications to which you are mailing your release.

Consider the following areas to help identify your key readers:

✔ **Job title:** Engineers are interested in your compressor's reliability and performance, while the purchasing agent is more concerned with cost. A person's job influences her perspective of your product, service, or idea. Are you writing for plant engineers? Office managers? CEOs? Machinists? Make the tone and content of your writing compatible with the professional interests of your readers.

✔ **Education:** Is your reader a PhD or a high-school dropout? Is he a chemical engineer? Does he understand computer programming, thermodynamics, physical chemistry, and the calculus of variations? Write simply enough so that even the least technical of your readers can understand what you're saying.

✔ **Industry:** When engineers buy a reverse-osmosis water purification system for a chemical plant, they want to know every technical detail down to the last pipe, pump, fan, and filter. Marine buyers, on the other hand, have only two basic questions: "What does it cost?" and "How reliable is it?" Especially in promotional writing, know what features of your product appeal to the various markets.

✔ **Level of interest:** Is your reader interested or disinterested? Friendly or hostile? Receptive or resistant? Understanding her state of mind helps you tailor your message to meet her needs.

Shunning "Corporatese"

Anyone who reads corporate documents knows the danger of "corporatese" — the pompous, overblown style that leaves your writing sounding as if it were written by a computer or a corporation instead of a human being.

Corporatese, by my definition, is language more complex than the concepts it serves to communicate. By loading up their writings with jargon, clichés, antiquated phrases, passive sentences, and an excess of adjectives, executives and bureaucrats hide behind a jumble of incomprehensible memos and reports.

To help you recognize corporatese (also known as *corporitis*), I've assembled a few samples from diverse sources. Note how the authors seem to be writing to impress rather than to express. All of these excerpts are real:

> *Will you please advise me at your earliest convenience of the correct status of this product?*
>
> —Memo from an advertising manager

> *All of the bonds in the above described account having been heretofore disposed of, we are this day terminating same. We accordingly enclose herein check in the amount of $30,050 same being your share realized therein, as per statement attached.*
>
> —Letter from a stockbroker

> *This procedure enables users to document data fields described in master files that were parsed and analyzed by the program dictionary.*
>
> —Software user's manual

How do you eliminate corporatese from your writing? Start by avoiding jargon. Don't use a technical term unless it communicates your meaning precisely. For example, never write "mobile dentition" when "loose teeth" will do just as well. Legal scholar Tamar Frankel notes that when you avoid jargon, your writing can be read easily by novices and experienced professionals alike.

Use contractions. Avoid clichés and antiquated phrases. Write simply. Prefer the active voice. In the active voice, action is expressed directly: "John performed the experiment." In the passive voice, the action is indirect: "The experiment was performed by John."

When you use the active voice, your writing will be more direct and vigorous; your sentences more concise. As you can see in the following samples, the passive voice seems puny and stiff by comparison:

Passive voice	*Active voice*
Control of the bearing-oil supply is provided by the shutoff valves.	Shutoff valves control the bearing-oil supply.
Leaking of the seals is prevented by the use of O-rings.	O-rings keep the seals from leaking.
Fuel-cost savings were realized through the installation of thermal insulation.	Installing thermal insulation cut fuel costs.

Avoiding Long Sentences

Lengthy sentences tire the reader and make your writing hard to read. A survey by Harvard professor D.H. Menzel indicates that in scientific papers, the sentences become difficult to understand when they're longer than 34 words.

One measure of writing clarity, the Fog Index, takes into account sentence length *and* word length. Here's how it works:

1. **Determine the average sentence length in a short (100- to 200-word) writing sample.**

   To do this, divide the number of words in the sample by the number of sentences. If parts of a sentence are separated by a semicolon (;), count each part as a separate sentence.

2. **Calculate the number of big words (words with three or more syllables) per 100 words of sample.**

   Don't include capitalized words, combinations of short words *(butterfly, moreover)*, or verbs that turn into three syllables by adding *–ed* or *–es (accepted, responses)*.

3. **Add the average sentence length to the number of big words per hundred words and multiply by 0.4.**

   This result gives you the Fog Index for the sample.

The Fog Index corresponds to the years of schooling you need to read and understand the sample. A score of 8 or 9 indicates high-school level; 13, a college freshman; 17, a college graduate.

Popular magazines have Fog Indexes ranging from 8 to 13. Technical journals should rate no higher than 17. Obviously, the higher the Fog Index, the more difficult the writing is to read. Scientific writing contains some of the densest fog, as in this 79-word sentence:

> In this book, I have attempted an accurate but at the same time readable account of recent work on the subject of how gene controls operate, a large subject that is rapidly acquiring a central position in the biology of today and that will inevitably become even more prominent in the future, in the efforts of scientists of numerous different specialists to explain how a single organism can contain cells of many different kinds developed from a common origin.

With 17 big words, this sample has a Fog Index of 40 — equivalent to a reading level of 28 years of college education! Obviously, this sentence is way too long. Here's a rewrite I came up with:

> This book is about how gene controls operate — a subject of growing importance in modern biology.

This rewrite gets the message across with a Fog Index of only 14.

Give your writing the Fog Index test. If you score in the upper teens or higher, it's time to trim sentence length. Go over your text, and break long sentences into two or more separate sentences. To further reduce average sentence length and add variety to your writing, you can occasionally use an extremely short sentence or sentence fragments of only three to four words or so. Like this one.

Short sentences are easier to grasp than long ones. A good guide for keeping sentence length under control is to write sentences that can be spoken aloud without losing your breath. (No cheating — don't take a deep breath before doing this test!)

Using Short, Simple Words

Business executives sometimes prefer to use big, important-sounding words rather than short, simple words. This is a mistake; fancy language just frustrates the reader. Write in plain, ordinary English, and your readers will love you for it.

The following table shows a few big words that occur frequently in technical literature. The column on the right shows shorter, and preferable, substitutions:

Big word	*Substitution*
Terminate	End
Utilize	Use
Incombustible	Fireproof
Substantiate	Prove
Eliminate	Get rid of

Use legitimate technical terms when they communicate your ideas precisely, but avoid using jargon just because the words sound impressive. Don't write that material is "gravimetrically conveyed" when it is simply "dumped."

In your writing, use the simplest word you can while still being accurate and specific. Don't be content to say something is good, bad, fast, or slow when you can say *how* good, *how* bad, *how* fast, or *how* slow. Be specific whenever possible.

General	Specific
A tall spray dryer	A 40-foot-tall spray dryer
Plant	Oil refinery
Unit	Evaporator
Unfavorable weather conditions	Rain
Structural degradation	A leaky roof
High performance	95 percent efficiency

The key to success in technical writing is to *keep it simple.* Write to express — not to impress. A relaxed, conversational style can add vigor and clarity to your work.

Formal style	Informal conversational style
The data provided by direct examination of samples under the lens of the microscope are insufficient for the purpose of making a proper identification of the components of the substance.	We can't tell what it is made of by looking at it under the microscope.
We have found during conversations with customers that even the most experienced of extruder specialists have a tendency to avoid the extrusion of silicone profiles or hoses.	Our customers tell us that experienced extruder specialists avoid extruding silicone profiles or hoses.
The corporation terminated the employment of Mr. Joseph Smith.	Joe was fired.

Sidestepping "Writer's Block"

Writer's block isn't just for professional writers; it can afflict nonwriters, too. Writer's block is the inability to start putting words on paper (or personal computer), and it stems from anxiety and fear of writing.

When people write, they're afraid to make mistakes, and so they edit themselves word by word, inhibiting the natural flow of ideas and sentences. But professional writers know that writing is a process consisting of numerous drafts, rewrites, deletions, and revisions. Rarely does a writer produce a perfect manuscript on the first try.

Follow these tips to help you overcome writer's block:

- **Break the writing into short sections, and write one section at a time.** Tackling many little writing assignments seems less formidable a task than tackling a large project all at once. This technique also benefits the reader. Writing is most readable when it deals with one simple idea rather than multiple complex ideas. Your entire paper can't be simple or restricted to one idea, but each section of it can.

- **Write the easy sections first.** Put in the page headers, section titles, cover page, and other boilerplate text. You'll feel an immediate sense of accomplishment, and the existence of a starting framework will make it easier for you to fill in the rest.

- **Avoid grammar-book rules that inhibit writers.** One such rule says every paragraph must begin with a topic sentence (a first sentence that states the central idea of the paragraph). By insisting on topic sentences, teachers and editors throw up a block that prevents people from putting their thoughts on paper. Professional writers don't worry about topic sentences (or sentence diagrams or ending a sentence with a preposition). Neither should you.

- **Sleep on it.** Put your manuscript away and come back to it the next morning — or even several days later. Refreshed, you'll be able to edit and rewrite effectively and easily.

Defining the Topic

Effective writing begins with a clear definition of the specific topic you want to write about. The big mistake many people make is to tackle a topic that's too broad. For example, the title "Project Management" is too all encompassing for a trade journal article. You could write a whole book on the subject. But by narrowing the scope, say, with the title "Managing Chemical Plant Construction Projects with Budgets under $500,000," you get a clearer definition and a more manageable topic.

Knowing the purpose of the document is also important. You may say, "That's easy; the purpose is to give technical information." But think again. Do you want the reader to buy a product? Change methods of working? Look for the hidden agenda beyond the mere transmission of facts.

Gathering Lots of Information

Okay. You've defined your topic, audience, and purpose. The next step is to do some homework and to gather information on the topic at hand. Most managers and entrepreneurs I know don't do this. When they're writing a release, for example, their attitude is, "I'm the expert here. So I'll just rely on my own experience and know-how."

That approach is a mistake. Even though you're an expert, your knowledge may be limited, your viewpoint lopsided. Gathering information from other sources helps round out your knowledge or, at the very least, verify your own thinking. And there's another benefit: Backing up your claims with facts is a real credibility builder.

After you cram a file folder full of reprints and clippings, take notes on index cards or a PC. Not only does note taking put the key facts at your fingertips in condensed form, but also reprocessing the research information through your fingers and brain puts you in closer touch with your material.

Writing, and Then Rewriting, Rewriting

After you gather facts and decide how to organize the piece, the next step is to sit down and write. When you do, keep in mind that the secret to successful writing is rewriting.

You don't have to get it right on the first draft. The pros rarely do. E. B. White, essayist and co-author of the writer's resource book *The Elements of Style,* was said to have rewritten every piece nine times.

Maybe you don't need nine drafts, but you probably need more than one. Use a simple, three-step procedure that I call SPP: Spit, Prune, and Polish:

- ✔ **When you sit down to write, just spit it out.** Don't worry about how the text sounds, or whether the grammar's right, or whether it fits your outline. Just let the words flow. If you make a mistake, leave it. You can always go back and fix it later. Some nonkeyboarding types find it helpful to talk into a tape recorder or dictate to an assistant. If you can type and have a personal computer, great. Some old-fashioned folks even use typewriters or pen and paper.

- ✔ **To prune, print out your first draft (double-spaced, for easy editing) and give it major surgery.** Take a red pen to the draft and slash out all unnecessary words and phrases. Rewrite any awkward passages to make them smoother, but if you get stuck, leave it and go on; come back to it later. Use the cut and paste feature in your word-processing program to cut the draft apart and reorganize to fit your outline, or to improve on that outline. Then print out a clean draft. Repeat the pruning step if necessary as many times as you want.

✔ **Polish your manuscript.** Check such points as equations, units of measure, references, grammar, spelling, and punctuation. Again, use the red pen and print out a fresh copy with corrections.

Being Consistent

"A foolish consistency," wrote Ralph Waldo Emerson, "is the hobgoblin of little minds." This may be so. But, on the other hand, inconsistencies in writing will confuse your readers and convince them that your products and company are as sloppy and disorganized as your prose. Good business writers strive for consistency in the use of numbers, hyphens, units of measure, punctuation, equations, grammar, symbols, capitalization, technical terms, and abbreviations.

Appendix
Recommended Resources

· ·

*T*aking advantage of the right resources can enhance your PR efforts. Use the information in this appendix to find some of the best resources you may need as you put into practice some of the tools and suggestions from this book.

Associations

Canadian Public Relations Society (CPRS)
Suite 346, 4195 Dundas Street West
Toronto, Ontario, M8X 1Y4
Canada
Phone: 416-239-7034
Web: www.cprs.ca

International Association of Business Communicators (IABC)
1 Hallidie Plaza, Suite 600
San Francisco, CA 94102
Phone: 800-776-4222 or 415-433-3400
Web: www.iabc.com

Institute for Public Relations
University of Florida
P.O. Box 118400
Gainesville, FL 32611-8400
Phone: 352-392-0280
Web: www.instituteforpr.com

National Investor Relations Institute (NIRI)
8045 Leesburg Pike, Suite 600
Vienna, VA 22182
Phone: 703-506-3570
Web: www.niri.org

Public Relations Society of America (PRSA)
33 Maiden Lane, 11th floor
New York, NY 10038
Phone: 212-460-1400
Web: www.prsa.org

Web Sites

- **Bloogz: Worldwide Blog (www.bloogz.com):** A search site for worldwide blogs.

- **Deadline Online (www.deadlineonline.com):** A resource for editors, reporters, and producers on deadline who are looking for source material for a story.

- **The Drudge Report (www.drudgereport.com):** Published by Matt Drudge, this site provides another perspective on the stories that you'll read in the newspaper; includes all press links.

- **MediaMap (www.mediamap.com):** Media people can post queries seeking sources, information, or experts from the PR community. PR professionals can post responses on the site.

- **MediaStudies.com (www.mediastudies.com):** Devoted to improving understanding between the media and the public. Brings journalists, academics, media executives, and the public together to examine media's effects on society.

- **The Museum of Public Relations (www.prmuseum.com):** Covers how ideas are developed for industry, education, and the government, and how they have been applied to successful public relations throughout the discipline's history.

- **TheNewPR/Wiki (www.thenewpr.com):** A repository of relevant information about how the PR practice is changing.

- **PSA Research Center (www.psaresearch.com):** An online information library dedicated to public service advertising.

- **The Viral Chart (www.viralchart.com):** Shows you which messages and video clips are being passed around the Internet

Books

- *The Associated Press Stylebook and Libel Manual,* by Norm Goldstein (Perseus Books)

- *The Copywriter's Handbook: A Step-by-Step Guide to Writing Copy That Sells,* by Robert W. Bly (Owl Books)

- *The Crisis Counselor: A Step-by-Step Guide to Managing a Business Crisis,* by Jeffrey R. Caponigro (McGraw-Hill)

- *A Dictionary of Modern English Usage,* by H. W. Fowler (Oxford University Press)

- *Find It Fast: How to Uncover Expert Information on Any Subject — In Print or Online,* by Robert I. Berkman (HarperResource)

- ✔ *Ideas & Research: Elements of Article Writing,* by Marshall Krantz (Writer's Digest Books)

- ✔ *I'll Get Back to You: 156 Ways to Get People to Return Your Calls and Other Helpful Sales Tips,* by Robert L. Shook and Eric Yaverbaum (McGraw-Hill)

- ✔ *Marketing Kit For Dummies,* 2nd Edition, by Alexander Hiam (Wiley)

- ✔ *Power Public Relations,* by Leonard Saffir with John Tarrant (NTC Business Books)

- ✔ *The Publicity Handbook,* by David R. Yale with Andrew J. Carothers (NTC Business Books)

- ✔ *Publishing Newsletters,* by Howard Penn Hudson (H & M Publishers)

- ✔ *Speechwriting: The Master Touch,* by Joseph J. Kelley, Jr. (Stackpole Books)

- ✔ *Successful Client Newsletters,* by Milton W. Zwicker (American Bar Association)

Periodicals

Bulldog Reporter
Infocom Group
5900 Hollis St., Suite L
Emeryville, CA 94608
Phone: 800-959-1059 or 510-596-9300
Web: www.bulldogreporter.com

Communication World
International Association of Business Communicators (IABC)
One Hallidie Plaza, Suite 600
San Francisco, CA 94102
Phone: 800-776-4222 or 415-544-4700
Web: www.iabc.com/cw

The Holmes Report
The Holmes Group
271 W. 47 St., Suite PHA
New York, NY 10036
Phone: 212-333-2300
Website: www.holmesreport.com

Jack O'Dwyer's Newsletter
J.R. O'Dwyer Company, Inc.
271 Madison Ave., Suite 600
New York, NY 10016
Phone: 212-679-2471
Web: www.odwyerpr.com

Partyline
35 Sutton Place
New York, NY 10022
Phone: 212-755-3487
Web: www.partylinepublishing.com

PR Week
220 Fifth Ave.
New York, NY 10001
Phone: 877-389-3862
Web: www.prweekus.com

The Public Relations Strategist
33 Maiden Lane, 11th floor
New York, NY 10038
Phone: 212-460-1400
Web: www.prplace.com

Public Relations Tactics
33 Maiden Lane, 11th floor
New York, NY 10038
Phone: 212-460-1400
Web: www.prplace.com

The Ragan Report
Lawrence Ragan Communications, Inc.
111 E. Wacker Dr., Suite 500
Chicago, IL 60601
Phone: 800-493-4867 or 312-960-4100
Web: www.ragan.com

Media Directories and Distribution Services

All-in-One Media Directory
Gebbie Press
P.O. Box 1000
New Paltz, NY 12561
Phone: 845-255-7560
Web: www.gebbieinc.com

Bacon's Media Directories
Bacon's Information, Inc.
332 S. Michigan Ave.
Chicago, IL 60604
Phone: 866-639-5087
Web: www.bacons.com

Burrelle's Media Directories
75 E. Northfield Rd.
Livingston, NJ 07039
Phone: 800-631-1160 or 973-992-6600
Web: www.burrellesluce.com

College Media Directory
Oxbridge Communications, Inc.
150 Fifth Ave.
New York, NY 10010
Phone: 800-955-0231 or 212-741-0231
Web: www.oxbridge.com

International Publicity Checker
Bacon's Information, Inc.
332 S. Michigan Ave.
Chicago, IL 60604
Phone: 866-639-5087
Web: www.bacons.com

Media Alerts
Bacon's Information, Inc.
332 S. Michigan Ave.
Chicago, IL 60604
Phone: 866-639-5087
Web: www.bacons.com

MediaMap
Bacon's Information, Inc.
332 S. Michigan Ave.
Chicago, IL 60604
Phone: 866-639-5087
Web: www.mediamap.com

Mediamatic (Calendar of Editorial Information)
Media Distribution Services, Inc. (MDS)
307 W. 36th St.
New York, NY 10018
Phone: 800-MDS-DATA or 212-279-4800
Web: www.mdsconnect.com

Radio/TV Directory
Bacon's Information, Inc.
332 S. Michigan Ave.
Chicago, IL 60604
Phone: 866-639-5087
Web: www.bacons.com

Broadcasting and Cable Yearbook
Web: www.reedref.com

R.R. Bowker LLC
630 Central Ave.
New Providence, NJ 07974
1-800-526-9537 or 1-908-286-1090
Web: www.bowker.com

Newswires

Associated Press Information Services
450 W. 33 St.
New York, NY 10001
Phone 212-621-1500
Website: www.ap.org

Business Wire
44 Montgomery Street, 39th Floor
San Francisco, CA 94104
888.381.WIRE (9473) or 415.986.4422
Web: www.businesswire.com

Collegiate Presswire
1191 Valley Rd., Suite 2
Clifton, NJ 07013
Phone: 888-621-7721 or 973-746-4446
Web: www.cpwire.com

PR Newswire
810 Seventh Ave., 32nd floor
New York, NY 10019
Phone: 888-776-0942
Web: www.prnewswire.com

U.S. Newswire
National Press Building, Suite 1230
Washington, DC 20045
Phone: 800-544-8995 or 202-347-2770
Web: www.usnewswire.com

Index

• *C* •

USINESS, CAREERS & PERSONAL FINANCE

0-7645-5307-0

0-7645-5331-3 *†

Also available:
- Accounting For Dummies †
  0-7645-5314-3
- Business Plans Kit For Dummies †
  0-7645-5365-8
- Cover Letters For Dummies
  0-7645-5224-4
- Frugal Living For Dummies
  0-7645-5403-4
- Leadership For Dummies
  0-7645-5176-0
- Managing For Dummies
  0-7645-1771-6

- Marketing For Dummies
  0-7645-5600-2
- Personal Finance For Dummies *
  0-7645-2590-5
- Project Management For Dummies
  0-7645-5283-X
- Resumes For Dummies †
  0-7645-5471-9
- Selling For Dummies
  0-7645-5363-1
- Small Business Kit For Dummies *†
  0-7645-5093-4

OME & BUSINESS COMPUTER BASICS

0-7645-4074-2

0-7645-3758-X

Also available:
- ACT! 6 For Dummies
  0-7645-2645-6
- iLife '04 All-in-One Desk Reference
  For Dummies
  0-7645-7347-0
- iPAQ For Dummies
  0-7645-6769-1
- Mac OS X Panther Timesaving
  Techniques For Dummies
  0-7645-5812-9
- Macs For Dummies
  0-7645-5656-8

- Microsoft Money 2004 For Dummies
  0-7645-4195-1
- Office 2003 All-in-One Desk Reference
  For Dummies
  0-7645-3883-7
- Outlook 2003 For Dummies
  0-7645-3759-8
- PCs For Dummies
  0-7645-4074-2
- TiVo For Dummies
  0-7645-6923-6
- Upgrading and Fixing PCs For Dummies
  0-7645-1665-5
- Windows XP Timesaving Techniques
  For Dummies
  0-7645-3748-2

OOD, HOME, GARDEN, HOBBIES, MUSIC & PETS

0-7645-5295-3

0-7645-5232-5

Also available:
- Bass Guitar For Dummies
  0-7645-2487-9
- Diabetes Cookbook For Dummies
  0-7645-5230-9
- Gardening For Dummies *
  0-7645-5130-2
- Guitar For Dummies
  0-7645-5106-X
- Holiday Decorating For Dummies
  0-7645-2570-0
- Home Improvement All-in-One
  For Dummies
  0-7645-5680-0

- Knitting For Dummies
  0-7645-5395-X
- Piano For Dummies
  0-7645-5105-1
- Puppies For Dummies
  0-7645-5255-4
- Scrapbooking For Dummies
  0-7645-7208-3
- Senior Dogs For Dummies
  0-7645-5818-8
- Singing For Dummies
  0-7645-2475-5
- 30-Minute Meals For Dummies
  0-7645-2589-1

NTERNET & DIGITAL MEDIA

0-7645-1664-7

0-7645-6924-4

Also available:
- 2005 Online Shopping Directory
  For Dummies
  0-7645-7495-7
- CD & DVD Recording For Dummies
  0-7645-5956-7
- eBay For Dummies
  0-7645-5654-1
- Fighting Spam For Dummies
  0-7645-5965-6
- Genealogy Online For Dummies
  0-7645-5964-8
- Google For Dummies
  0-7645-4420-9

- Home Recording For Musicians
  For Dummies
  0-7645-1634-5
- The Internet For Dummies
  0-7645-4173-0
- iPod & iTunes For Dummies
  0-7645-7772-7
- Preventing Identity Theft For Dummies
  0-7645-7336-5
- Pro Tools All-in-One Desk Reference
  For Dummies
  0-7645-5714-9
- Roxio Easy Media Creator For Dummies
  0-7645-7131-1

Separate Canadian edition also available
Separate U.K. edition also available

vailable wherever books are sold. For more information or to order direct: U.S. customers visit www.dummies.com or call 1-877-762-2974.
.K. customers visit www.wileyeurope.com or call 0800 243407. Canadian customers visit www.wiley.ca or call 1-800-567-4797.

SPORTS, FITNESS, PARENTING, RELIGION & SPIRITUALITY

0-7645-5146-9

0-7645-5418-2

Also available:
- Adoption For Dummies
  0-7645-5488-3
- Basketball For Dummies
  0-7645-5248-1
- The Bible For Dummies
  0-7645-5296-1
- Buddhism For Dummies
  0-7645-5359-3
- Catholicism For Dummies
  0-7645-5391-7
- Hockey For Dummies
  0-7645-5228-7

- Judaism For Dummies
  0-7645-5299-6
- Martial Arts For Dummies
  0-7645-5358-5
- Pilates For Dummies
  0-7645-5397-6
- Religion For Dummies
  0-7645-5264-3
- Teaching Kids to Read For Dummies
  0-7645-4043-2
- Weight Training For Dummies
  0-7645-5168-X
- Yoga For Dummies
  0-7645-5117-5

TRAVEL

0-7645-5438-7

0-7645-5453-0

Also available:
- Alaska For Dummies
  0-7645-1761-9
- Arizona For Dummies
  0-7645-6938-4
- Cancún and the Yucatán For Dummies
  0-7645-2437-2
- Cruise Vacations For Dummies
  0-7645-6941-4
- Europe For Dummies
  0-7645-5456-5
- Ireland For Dummies
  0-7645-5455-7

- Las Vegas For Dummies
  0-7645-5448-4
- London For Dummies
  0-7645-4277-X
- New York City For Dummies
  0-7645-6945-7
- Paris For Dummies
  0-7645-5494-8
- RV Vacations For Dummies
  0-7645-5443-3
- Walt Disney World & Orlando For Dummies
  0-7645-6943-0

GRAPHICS, DESIGN & WEB DEVELOPMENT

0-7645-4345-8

0-7645-5589-8

Also available:
- Adobe Acrobat 6 PDF For Dummies
  0-7645-3760-1
- Building a Web Site For Dummies
  0-7645-7144-3
- Dreamweaver MX 2004 For Dummies
  0-7645-4342-3
- FrontPage 2003 For Dummies
  0-7645-3882-9
- HTML 4 For Dummies
  0-7645-1995-6
- Illustrator CS For Dummies
  0-7645-4084-X

- Macromedia Flash MX 2004 For Dummies
  0-7645-4358-X
- Photoshop 7 All-in-One Desk Reference For Dummies
  0-7645-1667-1
- Photoshop CS Timesaving Techniques For Dummies
  0-7645-6782-9
- PHP 5 For Dummies
  0-7645-4166-8
- PowerPoint 2003 For Dummies
  0-7645-3908-6
- QuarkXPress 6 For Dummies
  0-7645-2593-X

NETWORKING, SECURITY, PROGRAMMING & DATABASES

0-7645-6852-3

0-7645-5784-X

Also available:
- A+ Certification For Dummies
  0-7645-4187-0
- Access 2003 All-in-One Desk Reference For Dummies
  0-7645-3988-4
- Beginning Programming For Dummies
  0-7645-4997-9
- C For Dummies
  0-7645-7068-4
- Firewalls For Dummies
  0-7645-4048-3
- Home Networking For Dummies
  0-7645-42796

- Network Security For Dummies
  0-7645-1679-5
- Networking For Dummies
  0-7645-1677-9
- TCP/IP For Dummies
  0-7645-1760-0
- VBA For Dummies
  0-7645-3989-2
- Wireless All In-One Desk Reference For Dummies
  0-7645-7496-5
- Wireless Home Networking For Dummies
  0-7645-3910-8